Telling the Story

Gospel, Mission and Culture

ANDREW WALKER

First published in Great Britain 1996
Society for Promoting Christian Knowledge
Holy Trinity Church
Marylebone Road
London NW1 4DU

British Library Cataloguing-in-Publication Data
A catalogue record of this book is available from the British Library

ISBN 0-281-04726-X

Typeset by Simon Jenkins Associates
Printed in Great Britain by The Longdunn Press, Bristol

For Metropolitan Anthony, Bishop Lesslie Newbigin,
Cardinal Leon Suenens: three wise men who heard
the story and passed it on.

Contents

Acknowledgements

I would like to thank Naomi Starkey at SPCK for her heroic patience in waiting for this book. I am also grateful to the Bible Society for providing me with a research assistant at King's College London, which allowed me the extra time necessary to complete this book. Thanks too to David Mackinder, who put in sterling and exacting work on the bibliography. Iwan Russell-Jones and Michael Roberts helped me in conversation to understand more about media and culture. A special thank you to Simon Jenkins for his advice, reflections and friendship, and for editing this book.

Andrew Walker

Preface

This is a book about the Christian gospel and modern culture. It is not written with the academic specialist in mind, although like C.S. Lewis's apologetics books of the 1940s it is intended for the intellectually curious. Perhaps we should call the style 'academic journalism', and this means that there will inevitably be over-simplification of extremely complex issues. Readers are directed to the bibliographical essay at the end of the book if they wish to go beyond the sketches, glosses and impressions presented here to a deeper scholarship.

Telling The Story is a contribution to the movement known as Gospel and Culture, which is centred around the writings of Bishop Lesslie Newbigin. Indeed, the primary purpose of this book is to continue the debate so eloquently begun by Newbigin in *The Other Side of 1984*, and continued in *Foolishness to the Greeks* and *The Gospel in a Pluralist Society*.

Gospel and Culture is essentially a missionary initiative to the First World of advanced industrial societies. It rests on a number of premises, or 'faith commitments'. These are:

- The gospel is not private opinion, but public truth 'once delivered to the saints'. It needs to be re-presented and discovered anew in every historical epoch and national culture.
- This historical gospel has been muzzled by the timidity of the modern Churches in accepting many of the presuppositions of the philosophical Enlightenment which inform contemporary culture.
- Modern culture is itself based on certain often untested

presuppositions, or faith commitments, which themselves need to be tested and tried by the Church in the light of the gospel.

Telling The Story accepts these premises, but it also adds to them two assumptions:

- Consumerism and mass communication are more influential in contemporary culture than academics in universities or scientists in their laboratories.
- Modernity, the scientific-rationalist-industrial culture of the last 200 years, is not merely in advanced decay, but in a process of cultural transition.

If this final assumption is correct, it means that many of the recent popular Christian books on modernity, ranging from Os Guinness's *The Gravedigger File* (1983), my own *Enemy Territory* (1987), and Lesslie Newbigin's *The Gospel in a Pluralist Society* (1990) already begin to read like obituaries for modern culture, rather than contemporary analyses of it. I believe that Professor Thomas Oden has struck the right retrospective note for our passing culture in his book, *Two Worlds: Notes on the Death of Modernity in America and Russia*, while Lawrence Osborn sounds the right note of hope for what is to come in *Restoring the Vision: the Gospel and Modern Culture*.

With their examples in mind, *Telling The Story* looks to the gospel in the future, as well as trying to make sense of both the present and the past.

A Story to Live By

In March 1993, *The Sunday Times* held an open forum at the Dominion Theatre in London to discuss the issues raised by Michael Medved's book, *Hollywood vs. America*. Despite his contentious claims, Medved had successfully brought to the public's attention the value system of a film industry hell-bent on saturating popular culture with images of sex and violence, even though these are often at variance with what many ordinary people want to see.

A lively debate ensued at the Dominion, with *Death Wish* director Michael Winner not surprisingly refusing to accept a link between violent films and anti-social behaviour on the streets. The producer of *Chariots of Fire*, David Putnam, was prepared to accept many aspects of the Medved thesis, and the BBC film critic, the equivocal Barry Norman, conceded that the author of *Hollywood vs. America* might be on to something.

The 'something' that Medved is on to is not that film violence causes real physical assault. It may very well do so, but the many sociological and psychological studies on the causal link between screen violence, street muggings, and domestic batterings are ambiguous and inconclusive. The 'something' is less tangible, but no less insidious, because the suggestion Medved makes is that a continual bombardment of anti-social – and especially violent – images permeates popular culture with a value system at odds with traditional morality.

The problem is not actually that of a new value system versus an old one: the problem is that modern, popular culture champions any and all values. This is so because in a free, consumer-led market, the market, which is amoral, promotes any values so long as they have a market price. Furthermore, the 'right to free expression' habitually overrides community ethics which are not perceived by many citizens as either binding on their lives or as even legitimate. Indeed, it is doubtful whether 'the community' has any meaningful significance in the modern world of individual freedoms. When rights are talked about today, they are perceived as either the ideological 'rightism' of minority cultural interests, or the 'natural rights' of individuals.

But to return to the Dominion theatre debate. One father of three small children voiced an opinion that echoes the concerns of many parents who are confused and bewildered in a morally pluralistic world. He said:

> I feel that all the major institutions are failing me in the task of bringing up my children. The film industry, too, is trying to squirm out of responsibility. What I am asking is: who will give some help to me as a family man to bring up my children with positive values? We form these values through stories. Where are the stories that tell us what kind of people we are as human beings?

Telling The Story is one response to that question. For there is a story, once widely known, that tells us who we are, where we came from, and where we are going. It is a story that was once the official ideology of many an emperor and government (although this in itself is no recommendation, and does not make the story legitimate in any way). More significantly, it is a story that was once celebrated in villages and towns throughout the western world, and gave meaning and hope to millions of ordinary men and women. This story is told by Christians and it is called the gospel. The gospel is the good news of the kingdom of God which has been revealed to us by the birth, life, death and resurrection of Jesus of Nazareth.

In the modern world, this story is now either forgotten, half-remembered, distorted, fragmented, or misrepresented. Alasdair

MacIntyre in his book, *After Virtue*, can help us make some sense of this with the aid of a useful analogy. He asks us to imagine that the natural sciences suffer a catastrophe: a series of environmental disasters are blamed by the public on scientists. Riots occur, scientists are lynched, laboratories are torn down, and books and instruments are burned.

Shortly after these events, a 'know nothing' political movement takes over western culture and abolishes science teaching in schools and universities. The last few scientists are imprisoned and executed. However, over time there is a reaction against this wave of destruction, and a more enlightened generation seek to revive science, although they have largely forgotten what it was.

The problem is that they only possess fragments of the scientific tradition – odd formulas here and there, half-existent chapters from text books, broken instruments, theorems, some calculus. In time, they try to reorganise science around the disciplines of physics, biology and chemistry. Fierce debates rage over the respective merits of relativity theory and evolutionary theory – although they possess only a very partial knowledge of these theories. Cut off from the scientific tradition in itself, and from its canons of consistency and coherence, they are not really doing science in any proper sense at all. They will probably never be able to make sense of what they are doing, and true, natural science will perhaps be irretrievably lost.

Apocalyptic as this might sound, for MacIntyre something like this has already happened to ethics and morality in the modern world. By extrapolation, I think we can say that something akin to this is happening to Christianity.

Of course, analogies are always limited in their application. We cannot say with accuracy that governments are systematically eliminating Christianity from contemporary culture; although we could with some certainty insist that Christian faith has been driven from public life into a privatized world of personal choice and leisure pursuits. In such a domain, private opinion rather than public truth rules, and Christian tradition and canon become increasingly difficult to maintain.

If we move from analogy to history, we can make similar judgments about Christian decline. After all, there was once a time when the Christian story had few competitors in the West, and its ideological dominance was assured. Now, in a pluralistic society, it is merely one story among many in a culture which is overflowing with stories. However, in a world of 'soaps' and commercial advertising, where brand loyalty is notoriously difficult to establish, the stories we tell that are so crucial to our cultural identity, and which are so important in giving us values to live by, are easily disposed of or exchanged for others.

We might say that Christianity has become tangled in the mix. It has had to come to terms with the fact that it can no longer insist – with any realistic hope of being listened to – that its story is *the* story to live by. Christendom certainly no longer exists as a living backdrop against which institutional Christianity can claim protection and support. Vestiges of our Judaeo-Christian heritage can be said to survive in the West – in jurisprudence and common morality, for example – but like MacIntyre's story of science in the future, it is truncated and disconnected from the historical tradition.

The French philosopher, Jean-François Lyotard, has argued that after the eighteenth century, it was no longer possible to talk of our culture as being driven by what he calls 'narratives' such as the Christian gospel – or any narrative that claimed to explain the meaning of life in symbolic or mythical terms. The rational dominance of modernity rendered such narrations impossible. For Lyotard, the Enlightenment generated its own 'myths' of progress, which he calls 'master' or 'meta' narratives, and these myths are no more tenable as stories to give meaning to our lives than their more ancient rivals and precursors.

Strictly speaking, by metanarrative Lyotard has in mind a second-order legitimation of reality, one that begins as a rational account of the world, but ends up as a world-view or as a grand theory of historicist dimensions – Hegelianism in its many forms comes to mind.

In this book, I want to resist the collapse of narratives and support the idea of a 'master narrative', though by that I mean not a second-order philosophical gloss on reality, but what I call a 'grand narrative' – a mythopoeic story that gives meaning and direction to life. This is not historicist in the sense that such a story claims to have found a key to interpret history, like Hegel's dialectic or Evangelical dispensationalism, but it is teleological in the sense that the story, in Tillich's language, is of 'ultimate concern'. In more traditional Christian language, we might say that such a story is turned towards ultimate fulfilment, or towards eschatology – the 'final things'.

The necessity for *homo sapiens* to tell and hear stories, according to Reynolds Price's celebrated essay on narrative, is second only to nourishment. If Price is right, the loss of a mythopoeic or grand narrative for our culture is serious indeed. While we tell endless stories of almost narcotic escape and personal angst, what we are really looking for, Price believes, is something else:

> … credible news that our lives proceed in order towards a pattern which… is ultimately pleasing in the mind of a god who sees a totality and *at last* enacts His will. We crave nothing less than perfect story; and while we chatter or listen all our lives in a din of craving – jokes, anecdotes, novels, dreams, films, plays, songs, half the words of our days – we are satisfied only by the one short tale we feel to be true: *History is the will of a just god who knows us.*

For Christians, 'the one short tale we feel to be true' is the gospel. It is our grand narrative, and one that we wish to recommend to the modern world as a story to live by. The gospel is not, however, the sort of story that we should – even if we could – impose upon western society as official ideology. Christianity has tried this approach since the time of the Roman Emperor Constantine, and the results have at best been mixed.

In biblical times, the good news of the gospel was preached first at Jerusalem before it was taken to the four corners of the world. This is a reminder to us that story-telling, like charity, begins at home. Christians must begin with parochial commitments before gossiping their story abroad, because one of the underlying problems of the modern Churches is that they have forgotten their own story. Reviving the gospel as a grand narrative is a fundamental necessity of Christian identity. Wittgenstein believed that we all need a 'form of life' to live by, but a form in this sense is not an abstract philosophy or a coherent set of principles, it is a way of life, a narrative of belonging. If Christians cannot remember to whom they belong, how can they pass their story on?

Modern society seeks to assimilate all citizens into the mass culture of free-wheeling choice, where community commitments are notoriously difficult to maintain. In this respect, Christians are no different from Jews, Muslims or Mormons, apart from the fact that Muslims and Mormons seem to be more successful in seeing the importance of their story for maintaining cultural identity.

However, the Christian story, essential though it is for maintaining cultural identity in a world which is hostile to the absolute claims of organized religion, is also a story that is meant to be shared with others. This is not to say that all other stories are to be rubbished, or to say (to paraphrase the Anglican prayer book) that there is no health in them, but it does mean that the Christian story is one which Christians believe has universal significance. In this respect, it is odd to suggest, as some do, that Churches should not engage in mission or evangelism, for the story is good news for a despairing world.

With these thoughts in the background, this book focuses on telling the gospel story as mission to western contemporary culture. Part one begins by suggesting that the gospel needs to be understood as a story of hope for the world. We begin with hope, for it is the conviction of the Gospel and Culture movement that mission activity should be determined by the content of faith and not the context of culture. Too much attention to culture distorts the message, and Christianity becomes not inculturated but domesticated.

We need, as missionaries, to see the culture in which we live from inside the narrative of our story, and not as strangers to our own tradition. Perhaps for a Muslim this is obvious, but for a westerner, this has become a very strange idea.

Part one continues by providing historical snapshots of the transmission of the gospel to the present day, paying attention to the larger cultural context and its effects on that transmission. This section applies Walter Ong's thesis of *Orality and Literacy* to the telling of the gospel. Ong shows how the invention of printing radically altered the communication of earlier cultures, which were essentially oral in nature. He also suggests – although he devotes only two pages to it in his book – that electronic processes are now altering the nature of literary culture.

With the help of Neil Postman's *Amusing Ourselves To Death*, and with some insights from the postmodernist sociologist Jean Baudrillard, Ong's thesis is extended to include the gospel and electronic culture – although we will leave consideration of electric culture as mass culture to part two. Part one ends with a reconsideration of the significance, and possible primacy, of oral culture for the Christian story. This issue is explored in the context of a world where literary culture is being overtaken by an electronic culture, which Ong calls 'the second orality'.

To insist that Christian mission should be driven by the gospel story does not mean that we can remain indifferent to our cultures. Clearly, too little attention to our cultural context leads to a failure of communication. Part two, therefore, switches its attention to examining the nature of modernity as the cultural epoch in which our grandparents, we ourselves, and our children have lived their lives. In particular, we will be drawing on the sociology of knowledge approach associated with Peter Berger, Thomas Luckman, and James Davison Hunter. We will see in what ways modernity thwarts the gospel, and, in turn, in what ways the gospel can speak to the situation of today.

Following this examination, we will sift the evidence that modernity is itself now in transition to postmodernity, and what this tells us about the future of western mission. Lastly, we will explore the idea that the Christian story is a gospel of hope for a world that no longer has any story to live by. The gospel should not be seen, however, as a grand narrative whose sole purpose is to shore up western civilization – however laudable an aim this might be. Arguably, Schleiermacher, with his 'perpetual alliance' between Christianity and culture, and Troeltsch, with his 'creative compromise' of Church and state, tended to forget that the purpose of the story is not to improve the world but to turn people away from its false hopes and self-delusions. Christianity is in effect a rescue mission for humankind, for through the telling of the story, people find themselves enabled to indwell it, make the story their own, and discover in it ultimate concern – their true end.

PART ONE

The Gospel Story and its Cultural Transmission

1

The Gospel as Story

In 1983, Lesslie Newbigin's first draft for his book, *The Other Side of 1984*, was being discussed in the British Council of Churches by a distinguished group of churchmen and women, including bishops and leading theologians. The question arose: 'Well, what is the gospel anyway?' Only two of the people present were prepared to hazard a guess.

This is shocking, but it is not so surprising. It is a feature of much biblical scholarship these days that hermeneutical, literary and historical methods unravel the scriptures in such sophisticated ways that while we can now identify a midrash, Q source, or the hand of a late interpolator in the pastoral epistles, we find it increasingly difficult to find a central message in the Bible.

Losing the wood for the trees

The emphasis on the good news of the scriptures, which was once so central to the early Church, has been replaced today by a packet of fragmented evangels. Where once the Fathers could call the books of the four evangelists 'the gospel', on the grounds that they bore witness to a single, though developing, story, today we analyse in what ways Matthew, Mark, Luke and John are different Gospels.

Of course, not everyone feels that the gospel as the good news is entirely lost in the Rorschach blot of New Testament scholarship. Others have peered deep into the scriptures and found what they think is the essence of the *kerygma*, which they have re-appropriated and translated into the gospel of process metaphysics or the existentialist gospel. Alternatively, the good news has been transformed into the radical political terms of liberation – of the poor, the ethnic group, or the oppressed sex.

This is not to say that the gospel is not concerned with these things, but it does mean that in themselves these are not the gospel of Bible and Church as understood by historic and credal Christianity. Perhaps this is also another way of saying, in the words of Gabriel Josipovici, that modern readers of the Bible no longer understand it to be 'the book of God' in which the Creator reveals to his creatures his purposes for the world. The very fact that many of us now approach the Bible with the same scientific curiosity as any other interesting object of study has led to an inability to read the ancient writings as a sacred text. Our archaeological and increasingly literary approaches to the Bible bring us ever new insights into its sources and construction, but these gains have to be balanced by what Georges Florovsky has called 'the loss of the scriptural mind'. This loss, this failure to see the wood for the trees, is endemic in the modern Church. We no longer know what the gospel means.

The creation of the gospel story as the grand narrative of the Church

Walter Brueggemann has recently reminded us, in a useful *aide memoire*, that the noun 'gospel' in the Bible, *euangelion*, is not merely a rhetorical declaration of glad tidings but a message of great import. This message he says is linked to the Hebrew verb, *bissar*, 'tell the news'. The gospel, therefore, is not only the central message of the Christian faith: it is both the story and its telling. It is only by telling the story that the message becomes gospel: 'How then shall they call on him in whom they have not believed? and how shall they believe in him of whom they have not heard? and how shall they hear without a preacher?' (Romans 10.14).

Historically, the gospel as a grand narrative was predicated – not overnight, but over a protracted period of history and experience – upon a number of interlinked Old and New Testament narrations. This also included both the ordering of these narrations, and theological reflection upon them by the apostles, Fathers, and doctors of the early Church.

There was a certain amount of jostling in the order, not least because of the tension between Jews and Gentiles in the first Christian centuries. Jesus as a Jew was seen by many Jewish followers as the Messiah of Israel; and yet as Emmanuel – God with us – he was also seen to be a figure of universal significance. The story was also not an *idée fixe*. This is not quite to say that it was a moveable feast – the sweep of the story was clear enough – but it was a story rich in narrative possibilities and subtle interpretations. Origen's imaginative and brilliant typological hermeneutics, for example, greatly influenced the Church's homiletics from the second century. More straightforwardly, the story took time to be fully explicated, although it was operational from the time of the apostles. This is understandable when we consider that it took the Church Fathers nearly five centuries to hammer out an authoritative doctrine of the person of Jesus, a process which culminated in the Council of Chalcedon in AD 451.

Given these caveats, and granting that there is more than one way to tell a tale, we can identify the interpretative narrations – the chapters – which when interleaved together formed the grand narrative:

1. Outside time and space there is God who is good and lives in loving and perfect communion as Father, Son and Holy Spirit.
2. God calls time and space into existence with the creation of the cosmos out of nothing, and like its creator this universe is also very good.
3. Creation includes the formation of our world, where human beings are made in the image of God. This gives them the power freely to follow God or reject him.
4. Humankind, however, wilfully rebels against God. This results in enmity between people and God and the estrangement of all

creation from its source – this is so because human beings, as 'matter made articulate', betray all of creation.

5. God takes the initiative to end this estrangement, because his nature is love. First he chooses a human tribe, the Jews, and establishes a special relationship with them in order to demonstrate his desire to restore communion with the human race. Second, after several hundreds of years of favoured treatment, to show that he wishes to extend this special relationship to the whole world, he enters the physical universe through the incarnation of his eternal Son. He is joined to created matter – human nature – in the person of Jesus of Nazareth.

6. Jesus achieves God's desire to restore the broken communion between himself and creation through his birth, life, death, resurrection and ascension.

7. During his lifetime, Jesus Christ calls disciples as the authentic witnesses to and co-participators of his work. Through them he *institutes* a Church, an *ecclesia* – the people of God. The people of God, in all generations, do not merely follow their founder, but are organically linked to him by divine favour, though not by nature. This is accomplished by the Holy Spirit, who is sent by Jesus from his Father after the resurrection. The Holy Spirit *constitutes* the Church.

8. The people of God, under the Spirit's guidance, are the bearers of the good news of God's restoration of the world through Jesus. They are bearers in the double sense that they are guardians of the apostolic 'deposit of faith', and the tellers of the story.

9. The good news will not end like the final chapter of a book, because it is a never-ending story which continues beyond time in everlasting communion with God. But it will reach its fulfilment at the end of time, when Christ will return in glory so that 'God may be all in all'.

These narrations, or chapters, of the story, centred as they are around the Christ event, can be (and have been) differently arranged in many respects. They have been embellished, added to, and subtracted from. The early Church, for example, made much of the role of 'the Evil One' – the fallen angel, Lucifer – highlighting the conflict of good and evil in the universe. This ran the risk of overplaying the Devil's hand in what we might see today as a heightened dualism. Or again, the way in which Jesus achieved human redemption or reconciliation through his life and passion varies from Church Father to Father. Many different theories of atonement are available to us from Irenaeus, Augustine, and the other Fathers.

Nevertheless, despite the flexibility of the story, its various orderings and differing interpretations, the narrations as chapters of the master narrative of the Church were in place from apostolic times. Some chapters, such as the resurrection narrative, were already well developed in the New Testament, while others, such as the understanding of God as Trinity, were more sketchy. If we want to say that the apologetical and patristic ages rounded and developed a fuller version of the master narrative, then we must recognize that this also means that from the earliest centuries Christians knew the gospel story and allowed it to form their identity and character as the people of God.

To claim, however, that the gospel is the grand narrative of the Church does not mean that it can be heard and read like a detective novel, a fairy tale, or a Norseman's saga (although parts of it can be translated into these literary genres). Nor is it to say that the story is simply a plain factual narrative – the gospel is certainly not a documentary of historical events. To say that the gospel is story is to suggest that it is more like a story than any other kind of discourse. It is not the banter of everyday conversation, though it may be the subject of gossip. Neither is it philosophy, psychology, or literary criticism – though it has provided enticing speculation in these, and other, academic fields of enquiry.

Admittedly, the gospel as story does not leap off the pages of the Bible ready-made. As we have seen, the story is the grand narrative of the people of God, and this narrative is gleaned from the scriptures.

Under the inspiration of the Spirit, so the people believe, the story takes shape. However, just because the Bible is not like a pop-up book does not mean that the gospel is hidden and trapped in the text, waiting to be released from the restricting overlays of dogma by some gnostic know-it-all. The gospel may not be located in the text, but it is focused there in Jesus of Nazareth, the person identified by St John as 'the Word': the telling-forth, or self-revealing of God. This self-revelation of God comes from his very being, in the way that an only son uniquely participates in the nature of his father (John 3.16).

Because God reveals himself in Jesus, we might say, in Lesslie Newbigin's memorable phrase, that the gospel is an 'open secret': it is open to all who have ears to hear. This open secret turns out to be nothing less than the story of – and the story behind – the life, words and person of God's Son. John, in concert with the synoptic Gospels, also identifies this Son and Word of God as the Christ, which brings together the Hebrew and Christian narrations into one grand story: 'For the law was given by Moses, but grace and truth came by Jesus Christ' (John 1.17).

If we follow John, as the early Church followed him, then telling the story of Jesus has the character of great myth and history intertwined, because the gospel takes us from metahistory to history. We find that the story of Jesus is also God's own story. It is the story of his personality and his relationship to the world.

Many modern theologians prefer to begin with the Christ of history, and try to work upwards towards understanding in what way we may say that Jesus is divine. However, this approach is really a function of modern sensibilities. The anthropological Jesus is the logical place to start, rather than the Christ of faith, if one's theology is determined by the methods of historical research, rather than by a belief in God's self-disclosure to us through his Son.

The idea of the incarnation as a divine event suggests that something happened from God to us. This approach is quite different in character to one which tries to grasp the incarnation as a mythological rendering of history, or as a metaphor that speaks to us of the encounter of the human and divine in one personality.

The early Church Fathers did not understand theology to be a primary function of reason any more than they worked with a concept of a divine Jesus over and against a human Jesus. They believed that the gospel, as a whole, pointed to Jesus as the unique revelation of God-in-man.

Telling the story, however, is more than a tale about the life of the God-man. It is to discover that its central focus, Jesus himself, is also knowable – unlike the characters in a work of fiction or a history book. This is possible, so the story goes, because although Jesus as a figure of history is the object of the story, he is also, as God's Word, the author of the story. As author and originator of the story, he transcends history as the Christ of faith. Following him in faith is to be drawn in to God's story, which then becomes our own.

The gospel therefore begins for us as a story, and becomes not only a living drama in which we can play our part, but also takes on the numinous quality of a great myth, where we become more like gods than fallen mortals.

Such a high-sounding myth takes on the character of a great cosmological epic – which is one legitimate way to see it. However, in order that we should understand the down-to-earth seriousness and life-transforming experience of the story, we find that the New Testament often talks of the gospel as something which needs to be 'announced' (*anangello*) or 'proclaimed' (*kerygma*). There is a 'hear ye, hear ye' tone that is unmistakable. The gospel is not a call to a fantasy existence, but a call to people everywhere radically to change direction – to abandon old stories and become a living part of God's story. 'The time is fulfilled, and the kingdom of God is at hand: repent and believe in the gospel' – these are the opening words of Jesus' ministry (Mark 1.15).

The good news message has an objective character about it, as if the story is not merely arresting, but binding on those who listen and believe. St Paul tells us that he stands under the judgment or authority of the gospel (Galatians 1.8). It is true that faith comes through hearing, but the ability to hear aright is a function of the objective character of the word of God (Romans 10.17).

This objective character of the evangel is reflected in the fact that the New Testament contains accounts of the story which see God's appearance in it as a shock – a rupture of normal events – which confirms the authenticity of the story. What can be more shocking for the author of an epic drama to stride onto the stage half-way through its production and declare before the final curtain call that the end is not merely in sight, but already here in person!

Metaphorically, we might say that if it were possible, the hills would have clapped their hands and the stones cried out to announce God's coming into the world. And yet, beyond metaphor, and with respect to the German theologian Rudolf Bultmann, there is also an ecclesial realism at work in the gospel story that undergirds its objective character.

The incarnation is presented to us in St Luke and St Matthew not only like a fairy-tale account of the story's origins, but also as an event in space and time that enabled God's story to become our own. St Mark's gospel in particular is clearly a form of narrative history – admittedly edited – in which we are presented with reportage of actual events which are markedly different from the a-historical, once-upon-a-time stories of Esther or Job.

Neither the Fathers, the Catholic divines, nor the Reformers doubted the objective and realistic character of the gospel story, although they did not see it merely as an historical or empirical story. It remained for them both metaphysical and an historical reality of the material world. They realized that while the story in reality began beyond time, by the interpenetration of that reality in creation through the incarnation, it took on the phenomenal characteristics of space and time, of history and place, and of the chronology of observable events.

It is precisely because the gospel emerged in history that we have to understand it as also incarnated in a culture. It did not fall from the skies with the swiftness of a meteor, nor was it received from space like a radio signal. Bishop Rowan Williams is quite right to insist that we will look in vain for a 'pure gospel', if by that we mean an original message as if wafted to earth from Gabriel's horn. The good news is both God speaking to us and us speaking of God, but it is also a cultural product – brought to life by the person and deeds of Jesus – and forged in the crucible of cross-cultural developments. Strictly speaking, it is not even a Jewish product, because the gospel comes to us from Israel under Roman tutelage, and in the language of the Greeks.

Can the story stay the same over time?

The gospel as a story is both a product of early Christian culture and the grand narrative that drives that culture, but stories change over time. Is it reasonable to assume that the gospel story of the early centuries is still the same today? This is an important question, because a story is not like a simple mathematical theorem. There is a logical constancy, for example, in the formula $2+2=4$ that holds across cultural and historical boundaries. But the gospel, as we have already noticed, is not lodged in a text: it resides in a person. The 'what think you of this man?' calls for an existential response, and such a response will be influenced by the culture of the respondent.

We can see the different ways in which cultures have responded to Jesus in their religious iconography. The ancient Syrian Church of South India, for example, presents Jesus as the guru complete with turban. Quite naturally, the Ethiopian Jesus is black, and the Russian Orthodox Christ is Russified and noticeably softer and more recognisably human than the stylized and stern Jesus of Byzantium.

The fact that Jesus and his story are responded to in various ways by people in different societies is a reflection of the diversity of human culture and human personality. But does the story as a story remain much the same? Although the story did not emerge overnight, and has changed in emphasis and detail over time, it has remained remarkably constant – at least until the modern era.

This is so because the story as grand narrative has special features which have enabled it to ride the roller coaster of cultural change without serious loss of content. Many stories are quickly distorted in the telling, such as the whispered sentence in the party game which soon mutates into something which sounds the same but has lost its original content. If, however, stories have a deep moral seriousness, and more importantly an obvious mythic and sacred quality, this militates against mutation and transformation. At least, it does this if the content of the story is remembered and repeated in a form which helps maintain the integrity and intention of the storytellers.

Two features of the telling of the story were crucial for the development of the gospel. One was the fact that the evangel emerged and spread in a culture that was primarily oral. Contrary to popular imagination, oral culture, as we will see, facilitates repetition and faithful remembrance. Secondly, although Christianity developed in cultures which were essentially pre-literate, the Church's story was always warranted by the scriptures, and facilitated by liturgies which had the special character of being not merely serious but sacred.

It is unwise to try to separate Bible from worship in the early Church. The liturgical, credal, and scriptural canons emerged together, and together they became the crucible in which the grand narrative was forged. But in order to see how the gospel story was successfully handed down through the ages, we must turn to its progress from oral to literary culture.

2

Handing the Story On

Oral cultures rely for their continuity, their cultural transmission, on personal reminiscence and the art of remembrance. This art is the re-telling of stories in ceremony, ritual, symbol, solemn repetition and poetry. It is, in fact, all those things that our modern cultures think of as peripheral, redundant, or epiphenomenal to cultural life. Not that we know nothing of these things. Every British school girl and boy knows that we 'remember, remember the fifth of November' – and not because we look up our history books to read how in 1605 there was a failed Catholic plot to blow up the Houses of Parliament. We remember it because every 5th November we build a bonfire, burn the guy, and celebrate with fireworks.

Another vestige of an earlier era is the use of mnemonic devices for learning: 'remember remember…' is itself one. Another is: 'Thirty days hath September, April, June and November…' Some people still tie a knot in their handkerchief so that they will not forget something of importance.

But we have to make a great effort of imagination to realize that before the invention of printing – the technologizing of the word – and the Renaissance and Reformation periods of western civilization, most ways of remembering, learning and understanding took place in a context in which texts were virtually absent from the general populace. When texts were available, they were often considered to be of a sacred and authoritative nature and were to be housed in a sacred place – namely a church or monastery.

Oral culture and storytelling

Christianity developed in the early centuries in much the same way as it had begun in Aramaic oral culture. To our knowledge, there never was an Aramaic text of the gospel, and Jesus as the source of the Christian story left no written records about it. In so far as texts played a significant part in early Christianity, they did so because they were already recollections of the sayings and events of Jesus and the apostles. The Bible takes on its sacred character for the Church not because it is dictated by God, but precisely because it is the inspired doctrine of the apostles who had received it, as it were, from the horse's mouth.

Of great importance, too, was the conviction of the Church Fathers that there was an unbroken continuity between the apostles and the developing Church. In the second century, for example, Irenaeus believed that he was a direct descendant of the apostles, for he was a student of Polycarp, who was himself a disciple of St John. It is this continuity with the tradition handed down that became inextricably linked with an attempt to reconstruct it in such a way that it would not be distorted or forgotten. Apostolic succession in the early centuries of the Church was not so much an entitlement, through the laying on of hands, as a duty to hand on the doctrine of the apostles.

We can see here the absolute distinction between ancient and modern cultures. For the ancients, tradition is sacred, sacrosanct, inviolable. For the early Christians, the story, including the events recorded in the Old Testament, must not be forgotten because it is God's story. To falsify it was to betray the apostles. For moderns, and modernism in particular, tradition is the enemy of progress, reason and rational development.

For many modern Christians, the gospel story is no longer sacred in itself, a vehicle of grace and revelation. Its very ancientness makes it historically suspect, and its miraculous and supernatural narrations jar with modern sensibilities, which have been force-fed in a hothouse of realistic narratives. Read of miraculous happenings, and we translate either to the rational category 'false', or to the literary category 'fairy story'. In both cases we read 'unhistorical'.

However, oral traditions in themselves cannot be dismissed as unhistorical so easily. Admittedly, they do present obvious problems for the historian, but in recent years, in the light of ethnomusicology and anthropological studies, greater credence has been given to their historical veracity. Much has been learned, for example, from the folk songs and slave tales in the pre-Civil War period of North American history. In Levine's book, *Slaves and Black Consciousness*, we discover that slave stories were remembered by the slaves because for them to remember was to be reminded of who they were. No doubt stories were embellished in the telling, but grandmother's knee was the place that many a slave child, and later free African-Americans, learned to remember and relive the horror of slavery and sing again the songs of freedom.

The telling of tales in oral cultures is so crucial because, to reiterate an earlier point, continuity of culture cannot rely on anything other than memory and internalizing the habits and mores of tradition through rote and mimicry. If the tradition is not accepted as authoritative through faithful copying or reconstruction, the culture will die.

What Levine calls 'the sacred world of the slave', with its unique and impressive liturgy, failed to survive once slavery was abolished, and the necessary conditions for a sacred, though closed, society disappeared. Racial or tribal memory, in order to be faithfully conserved, has to be handed down in a culture which is relatively static and receptive to its history. It needs also to be couched in a form which is both recognizable and repeatable. The 'trickster' tales of American slavery, such as *Brer Rabbit*, for example, became a favourite genre of the slaves, for they were not only good stories but coded ones: Brer Rabbit represented the smart African-American who could outwit his white enemies. Today, a distorted and distant trickster tradition still lingers on in mainstream America in the 'trick or treat' of Hallowe'en.

Another successful medium of cultural transmission in many oral cultures is the mythopoeic storytelling which we call epic, or saga. The metre and rhythm of such poetry is self-consciously formalized and repetitious, so that in its recital or singing, the story can be clearly and faithfully retold. Homer's *Odyssey* and *Iliad* are perhaps the best-known examples from antiquity. The Christian grand narrative also lends itself to epic representation: God the Father sends his Son to redeem the world; the world rejects him, yet he defeats death by death, rises from the grave, and returns triumphant to his Father; now he waits to return to the world, which this time will acknowledge him as Lord.

A rendition of an epic or saga in oral culture was not a time for excessive innovation, or individual embellishment. Instead, it was a time for the bard to retell with accuracy but intense feeling the old, old story. Parents today know full well how children can be upset if they do not hear their favourite nursery stories told they way they like it.

Similarly, the pleasure of hearing the saga retold in the past was to hear it faithfully repeated over and over again. We must realize, however, that this was not just a question of conventional wisdom or good form: it was essential to the literary genre. Introduce excessive novelty into the story, or pepper the narrative with transient idioms, and the poem can no longer be remembered and transmitted. This, no doubt, is why the Good News Bible is so notoriously difficult to commit to memory.

The way in which the Church developed its storytelling in oral culture in the early centuries was not through camp-fire sagas, but through the drama of liturgy. And in this area, as in so much more, Christian liturgical drama owes much to its Jewish heritage. This is not only true in terms of sacred text and the appropriation and adapting of temple and synagogue worship. It is also true because of the significance in Jewish culture, even today, of learning to remember.

When you hear people say such things as: 'I do wish the Jews would not go on about the holocaust', you might as well ask them to cut off their right arm. Remembering those evil days, keeping them alive so that the injustice and pain will never be forgotten, is very deeply ingrained in Jewish consciousness. Perhaps we forget that Judaism has always been a religion of a people chosen by a God who acted in history through great events of sorrow and triumph.

The history of Israel from the beginning was one of promise, pilgrimage, possession of land and power, exile, and return. This almost cyclical sense of history – although for the Jews, time was not circular as it was in antiquity – has a spiritual counterpart: obedience, rebellion, apostasy, repentance and renewal. It is necessary for the Jews to remember these stories because, like the descendants of the American slaves, recollecting tells you who you are. Who you are is a function of where you come from; and from whence you came is the source of hope that tells you where you are going; and the going hence is to turn again either to a literal homeland or your spiritual home – the heartland.

In terms of the Christian story, the gospel of hope, which is prospective, is based on what God has done in history, which is retrospective. Hope, without foundation in what God has already done, is void: 'But if there be no resurrection of the dead, then is Christ not risen: And if Christ be not risen then is our preaching vain, and your faith is also vain' (1 Corinthians 15.13-14).

In the early Christian centuries, the gospel story, despite all its Hellenistic mysteries and Latin legalisms, and notwithstanding its analogical, philosophical theologizing and its neo-Platonism, never lost the Hebrew necessity for remembrance, nor its art of doing so. This art of remembrance is how we preserved the story – how it was handed on.

Oral culture and sacred liturgy

Jewishness survives in Christian liturgy in a quite direct way. Early Christian worship, for example, was the 'meeting' or *synaxis* of the synagogue – with its greetings, lections, homily, psalmody and benediction – plus the eucharist. The Torah was replaced by the readings from the gospel, epistle, and Hebrew scriptures. Deacons took the place

25

of cantors, and even the central sacraments of baptism and communion had their origins in Jewish practices.

It is true that anti-Semitism existed in the Church from the beginning, but as the holy orders of bishops, presbyters and deacons began to take shape in the first two centuries after Christ, there emerged what amounted to a re-invention or reconstruction of the priesthood of the tabernacle and early temple worship. By the time of Constantine, the increasing use of vestments was legitimized by an almost slavish copying of Old Testament priestly garments – although vestments themselves initially developed from the *haute couture* of the aristocratic classes of the Roman Empire.

To be exact, what developed in the great liturgies of Constantinople and Rome from the third to the fifth centuries was a strange amalgam of a reconstructed Levitical priesthood, with the trappings of the Roman emperor and his entourage. The 'holy doors' in the centre of the iconostasis, which separated the sanctuary from the people (the tabernacle motif is clear here), are also known as the 'royal doors', for only the emperor and the bishop could pass through them. This echoed the temporal and spiritual powers, as represented by the Davidic and Levitical dynasties. Perhaps this is the origin of the Erastianism that has so bedevilled the eastern Churches.

And if in the East and West the ark of the covenant was replaced behind the altar screen by the 'holy table' of eucharistic sacrifice, in Ethiopia the sanctuary contained a replica of that ark. But now the shekinah glory of Yahweh was understood to be the uncreated light of the transfigured, resurrected and ascended Christ, who still resided with his people in the 'holy mysteries'.

These snapshots of early liturgy remind us that Christianity has to be properly seen as a Jewish-Gentile hybrid, and not as a pure Jewish offshoot. If Judaism was essentially a religion of the ear, as Islam and Protestantism would later be, early Christianity developed a healthy balance of the eye and ear. Or to be exact, at its best it did so. We will later argue that what Camille Paglia has called the 'western aggressive eye' shifted medieval Europe towards pagan decadence – a view, ironically, shared by high Puritans and the Eastern Orthodox.

For now, it is sufficient to stress that although oral cultures do not rely for their continuity on written texts – even if written texts exist, as they did with Christianity – this does not mean that they persist only through the spoken word. Indeed, most pre-industrial cultures are replete with art, symbol, totem, and religious artefacts. Christian culture combined the oral austerity of its Jewish past with the visual artfulness of pagan antiquity. That was its original cultural genius.

This does not mean that there was absolutely no biblical basis for an iconic presentation of the gospel. We often forget, for example, that although St John talks of Jesus as the *logos*, or 'Word', St Paul prefers the language of *eikon*, or 'image' of the Father (see 2 Corinthians 4.4 and Colossians 1.15). The author of the book of Hebrews writes of God's Son as 'the brightness of God's glory, and the express image of his person' (Hebrews 1.3).

This combined use of ear and eye meant that the Christian grand narrative was not so much preached or recited in the liturgy: it was presented dramaturgically with costumes, lights, food, music, and in some cases sacred dance. Music was hotly disputed in the early Church – the Desert Fathers in the fourth century saw it as 'demonic theatre'. But it was the creation of heretical popular songs, such as Arius's 'Thalia' in the fourth century, that forced the Church to retaliate with its own versions.

The early Christian liturgies were a re-telling of the divine drama of salvation, centred upon a re-presentation of the main events of the life of Christ, the apostles, and the patriarchs and prophets of old. This drama was housed in an appropriate 'theatre', which was reflected in the very architecture of the church building. In the East, for example, during the first millennium, the ideal church was round, representing the cosmos. The painted Jesus who looked down from the domed ceiling was the *pantokrator*: the ascended Lord and judge of the universe. In western (and some eastern) churches, the narthex represented the fallen world, the nave stood for heaven, and the separated sanctuary signified God's holiness and transcendent glory.

When in the East the people gathered to worship at the great eucharistic feast, the deacon began with the solemn announcement, 'blessed is the kingdom…', for it was assumed in the sacred space of the consecrated church that God was indeed present in an act of self-disclosure. To enter church was to remember the passion of Christ, and yet to be with him in the present. If the liturgy was not quite yet heaven, it was understood to be a foretaste of the kingdom to come. 'O taste and see that the Lord is good' was an invitation to the banqueting meal of the heavenly bridegroom, where God, his angelic creation and his people met in communion.

For the Fathers, just as Jacob's ladder in the book of Genesis witnessed a two-way traffic of angels on the ladder between heaven and earth, so too was the earthly Church literally surrounded by a heavenly 'cloud of witnesses'. This eschatological or kingdom sense of coming together is reflected in the fact that the distinction between Church militant and Church triumphant is foreign to the eastern Churches.

In both the early western and eastern liturgies, the story of salvation was woven into the very structure of the Church services, for it moved inexorably from God the Trinity to the passion and death of God in Christ, and ended with the triumph of resurrection. The structure of movement from life, to death, to new life was punctuated by the readings from the sacred Hebrew and Greek texts. Throughout the liturgy, there was the celebration of God through the chants of the old Psalter and the songs of the new covenant.

The movement of the priest from the sanctuary to the larger auditorium represented God's decisive action in the incarnation. The holy of holies existed but it was breached: the doors were opened, just as the way was now open from God to humankind.

Throughout the Middle Ages in both East and West, the people responded to the events and movements of the liturgy in both a formal and subjective way. When the Bible was brought out of the sanctuary, worshippers inclined their heads in veneration, for God's own story was being audibly told. In the East, when they partook of holy communion, they crossed their arms and kissed the cup of blessing.

During the frequent calling on God's name, the congregation crossed themselves, an action which reminded them simultaneously of the cross and of the divine Trinity. They might also have wept, knelt or prostrated themselves when they were overcome with sorrow or joy. They would not have been condemned for emotional display, within culturally acceptable bounds, for the objective structure of the liturgy was not affected.

Inside the eastern church, peasants could wander from icon to icon, which was for them their contact with 'theology in colour' – for virtually every nuance and brush stroke of the painting had its theological significance. The priest would explain the stories of Jesus and the saints to the congregation through the icons, much as children in Protestant Sunday schools used to be taught by the 'flannelgraph' from the First World War until very recently. More tellingly, for the early Christians the icons were windows onto heaven, just as the Bible opened the way to the living Word.

Both word and image in early liturgy expressed the dogmatic teaching of the Church. Icons, like plainsong, were designed to enhance the word, and not to detract from it. Nowhere is this more clear than in the icon of Jesus as the Logos, where we see that our Lord is holding the Gospel of St John open at chapter 14, verse 6: 'I am the way, the truth, and the life: no man cometh unto the Father, but by me.'

Being in church, with its food, smells, lights, body language, Bible stories and homilies, was to be rooted in the material world with its linear time and structure. And yet the liturgy, with its many component rites and customs, was seen in itself to be a living symbol of God's kingdom. To adapt Lampert's use of symbol and apply it to liturgy, we might say that, 'though it is immersed in the world of empirical existence and is perceived empirically, it is yet essentially turned towards the transcendent, transcends the given reality and at the same time immanentizes the transcendent, thus realising and revealing it.'

The Fathers called the liturgy the 'divine liturgy', precisely because it was where God and his people met as if the end had already come. It was where eschatological time had replaced the necessary time of created existence. This is more important than it appears, for Christian liturgy, unlike most pagan services, was more concerned with redeeming time than creating a sacred space in the world. If we can properly say that church was a sacred place, this was not because of some kind of animist conception of divinized matter, but because it was where God was encountered.

The weekly eucharistic liturgy, celebrated everywhere on Sunday by the end of the second century, was buttressed every other day with prayers and songs for morning and evening. These prayers within the church, and supremely in the monasteries, became also the prayers of the people at home. The extension of the Church into the home was another direct link with the earlier oral Jewish tradition.

The Sunday liturgy was really a microcosm of the liturgical year, which not only followed the natural pattern of nature – spring, summer, autumn, winter – but also captured the great events of salvation. The doxology of yearly worship was thus punctuated by the periods of Lent, the great celebrations of the Annunciation and Advent, Christmas, Epiphany, Easter and Pentecost. Other events crowded in, such as the transfiguration of Christ, and the celebration of the martyrdom of Stephen.

In time, every day became a remembrance day of little narrations, which made up the grander narrative of the liturgical calendar. Such narrations were not only of the life of Jesus, the patriarchs of Israel, and the apostles, but also of the martyrs and saints of the Church. Just as the epistle to the Hebrews retold the great stories of the faithful saints of the Old Testament, the Church remembered its post-biblical heroes and stories. In eastern and western Churches, birthdays were less significant than 'naming days', when the children, always named after a hero of the faith, would celebrate their saint's day.

The Church and the wider culture

The telling of the story in oral culture was faithfully to remember and re-enact through liturgy the events of salvation. But there were also elaborations on the great themes of redemption, as well as indulging the medieval passion for hagiography. Church customs and stories spilled over into the larger folk culture and become adulterated with existing pagan rituals. We see this tendency even today, in the sun-worshipping cults of Peru, for example, or voodoo in Haiti.

Conversely, many pagan symbols entered the Church. They were not rejected, because it was believed that unless they were intrinsically evil, they could be transfigured and made into signs of the kingdom. In Celtic Britain, even the Druidic symbols were exorcized, Christianized, and incorporated into the Christian cross. The solstice celebrations of pagan Rome were turned into Christmas, which was the last of the great Christian festivals to be incorporated into the Church.

Sometimes folk tales were added to the gospel to bring greater texture and colour to the story. Even after the Reformation, we can recall Luther's carol of the infant Jesus, 'Away in a Manger', with its lowing cattle, even though there is no biblical basis for this much-loved rural tableau. Admittedly, the Middle Ages also saw the beginnings of the cult of Mary as *theotokos*, the 'God-bearer', although there were no dogmatic doctrines attached to the pious traditions surrounding her. It was not until the fifteenth century, when the Middle Ages had waned and decadence abounded in the Catholic Church, that widespread heresy emerged concerning the 'mother of God' among the peasantry. A popular representation of the Madonna was a statue of her which opened to reveal in her womb the Father, the Son and the Holy Ghost!

The Church may have been a cult within the wider culture, a world within a world, but it was never a closed world unto itself. It inherited not only the songs and folk tales of popular culture, but also borrowed the pomp, splendour and mystery from the courts of the Roman emperor. To this day, the Eastern Orthodox Church marries husband

and wife in imitation of the splendid coronation of Byzantium. The exchange of crowns is a wonderful symbol of both stewardship and kingship, and yet is not in itself directly gleaned from the story of Israel and the coming of the Messiah.

Similarly, both Catholics and Protestants have inherited a marriage ceremony that harks back to the legal contracts of ancient Rome. The legalism of 'till death us do part' is both foreign to the Greek East and to the New Testament, but it is not noticeable that western Christians think of it as odd or in contradiction of *sola scriptura*. More to the point is that all these embellishments and additions to the story did not affect either the sweep of the divine drama, or break up the grand narrative in any way. Some might want to say that they detracted from it, or even distorted it, but there is no legitimate case for saying that they were able seriously to subvert it.

Up until now in this section, we have been looking at what amounts to a highly selected, compressed and idealized ethnography of early gospel culture. We have not been following the great political events of Christendom, for it is important to recall that there was a culture of Christian life that operated at the village and local level that was not dependent on the politics of history, but rather existed through the exigency of liturgy and local custom. Until the Reformation, it was liturgy that conserved the gospel as story and, along with the magisterium of the Church, interpreted it for the masses, even though popular piety was often heretical, if not pagan. This was so because oral cultures are friendly to all religions, and not only to the Christian faith.

Most people in medieval Europe were peasants. For them, the gospel story was not supremely the official story of the empire: it was the story that gave meaning to their community, their village or small town, their world. Pre-industrial and feudal societies change little over the centuries. For them, time is cyclical like the seasons, and not linear, as it becomes in the modern world which believes in progress.

The gospel story was conserved, then, and successfully transmitted by oral tradition. We cannot say that this was a pure oral tradition, because writing (chirography) was in existence before the birth of Christ, and sacred texts reinforced the orality of the Christian story. Nevertheless, only a small proportion of the Christian population could read, and the Middle Ages remained predominantly an oral rather than a literary culture.

During this time, the very fact that the gospel was seen to have been handed down 'from the beginning' gave it added legitimacy. The story was, as we have admitted, embellished in the telling as it was in the making. It also had to compete with many handed-down local traditions and pagan rituals. A theology of culture will tell us that we should not expect Christianity to be miraculously immune from the normal processes of cultural development. The Word of God himself appeared not merely in human form and Jewish context, but in fallible flesh. Therefore, to insist on the divine inspiration of the Bible, and what we might call the Spirit's expiration through the spreading of the gospel, is not to deny the positive and necessary role of human creativity. This creativity can be seen in the writing of sacred texts, in preaching, in the development of oral liturgies, and in remembering.

But in the Middle Ages, people were suspicious of too much innovation. They wanted not change but constancy, not the new but the old, not upheaval but permanence, not novelty but the familiar. Liturgy itself slowly changed over time but, like a fugue, its inventive variations were always centred on the same theme. This sometimes led to the downside of traditional authority, for liturgy could degenerate into legalism, where the spirit of the story became ensnared in the letter of rite and canon. And yet, rite and canon, precisely because of their sacred and authoritative character, presented medieval Europe with a normative standard of belief and behaviour.

The fact that so many potentates, friars and priests flouted the standard was due no doubt to hypocrisy. The feudal aristocracy also ignored the rules of courtship and courtesy as set out in the ideals and customs of chivalry during the Middle Ages, but this does not invalidate the normative status of such ideals.

The liturgies of medieval Europe appeared to satisfy all social strata from slaves, to serfs, to lords and bishops. To look at it in purely utilitarian terms, the liturgies survived for so long because they worked for the majority of the people most of the time. They provided stability and meaning in a world that was subject to great cruelty, war, famine and uncertainty.

This is not to deny that worship also played a negative function in social control. Under the authority of the magisterium, Christian liturgy was used to mediate feudal culture with its elements of power and oppression – just as today liberal clergymen abuse their pulpits to ride their favourite hobby horses, and televangelists use their cable networks to further the aims of the religious right. In order to avoid romanticism about the pre-modern era, we might say that the inculturation of the gospel in feudal times was incomplete. For although the story was successfully handed down in oral culture and may have become official ideology in both court and village life, this was not synonymous with the story being lived to the full: serfs remained in bondage to their masters, the poor were not adequately provided for, great cruelty remained.

Christianity, which had begun as a Jewish millennial sect, and was subversive of social order, had become not merely part of the system, but its legitimating authority. Its official nature gave it the air of a taken-for-granted world view, an unexamined conventional wisdom, and a subliminal backdrop to everyday life. The Church had grown tired of playing the fifth column over the years, and had settled down as if the world was not enemy territory, but home. It joined in the power politics and social processes of cultural development, sometimes resisting the *status quo*, like the early Dominican and Franciscan orders, but usually supporting it.

Indeed, the creative tension between the militant Church – of the monasteries, of the divine liturgy itself – and the worldly Christendom of medieval Europe, resulted in the highest culture the western world had known since Greek antiquity. This is not to deny the medieval legacy of thumbscrews and indulgences, of superstition and ignorance, but it is to affirm the achievements of Romanesque cathedrals and Renaissance art, of Chaucer and Rabelais, of scholastic learning and the viability and strength of oral culture.

The Reformation and the beginnings of literary culture

From the perspective of the late twentieth century, we are perhaps at a sufficient distance from the Reformation neither to rush in with a defence of it as 'the great recovery' of Christianity, nor to attack it as the betrayal of Christendom. As we have seen, Catholicism preserved the gospel as its grand narrative, but it could be argued that late medieval Christianity had become increasingly decadent. Like the Russian icons of the eighteenth century, with their silver filigree choking and masking the personality of *theotokos* and child, feudalism began to bury the gospel beneath the weight of its own contradictions and pagan encrustations.

Few Catholic historians today would deny that the Church as an institution had become corrupt. At the very least, the scandal of cut-rate relics and luxury indulgences demanded that the Church clean up its act. Initially, this is what Protestantism was, a protest against the apostasy and degeneracy of a dominant, monopoly religion, that in making the world its home had forgotten the imperatives of the gospel.

It was not inevitable that the Reformation should create a major schism in the western Church. The Council of Trent, which ended in 1563, suggests that a compromise between the Reformers and the counter-revolutionaries may have been possible. Protestants usually remember that Trent raised the authority of tradition to an equal status with the Bible – although this is not without ambiguities – but they sometimes forget that it also upheld the Reformation's emphasis on justification by faith. We owe a debt to Alister McGrath for reminding us that, far from being a Protestant doctrine, justification by faith was in fact a Catholic theme from patristic times.

Major reformation of Catholicism was inevitable, however, because the oral culture which had nurtured the rise of Christendom was in disarray by the fourteenth century, and consequently the story was in grave danger. Jacques Ellul rightly points to the fourteenth century as the 100 years in which the hegemony of Catholicism began to disintegrate, and feudalism entered a period of great instability.

As we have already seen, oral culture relies for its successful transmission on stability, and a relatively static and homogeneous community. In the fourteenth century, and persisting into the fifteenth, Europe underwent a series of great crises which can be said to have militated against both the continuity and the veracity of the Christian story. Not least of these crises was the Black Death, which resulted in the death of approximately one-third of the population of Europe.

Johan Huizinga tells us, in *The Waning of the Middle Ages*, that Europe lived under a deep cloud of pessimism during this time. People began to doubt either God's power or his goodness. The plague was accompanied not only by great European wars and the shifting fortunes of medieval princes, but also peasant revolts, and the emergence of restless nomadic herds of mystics and religious mountebanks. As Norman Cohn has brilliantly shown in his book, *The Pursuit of the Millennium*, the fracture of medieval stability led to hysteria, millennial longing, outbreaks of piety and powerful preaching.

Shifting and revolting populations are not good news for traditional oral cultures, and charismatic religious movements disrupt the *status quo*. During this period, European Christendom was split by the Hundred Years War, divided by the Avignon papacy, and confused by the great western schism. The net result of these seismic social and religious disturbances was not the decline of religion, but its proliferation and superfluity throughout civilization. We might say that Christianity's grand narrative almost disappeared beneath an explosion of popular piety that was out of control.

The Catholic Church seemed to lack either the will or the ability to maintain order. In particular, the fine balance between ear and eye in liturgy fell out of kilter and images, often of the most lurid and pagan kind, took over. The decadence of late medieval culture came about not because of oral culture, but because of its dissolution, through terror and social upheaval, into a syncretistic amalgam of Christianity and paganism.

Different scholars have stressed different aspects of this dissolution. For the Orthodox musicologist Dimitri Conomos, the rot began not in peasant culture but in the Catholic Church itself, and it started not with sculpture or art, but with music. Liturgical music in East and West (Gregorian chant is perhaps the best example) was never intended to decorate the word – the texts of scripture and prayer – but to reinforce it. In 1180, at Notre Dame in Paris, we see the beginnings of polyphonic organum, and the associated techniques of descant, *cantus firmus* and secular motet styles. We might say that the mathematization of music begins at this point. Music takes on a life of its own: no longer following the word, it follows the logic of its own form.

Plainsong can only follow a text, but harmonic and contrapuntal forms run the risk of overshadowing it by their sweetness and intricacy. In time, music became not merely decorative, but 'mood' music; performances for audiences rather than worship for congregations. By the fourteenth century, there was, according to Huizinga, virtually no difference between the musical character of sacred or profane music. The same could be said of the late twentieth century!

Leonid Ouspensky sees the same principle of music as decoration overtaking liturgical art, so that it ceased to represent the dogmas of the Church and became instead religious art. That is to say, this new art may have had a religious theme, but its form was sensuous, its style lurid, its content heretical. Western art certainly developed a more sentimental and world-affirming approach to church decoration than the art of the East. Renaissance art itself may have been a high art developed by the schools, but it was no longer informed by liturgy, following instead humanist principles and the aesthetics of Greek antiquity.

In this period, saints began to multiply in alarming numbers.

Through their familiarity in the wider culture, they become as reassuring as 'the sight of a policeman in a foreign city'. But perhaps they became almost too earthly, too enfleshed, to be of any heavenly use – more a crowd than a cloud of witnesses. Saints and biblical figures in early fifteenth-century religious art appeared dressed in contemporary fashion. So 'this worldly' did everything become – enhanced by the invention of perspective in painting by the late Middle Ages – that immanence, not transcendence, became the norm of piety. Sacredness spilled out of the churches and the *ecclesia* of the home, and ran amok in popular culture – in the sales of religious artefacts, statues, and a surfeit of fake relics. While this encouraged Europe's latent paganism, it did not socialize the population into the grand narrative of the gospel.

Many abbots and priests supported the new visual piety for rather the same reasons that some modern bishops support the demographics of Church Growth strategies: both clearly aid an expansion of religiosity. In the dying Middle Ages, however, the larger question was often ignored: what kind of religiosity was society getting? For the medieval Churchmen, like President Eisenhower in the twentieth century, they seemed to be content so long as society was being driven by some religion or other, rather than none at all.

Erwin Panofsky believes that cathedrals and churches themselves, as the supreme icons of medieval culture, became distorted images of the gospel with the ending of Romanesque architecture and the beginning of the Gothic style in the fourteenth century. Gothic cathedrals no longer provided a dogmatic architectural statement of the faith, but became decorative houses. We might want to say more modestly that Gothic structures were less obviously committed to a rational and orderly God. For Panofsky, once all theological control was lost of church building and art, the plastic nature of the new media inevitably led to the decadence of baroque, which today we might see as a precursor of playful postmodern architecture. Indeed, both carry within them the seeds of decadence, because they are a collapse of form and meaning into a fashion statement.

In some respects, both the Florentine Renaissance and the German and Swiss Reformation were a reaction against late medieval decadence. While the Renaissance sought its inspiration from classical antiquity, the Reformation turned to the Judaeo-Christian master narrative. Both movements were humanistic in their orientation towards individual expression in art and faith respectively. The Renaissance, however, was a flowering of reason, wrapped in the sensuous musculature of Greek narcissism and Dionysian extravagance, while the Reformation stood for freedom of conscience, but held on to the supremacy of divine revelation in human affairs with an almost Old Testament prophetic austerity. The Reformation was supremely a religion of the ear. The Italian Renaissance was essentially a revival of the Greek eye.

It was the Reformation which was to take hold of Europe in the sixteenth century, driving the Renaissance underground. The Renaissance eventually surfaced again through the philosophical Enlightenment of the eighteenth century, when it successfully challenged the Christian Reformation.

From the central perspective of this book, the Reformation is both good news and bad news. It is good news, because it rescued the story from pagan oblivion, and arguably led to the internal reforms of Catholicism after 1563. It is bad news, because it broke the bonds of catholicity and community that inhered in the grand narrative itself. Less obviously, in turning its back on pagan immanence, and re-establishing a hierarchy of ear over eye, it downgraded the sensuous faculties and undervalued the material world.

The banishing of images from churches, as happened in many a fine Anglican cathedral, reintroduced a lofty God secure in his heaven, but lost the intimacy of medieval communion and immanent presence. The Protestant solution to this lack was to substitute for it the religion of the heart, the religion of experience and spiritual assurance, initially through German and Moravian pietism, and later through Methodism and the Evangelical revivals. The possible long-term dangers in such a solution – anthropocentrism, docetism, and even gnosticism – would not be fully revealed until the late twentieth century, when once again a rampant paganism is loose in the world and the Churches find a religion of word and heart insufficient to attract a culture awash in a sea of images. However, we are anticipating later arguments in the next chapter and in part two.

More importantly for this chapter, however, we need to interpret the good-bad news of the Reformation within the understanding that it was part of the transformation of feudalism to capitalism, communitarianism to individualism, traditionalism to rationalism, and of oral culture to literary culture. It is to this latter development that we will now turn, because the emergence of a literary culture has had a profound effect on the telling of the Christian story.

Literary culture takes hold

When oral cultures become literary ones, both language and people change. In the predominantly oral culture of early and middle medievalism, communication was only possible by speaking directly to a listener or an audience. In this respect, communication was always personal; information was always information for somebody in particular. Of course, the Church already had her sacred texts which allowed the possibility of a wider audience than the immediate group of speaker and hearers, but these texts were located in the dramaturgical orality of liturgy. Written commentaries and theological reflection existed outside liturgies, but these were primarily written by and for the monks and the cultural elite of Christendom.

The invention of printing in the fifteenth century led to the dissemination of information outside the monasteries and clerical universities. It enabled the beginnings of a popular literary culture and the possibility of political and religious pamphleteering. Most importantly of all, the printed Bible began to pass out of the hands of monks to not only the educated aristocracy but also to the rising class of freemen and merchants.

What is it that widespread dissemination of books do to a culture? Let us start with reminding ourselves that unrecorded human speech is transitory and audience-specific. Liturgical discourse, or drama, works only in the sacred space of a church, or more accurately, in the *ecclesia* as congregation. Epic was made possible only because it was designed as a spoken medium of poetry to be learned off by heart and communicated to a gathered audience.

Human skills, beliefs and stories could only be handed down by word of mouth and/or by example. But with the invention of the printed word, that is typography, words are 'frozen' for all to see. Ideas can be wrenched out of their individual contexts, shared, discussed, disputed. The same is true with chirography, but handwritten texts are limited in their availability, and the individual styles of handwriting do not present the eye with the same standardized and objective sense of printed words.

Once words are set down in type, in a certain order and shape, they encourage, as Neil Postman puts it, the 'grammarian, the logician, the rhetorician, the historian, the scientist – all those who must hold language before them so that they can see what it means, where it errs, and where it is leading'. Printing aids precision of thought, facilitates reflection, opens numerous discourses to wider audiences, and assists the very process of reasoning. Imagine trying to follow the scientific method without being able to follow somebody else's experiments, or becoming an author without reference to a dictionary, or the literary styles of other authors.

We are not undermining the personalities, events and religious crises of the Reformation in suggesting that the invention of printing played a major role in religious development. It was a undoubtedly a moment of great historic importance when Luther nailed his protesting theses to the Wittenberg door in 1517. But we must not underestimate the significance of printing. It was through printing that Luther's theses were circulated to an audience far beyond the confines of a small cathedral town. We cannot say that there would not have been a

Reformation without printing, but it is certain that the Reformation would not have had the same impact without it.

Significantly, however, the Reformation through printing also added a new dimension to the gospel story. It might have been true that the Reformation disposed of pope and medieval iconography, but it preserved much of the Catholic liturgy, and enhanced, adumbrated or contradicted its theology. This is true not only for Lutheranism and Anglicanism, but also for Presbyterianism and early Methodism. Reformed liturgies may have been less colourful than the old ones, but they brought with them a new seriousness and literary appreciation of the gospel. Religious books also promoted private piety and helped to improve linguistic skills.

Preaching became a major way of proclaiming the good news, and it was informed not only by the rules of rhetoric, but also through the profundity of learned books. Epic and saga may not survive in literary cultures, but storytelling and oratory does. The age of Hooker and Baxter, Owen and Bunyan, the Caroline divines and Milton, was the first great religious stage in the English-speaking world of what Postman calls the 'age of exposition', in which literary culture had replaced orality as the dominant cultural form of communication.

Postman thinks that in the long run the rise of European literary culture has been beneficial both to civilization in general and Christian religion in particular. In the short term, however, he thinks that the Reformation encouraged individualism at the expense of community. The rub of the Reformation, we might say, is that it stood not only for *sola scriptura* and the dominance of ear over eye, but also for the right to interpret the Bible for oneself. This led to a division between Church and text, and the loosening of the communitarian ties that bound church and village together.

The Reformation championed the freedom of religious conscience in a world, to borrow a phrase from Kant, that had oppressed the 'autonomy' of the individual by collective fiat. But in fuelling individualism at the very moment of upholding the sacredness of scriptural text, the Reformation aided the break-up not only of the hegemony of the Roman Catholic Church, but also the sacred order of Christendom.

This was not necessarily bad, but new freedoms carry with them a price. We can see a parallel of the Reformation in Europe with the New England 'Great Awakening' of the eighteenth century. There, the revivalism of Jonathan Edwards fuelled a new religious consciousness and freedom, but at the expense of the old Puritan Commonwealth.

Politically, Protestantism did not destroy Christendom; it merely brought European societies under the auspices of a different legitimizing authority. For a time, the Protestant princes even helped to maintain the vestiges of feudalism. In the long run, however, the splitting of the religious community from its story – removing sacred text from sacred place – encouraged every man and woman to become his or her own pope. Once the story got away from the Church and became everybody's story, it ran the risk of becoming no one's in particular.

The Reformation got out of hand and became reformation *ad nauseam*, and the long history of Protestant denominationalism and sectarianism began. In this respect, religious pluralism is not a recent phenomenon of modernization, as some sociologists say, but a consequence of the ending of a homogenized medieval culture.

Other criticisms seem to be in order. A religion of the ear may destroy idols of the eye but not of the mind. The Bible itself can cease to be the focus of the grand narrative and become its locus: Jesus the Word becomes synonymous with the book of the word of God, and the Bible, not God, is now the source of all truth. Or again, the ear, as we have already suggested, can lead to an over-spiritualized, non-incarnational spirituality which is no longer rooted in the material world where God won our salvation.

To turn also from sacred liturgy to oratory as a means of passing on God's story is wide open to individual abuse, interpretation and falsification. As Studdert-Kennedy observed:

It has always been a matter of amazement to me that our forefathers – the Reformers of blessed memory – were able to believe that they served the cause of true religion when they turned the sculptor out of Church, and forbade him to praise his God in silent songs of wood and stone, threw out the painter with his proffered sacrifice of colour and line, very reluctantly and under severe restrictions admitted the musician, but put the orator up in a great big box bang in front of the altar, and bade him do his worst, which he has been doing ever since. Oratory is much the most dangerous of all the arts, the most commonly degraded and misused. It has, not without justification, been called the harlot of the arts, and yet they crowned it queen.

We can of course be far more positive. The Reformation may have been enabled by the rise of modern literary culture, but it did not destroy all that was most positive in oral culture for the Christian story – the art of remembering. It is important to recognize that the story was under real threat of extinction in the West, and the Reformation did keep it alive. Even if we think the balance from eye to ear was tipped too far in the direction of hearing, a radical speaking of the word of God was desperately needed in the closing days of feudal Europe.

Perhaps, also, because we have taken sides in the great schisms of Christendom, we have exaggerated our differences. Liturgy survived the Reformation and was enhanced by the printed lectionary. The creeds and the first four Councils of the Church were valued and promoted by Calvin and Luther. To conserve the Nicene-Constantinopolitan Creed of AD 381, albeit not in original form, was no small feat. As Dorothy Sayers was to recognize, the creed contains in itself neither a set of dogmatic formularies nor a string of doxologies, as many moderns would have it, but the structure of the story itself: 'the one short tale we feel to be true.'

Until the modern era, despite all their irreconcilable differences, the eastern and western Churches, both Roman and Protestant, preserved a family resemblance in so far as they maintained the objective content of the grand narrative of Christianity. This does not mean to say that they were in communion, or that we can avoid choosing one side over another, but it does mean that the story was not irrevocably lost.

How we began to lose it, to forget its sacred and binding character on our lives, is the story of our contemporary culture. It is not a culture that begins in the twentieth century, or even with nineteenth-century capitalism, but in the eighteenth century.

Unwittingly, the Reformation opened the door to the philosophical Enlightenment, because it took from feudalism more than the grand narrative of Christianity and the sacred text of scripture. It also, through its individualism and independent turn of mind, sneaked through the humanism of the Renaissance. If this seems too harsh, then shall we say that the price you pay when you establish a dynamic literary culture over a static oral one is that literature is no respecter of stories. The philosophical Enlightenment is the Renaissance back with a vengeance, but this time armed with critical tools of analysis which are a danger to any story, and in time will be fateful to its own.

Before we turn to the forgetting of the Christian story, let us end this chapter with an ironic parenthesis. The invention of printing and the beginning of literary culture had the opposite effect on Eastern Orthodoxy to that on Reformed Western Catholicism. Whereas the printed word prompted great change and upheaval in European countries, and was the major technological spur to religious reformation and secular enlightenment, in the East, where Constantinople had fallen to Islam shortly before the era of Luther and Calvin, printing was used not to print Bibles, but missals.

This had the effect of virtually freezing medieval liturgical developments and stultifying reform. Western Protestants pressed on to their New Jerusalem, but their Orthodox counterparts took their bearings from the patristic age. No doubt this was because the age of the Fathers was a golden age of innovation and philosophical daring; but it also offered historical legitimacy and meaning under Islamic colonialism. It is no coincidence that the Orthodox, who have still not been directly infiltrated by the philosophical Enlightenment, have never yet had a Reformation.

3

Losing the Story

Up until now we have been arguing that the gospel begins in and is maintained by oral culture, a culture that starts to break down with the upheavals of the later Middle Ages. We have further argued that the technologizing of the word in the fifteenth century began the long road of literary culture which has dominated western societies until recent times.

Initially, literary culture helped to achieve the success of the Reformation. In many ways, it has maintained not only Protestantism but has also become a successful medium for Christian development. However, although literary culture superseded oral culture, it did not obliterate it. Face-to-face communication cannot be entirely replaced by a bookish society any more than Christian liturgy can be entirely driven by textual resources. So to say that literary culture replaced oral culture is to make claims for its public authority and cultural pre-eminence, and not its ubiquity.

While the growth of literary culture – what Postman calls 'the age of exposition' – supported the Christian story, it also launched counterblasts against it. These counterblasts seriously undermined Christianity and set the scene for the long process of secularization and unbelief that we have seen over the last 150 years. However, we cannot claim that the development of literary culture caused the decline of Christianity in the West. In the first place, we cannot say with any certainty that the pre-modern era was more deeply religious than the present one. Secondly, even if we wanted to use Peter Berger's plausible argument, that people in pre-industrial societies, unlike us, lived in a world surrounded by a 'sacred canopy', we cannot lay the blame for modern indifference to Christianity on the shoulders of literary culture.

The origins of Christian decline can be traced to a multitude of causes, from demographics to economics, and from scientific methodologies to materialistic life-styles in consumer societies. What we can say about literary culture is that in promoting the cause of critical rationality, it provided the conceptual tools for unravelling the sacred narrations of the gospel story. And in order to say that, we have to start with the zenith of the age of exposition in the eighteenth century, which we more usually think of as the Age of Reason.

From reason to gospel amnesia

Walter Brueggemann, a contemporary master of narrative theology, shows that the modern age is an era which is long on information but short on narrative. He sees the intellectual culture that stemmed from the Age of Reason – the philosophical Enlightenment – as programmatically opposed to tradition, the preservation of cultural roots, and the remembrance of things past. It is with the Enlightenment that what he calls Christian 'amnesia' begins. For him, the problem with modern Christians is not merely that we are illiterate about our own faith. He sees this as a surface problem which betrays a deeper malaise: we have forgotten who we are.

As long as we continue to be forgetters and not rememberers of the gospel – and Brueggemann wants us to be good Jews in this sense – then no real missionary energy for our modern culture can be found.

It is here that the legacy of the eighteenth- and early-nineteenth-century philosophers has taken its toll within the Christian communities of the twentieth century. It may be argued that the Reformation unwittingly opened the door to the Enlightenment, but the Reformation, as we saw in the last chapter, conserved more of the Christian tradition than it destroyed. The Reformers held on to the creeds and councils of the Catholic era, and rescued the sacredness of the scriptural text from community neglect and ecclesiastical abuse. If it is true, as the Americans say, that Protestantism began to go 'every which way', each way it went it took with it the bare bones of the story, maintaining its mythical and numinous character. We can see this dimly in Spenser's *The Faerie Queene* in the sixteenth century, and clearly in Bunyan's allegory of *Pilgrim's Progress*, and in Milton's epic of *Paradise Lost* and *Paradise Regained* in the seventeenth century.

However, since the philosophical Enlightenment, the adequacy, not to mention the veracity, of the gospel story has been persistently called into question. With the rise of Deism and Unitarianism in the eighteenth century, there was a wholesale attack upon classical theism. The gardens of the court at Versailles in France and the landscapes of Capability Brown in England reflected a God of design and order rather than one of personal revelation. In philosophy, Kant's *Critique of Pure Reason* in 1781 undermined traditional metaphysics and by default the whole thrust of theology as revelation. By separating human knowledge into the noumenal realm of ideas (which was real but unknowable), and the self-conscious and sensate phenomenal realm (which was both real and knowable), a fundamental blow was struck against the story.

As a result of this attack, the Christian narrative was left with the anthropological and historical Jesus in the phenomenal world, casting him off from the eternal Son, who was left adrift in the noumenal sphere – like the hero in David Bowie's song, *Major Tom*, unable to get back to earth from his damaged spacecraft.

To accept Kant's divide of physics from metaphysics was, for the story, a disaster. Not only was Jesus as the God-man separated into two halves, but the whole mythical and epic dimensions of the story were lost. God was no longer allowed to be God, to be sovereign, as the Reformers insisted that he was. He could not enter the material world from beyond or outside, although Hegel valiantly tried to reintroduce God into the universe as the spirit of history. So the story had to go, and in its place was granted the right to discover historical information about Jesus of Nazareth. No wonder the nineteenth-century theologians were so obsessed with the quest for the historical Jesus: it was all that they had to go on, all they were allowed to pursue.

As the late eighteenth and early nineteenth century progressed, traditional modes of thought – from the credibility of miracles to the efficacy of ontological language – were subjected to rigorous thinking. The scientific determinism of philosophers such as Auguste Comte seemed to rule out of bounds the very possibility of supernaturalism. Even Kant had not gone this far, for the concept of the noumenal had not ruled out the supernatural as a matter of fact, but as a problem of language, and as a seemingly insurmountable difficulty for propositional truth claims.

In the face of the onslaught of critical reason, theologians and others sought both to defend Christianity and to transform it into a form relevant and acceptable to modernity. In the case of America's revolutionary leader, Thomas Jefferson, this amounted to editing the scriptures so that his Bible excised all the embarrassing supernaturalism and the primitive sacrificial motifs. His attempt to recreate Jesus as moral exemplar and philosophical ethicist, rather than as the focus of a Christian master narrative, found echoes in Tolstoy in Russia and Ritschl in Germany.

Schleiermacher, the most profound of the early modern theologians, bravely tried to transform the dogmas of historic Christianity into a form acceptable to the modern mind. His systematic theology was based not on the God of revelation, but on an 'absolute dependency' of God, located in the religious consciousness and 'affections' of men and women. Following Schleiermacher's ground-breaking studies, theological interests increasingly turned away from classical theism – with its tacit acceptance of the story – and towards historical studies, along with hermeneutical, epistemological, propositional, and sometimes foundational concerns. To use the language of conceptual analysis, we might say that 'first order' priorities, such as telling the gospel story, were replaced by 'second order' questions, such as finding adequate or new grounds for believing the claims of religion. In reality, this is often more 'first order' than it appears, as it so often leads to a reconstruction of the Christian faith altogether.

Much ink has been spilled on the problems of theological 'modernism', if we understand by that term 'a tendency or movement towards modifying traditional beliefs and doctrines in accordance with the findings of modern criticism and research' (*Oxford English Dictionary*). But it is sufficient at this point to assert with Hans Frei that the work of many scholars in the modern era, as brilliant as much of it has been, has eclipsed the gospel as narrative. Telling the story, the function of which is to reveal the Christ, has been replaced either by different gospels or by a critical re-evaluation of the grand narrative's constituent narrations. There has been a hermeneutical oppression whereby the story – now fragmented and disconnected – has had to await authentication from the critics in order to be told.

This hermeneutical oppression, often perpetrated by scholars who make little or no effort to reach out from the academy to the Churches, not only seems an affront to the Christ who can no longer move in his kingdom without the permission of the self-authenticating critic, but it also leads to an understandable hesitancy and timidity among priests and pastors when called upon to tell again 'the old, old story'. Wolfhart Pannenberg is quite blunt about the disastrous, long-term effects of secular Enlightenment thinking on the Christian Church in the contemporary world:

> Secularism's greatest success, however, is in the widespread demoralization in the ranks of clergy and theologians who are supposed to proclaim and interpret the truth of the gospel but delude themselves that they are achieving that purpose by adapting Christian faith and life to the demands of secularism. What the situation requires, I am convinced, is precisely the opposite of such uncritical adaption.

We can see, in hindsight, that for theology the legacy of the Enlightenment – and in particular the seminal influence of Kant, Hegel, and Schleiermacher – amounted to a radical shift from the historical tradition. In the first chapter, we suggested that the gospel had an objective and binding character about it. Luther could be said to represent this classical view when he says of anyone approaching scripture that one 'does not stand over the Bible and judge it, but below the Bible, and hears and obeys it.' For Kant, this amounted to what he called 'heteronomy' – an objectivized unfreedom. Following Kant, many modern men and women have preferred, in the matter of faith and morals at least, to opt for a more autonomous approach. It is now we who stand over the Bible and gospel and judge it by and for ourselves.

The radical shift in theological thinking from classical theism to post-classical theism has taken many contradictory forms since the Enlightenment – reasoned and romantic, scientific and mystical, objective and subjective, absolutist and relativist. In the nineteenth century, theologians reflected thinkers as diverse as Feuerbach or Strauss, Baur or Frazer. In our own time, we have seen the seminal influence of existentialism, neo-Marxism and, more recently, post-structuralism. The chances are, however, that those who have sought these new directions have been suffering from gospel amnesia.

Such forgetfulness, however, is not simply a question of swallowing modernism; it is also a function of modern intellectual specialization. Another consequence of Enlightenment literary culture for the Churches has been the break between academic theology and ecclesiastical authority. This not only holds for theology in secular universities, but also for many seminaries.

Academic theological studies reflect the general current of intellectual ideas in the larger society. There is nothing wrong with this in itself, for academic freedom is one of the great gifts of the Enlightenment to the modern world. It does mean, however, that the academy often sets the agenda for theology, and establishes its many sub-disciplines independently of the Churches. This agenda is not only sometimes subversive of Christianity, but often proceeds as if the Churches no longer exist. Don Cupitt's postmodern stories, for example, are predicated on the very fact that the Christian grand narrative is a fiction.

Even in colleges and seminaries formally dedicated to classical theology, the drive for specialization leads to a break up of the gospel story as narrative, so that New and Old Testament studies are often taught without reference to Church history or systematics. Students may become proficient in ancient languages, hermeneutics, and even homiletics, but still have little sense of the gospel as narrative. In many Bible schools, there is often very little attention given to historical studies, and virtually none to systematics. Even courses in evangelism can so concentrate on the demographics and psychometrics of Church Growth methodologies, that they have little to say about the content of the gospel – the story – to be proclaimed.

Of course, in the act of telling the story, modern theologians cannot make people believe it. What they can do, however, is to stand up for the story, and learn again to tell it in the way it was meant to be told. This means allowing the story to speak for itself. The gospel is not anything we choose, or the bits we enjoy, or those elements that affirm modern sensibility. It is the Church's grand narrative, which is essential not only for its own identity but for the salvation of the world. However, to insist on this is to risk the wrath of contemporary thinking. One of the features of life in an advanced industrial society is that absolute claims of any kind are anathema. This is why Christianity is tolerated by secularists as private opinion, but not as what Lesslie Newbigin has called 'public truth'.

We cannot blame the Enlightenment and literary culture for this. The humanist thought of the philosophers was not an open invitation to plunge into a sea of subjectivism. On the contrary, they were firmly convinced that public truth was obtainable, albeit based on reason rather than revelation. Perhaps what we are now seeing, as we approach the third millennium, is the failure of principled humanism to convince the modern world that it has a more believable story to live by than the older stories it has replaced.

In the wake of Enlightenment failure, however, many Christians seem to have absorbed the notion of truth as private opinion into their own ranks, rather than unlock their memories and offer their forgotten story to a world which still waits for 'the one short tale we feel to be true'. This may simply be a failure of nerve, or a modest sensibility in the face of a pluralist culture, but it may also be a function of unbelief.

When a member of a political party ceases to believe the party's central tenets, as normatively understood, she usually leaves. No doubt she stays for a while out of loyalty, but there comes a time when she can no longer truly endorse party beliefs. Christianity in the modern era, however, has become unashamedly revisionist to the extent that all its central tenets seem to have become negotiable products in a free market of ideas. Such openness to change is often praised as good in itself in modern culture, although it would have sapped the lifeblood of oral ones. Reacting no doubt against an unsavoury past of heresy-hunting and witch-baiting, we now praise tolerance, freedom of conscience, the right to free expression, and individual preference above all else. These are then played over and against outdated notions of public truth, group loyalty, community identity, tradition and dogma.

Historic Christianity, however, is more like a trade union than a society of free-thinkers. There is a *sobornost*, a common mind and spirit at work, which is not the oppression of a collectivity but the conviction of a community. The gospel is not what Andrew Walker thinks it is, nor Bishop Spong or Andrew Lloyd Webber: it is the message 'once delivered to the saints', which when faithfully retold becomes the grand narrative of the Church. This is not to say that reason does not need to comprehend it and has played no part in its construction, or that the gospel does not need to be imaginatively reconstructed for modern culture, but it is to say that it is not anything we choose.

This brief sketch of the Enlightenment and the beginning of gospel amnesia is a reminder that the habit of refashioning the Christian story according to the precepts of modern thinking is not some fad of the late twentieth century. It emerged in the intellectual and literary culture of eighteenth-century Europe. It may very well be that unbelief in society at large has more to do with the sociological process of secularization than with the philosophy of secularism, but this does not alter the fact that academic theology has drunk deep at the well of modern thought for over 200 years, and has only itself to blame for its present sickness.

From the eighteenth century to the present day, there have of course been Christians who have faithfully told the story. Their high view of scripture, commitment to evangelism as proclamation, and/or a traditional liturgical structure, has ensured that the gospel has not been entirely swamped by modernist thinking. Ironically, as we will see later, the Age of Reason, and its nineteenth-century incarnation as the age of steam, was also the age of religious revivals. But for now, if we turn to the larger society, we can see that literary culture has tended to create problems for the acceptance of the Christian story; problems that have been exacerbated by the establishment of rival stories.

Metanarratives and the displacement of the Christian story

Perhaps the supreme irony of the Enlightenment is this: it was predicated on modern critical reason that eschewed tradition and mythopoeic narratives of meaning; and yet it was unable to resist its own meta level of discourse that functioned in much the same way as the older mythopoeic narratives. These metanarratives have operated as legitimating ideologies for the modern world and have sometimes been seen as alternative world-views to religious ones.

Nowhere is this more apparent than in the nineteenth century, when intellectual discourse was dominated by the 'grand theory'. Grand theories were comprehensive explanations of social and cultural life. It was a feature of social theorists, such as Saint-Simon in France, and James Frazer in Great Britain, to be driven by the 'big idea'. What bound these theories together was faith in rationality and an optimistic belief in human progress. It may be true that Hume, sceptical to the last, was not an apostle of progress. Neither was Kant, for despite his seminal critiques of pure and practical reasoning, he remained pessimistic about the emergence of a truly just and moral society. But the general tenor of the Enlightenment was optimistic, from the reasoned natural religion of Locke, to the utopian dreams of Rousseau and Hegel.

The optimistic strain of developing literary culture was on one level quite diffuse. It was supported among the general population of Europe and the New World because of the empirical success of science and technology, through the democratization of feudalism, and by the economic success of capital economies. Diffuse it may have been, but it was also pervasive. The idea of the ever-increasing 'good life' has been encapsulated in no clearer way than in the 'American dream'. To be an American was to be free from tyranny and strife. To be an American was, since the late eighteenth century, to be a person who was paid fair wages for hard work. To be an American meant that in principle you could begin your life in a log cabin and end it in the White House, or go from rags to riches in a single lifetime. To be an American – and this belief is on the whole less prevalent among Europeans – is to have the right to be happy.

Such a diffuse optimism can be said to be a metanarrative only at the level of ingrained social attitudes, or 'habits of the heart'. They articulate themselves not in theory, but as 'vox pop'. 'Is America a great country or what?' is a sentiment you can still hear in the United States, from Pensacola in Florida, to Portland, Maine.

A less diffuse, but still not a full-blown metanarrative has been scientism. Scientism is not merely the acceptance of the efficacy of science. In its weak form, it claims that science is superior to all other methodologies and philosophies; in its stronger form, it claims exclusive rights to understanding reality. The stronger form has been located in philosophies hostile to metaphysics, such as Comtean sociology and Logical Positivism. The precursor of this philosophical scientism was the empiricism of David Hume:

When we run over libraries, persuaded of these principles, what havoc must we make? If we take in our hand any volume; of divinity or school metaphysics, for instance; let us ask, Does it contain any abstract reasoning concerning quantity or numbers? No. Does it contain any experimental reasoning concerning matter of fact and existence? No. Commit it then to the flames: for it can contain nothing but sophistry and illusion.

It is implausible, however, to suggest that such a philosophical scientism runs amok in society. The general public has been tacitly scientistic, not because of an appreciation of scientific research, or an understanding of Darwinism or Freud. They have been scientistic because of the wonder of machines, medicine and engineering. Mastery over nature induces awe and trust. Labour-saving devices, transport inventions and technological innovations of all kinds lead to thanksgiving, not intellectual curiosity.

In this respect, to believe in a scientific world view is not necessarily to accept truth claims about science; instead, it is the acceptance that science has the answers to the world's problems, based on the past performance of the prediction and control of the natural world. From the perspective of the late twentieth century, this view may seem incredible, looking back as we do on two technologically-dominated world wars, the ecological mismanagement of the planet, and the lengthening shadow of the atom bomb. But from the perspective of the age of steam, of the nineteenth century, progress seemed the stuff of the universe, and science was the key that could unlock the secrets of utopian bliss.

And it is here that the true metanarratives of the modern world came into their own. For Hegel, Marx and Comte, the architects of early-nineteenth-century grand theories, time was about to enter its final stretch. If it is true that medieval man saw himself at the bottom of a ladder reaching up to the stars and to the glory beyond, Enlightenment meta-theorists saw themselves at the apex of the ladder, at the top of the evolutionary scale of ideas. Their vision looked backwards and ended with themselves.

For Hegel, history was coming to a close, and he sought to bring civilization to fulfilment through the application of his own philosophical system. In the *Philosophy of Mind*, his dialectic of ideas and the synthesis of oppositional forces in history would usher in, he believed, the end of history and the cessation of human conflict. So too with Marx. Turning Hegel's dialectic on its head and grounding it in economy and polity, in his system, too, history was nearing its perfection in the classless society of Communism.

For Comte – forgotten now, but probably the greatest intellectual influence in Europe in the 1830s and 1840s – his evolutionary three stages of consciousness (from the fetishist, through the metaphysical, to the positivistic) ends triumphantly with his own philosophical system. The great Thomist philosopher Jacques Maritain wryly remarked that 'with Auguste Comte, as with Hegel, we have arrived at the end of time'.

These metanarratives of progress were ideological and historical challenges both to the philosophies of antiquity and to Judaic Christianity. Hegel the Deist, and Marx and Comte the atheists, all turn out to be historicists who through reason have discerned the hidden springs of social and human development. How ironic that the Enlightenment not only took up the mantle of Renaissance humanism, with which it suffocated the Reformation, but also turned again to the Hermetic tradition of the philosopher's stone and the *Kabbala* – only now it is reason, rather than magic and ancient mysteries, that unlock the universe's secrets.

Master narratives of progress – false myths, as C.S. Lewis saw them – continued sporadically throughout the nineteenth century. Darwin's *On the Origins of Species*, published in 1859, spawned a host of neo-Darwinisms, from Herbert Spencer's sociology to Fabian socialism. James Frazer's anthropology in *The Golden Bough* clearly followed in the footsteps of Strauss and Comte. And if Adam Smith's *Wealth of*

Nations, first published in 1776, did not quite live up to the status of a metanarrative, capitalism itself provided the infrastructure for a mythology of progress for the liberal democracies right to the end of the twentieth century.

Shortly after the collapse of the Berlin wall in 1989, for example, when it seemed that Marxism and all evolutionary ideologies had fallen with it, Francis Fukuyama told us in *The End of History and the Last Man,* that history in the Hegelian sense was over, leaving capitalist western democracies the outright winner. Lyotard could tell him that liberal capitalist democracies also flout their own meta-theories of progress. Fukuyama rather gives the lie to his own position when, in what is scarcely less than a gloat, he tells us that we will see 'Western liberal democracy as the *final form* of human government' (my italics).

This vignette from the end of the modern age is a reminder to us of how far-reaching the arm of metanarratives has been. The Age of Reason, born as it was out of a burgeoning literary culture, turned out to be Promethean. It overreached itself and fell prey to myths of its own imagination, both specific and diffuse, that could not be sustained by reason alone. Auguste Comte was perhaps the only grand theorist of the nineteenth century to realize this.

In his notorious 'subjective synthesis' and the foundation of his religion of humanity in the 1850s, Comte asserted that man could not live by rational narratives alone. There had to be a strong social order, but he came to believe that this necessitated religious rituals and personal 'emotional effusion' – his substitute for prayer – to ensure a stable and prosperous society.

Comte's disciples, such as J.S. Mill, abandoned him in droves, and the self-declared high priest of the new religion failed to convert any significant numbers to his cause. Comte failed primarily because his religion was no religion at all. He believed in the necessary and useful functions of religion, but rejected true religious experience and remained, somewhat like Don Cupitt in our own day, that strangest of oxymorons – a religious atheist.

But at least Comte came to see that metanarratives, created from reason alone, are in fact unreasonable, distorted realities. They are more like Frankenstein's monsters, we might say, than healthy children of the Enlightenment. In Mary Shelley's classic tale, before Hollywood recast it as Grand Guignol, the monster was not evil in itself but a folly of its creator, bearing in its unnatural body the stigma of Baron Frankenstein's deceit and pride. So too with the authors of the nineteenth-century grand theories. They denied Christian revelation as a legitimate source of knowledge and redemption, and then granted to their own meta-creations both redemptive and epistemological superiority to Christian faith.

It might be more appropriate to say, looking from inside the Christian grand story, that the Enlightenment ideologues look less like Gothic miscreants and more like glittering angels – 'morning stars' at the dawn of another Eden. 'You too can be as gods' has been a temptation for humankind since the dawn of time.

But if the Enlightenment was, as Paulos Mar Gregorios has described it, a 'light too bright' that dazzled and bedazzled humanity, so that blinded by the light we failed to see the shadow side of reason's stature, we must also recognize that the stature was genuine enough. Enlightenment thinking brought with it a new and brave critical rationality that would not have been possible in earlier oral cultures. Printing does not merely distribute ideas widely, it facilitates their gestation and germination. And lest we forget, it was from the fecundity of public knowledge, facilitated by print and heralded by the Age of Reason, that fresh ideals emerged of human freedom and justice in the western world. Such ideals aided the abolition of slavery, the modern birth of democracy, belief in universal truth, and the possibility of a peaceful accord between nations.

The problem with the Enlightenment was not so much a loss of confidence in the eternal verities or the *philosophia perennis* of the ancients – tainted as they were by their association with the traditions of the past – the problem was a displacement of God by reason, and the beginning of the modern absorption with self. If the Desert Fathers, satiated with prayer, were 'God-possessed', then Enlightenment men, drunk with the new knowledge of literary culture, became the shamans of a humankind in which men wished to be gods themselves. Or as Alexander Pope put it, in what could perhaps stand as the literary shorthand of the Enlightenment:

> Know then thyself, presume not god to scan,
> The proper study of mankind is man.

Revival, evangelism and the gospel

It might seem as if we have accumulated enough evidence to show that on the whole literary culture, after its initial boost to the Reformation, turned on the gospel through the critical developments of the Enlightenment and devoured it. However, the effects of literary culture on Christianity have been paradoxical. We often forget that the Age of Reason has also been an age of revivals, which set the scene for the growth of Protestant Evangelical movements down to the present day.

The First and Second Great Awakenings of North America (which began in the 1730s and the early 1800s respectively), together with the nineteenth- and twentieth-century revivals in Europe and the United States, are well documented. Evangelical literature, in particular, is replete with earnest history and hagiography. From the perspective of our consideration of gospel and culture, however, certain features of the revivals are significant and, rather like our all-too-brief glance at the Reformation, we can say that the revivals are both good and bad news.

But perhaps the most striking feature of the great revivals is not so much that they are good or bad, but that they are modern: they came into being with the dawn of the Enlightenment itself. This is not to deny the coming of the Spirit on the Day of Pentecost, or to downplay the significance of New Testament *charismata*, but it is to assert that we know few historical details about such 'signs and wonders', and we should resist the temptation to read modern Evangelical movements back in to the New Testament record. The same can be said of Montanism in the second century. This movement was certainly apocalyptic and visionary, but its hallmarks were asceticism and moral legalism, rather than heartfelt Evangelicalism.

We can properly say that there was moral panic and millennial excitation in the Middle Ages, but they were hardly mass revivals. Or again, we can talk of the commitment and martyrdom of the saints of the Reformation and Catholic Reformation, but these were not ages typified by revivalistic fervour. Even the English Civil War, with its Levellers and Diggers in the south, or Scottish Covenanters in the north, bear little in common with, say, the early nineteenth-century revival at London's Regent Square in 1832, or even the evangelistic piety of the Keswick Convention of 1875.

If we take the hallmarks of revival to be powerful and charismatic preaching, accompanied by intense emotion and mass conversions, or if we think of Evangelical awakenings as resulting in long-term impact upon the larger society, then we can say that in its modern form, revival began in the eighteenth century, and was facilitated by literary culture.

Furthermore, we cannot see the eighteenth-century revivals simply as conservative reactions to Enlightenment radicalism, because in many ways they were conducted by men of the Enlightenment. John Wesley and Jonathan Edwards, for example, who were both born in 1703, were scholars and admirers of science. Not only were Isaac Newton and John Locke a major influence on Edwards, but Edwards's own *Treatise on Religious Affections* overlapped with Schleiermacher's work, as well as foreshadowing the psychological studies of William James's *The Varieties of Religious Experience*.

Many of the great revivalists were men of the pen. Jonathan Edwards always wrote out his sermons in longhand, as did Scottish preacher Edward Irving in London's Hatton Garden and Regent Square, during the 1820s. Indeed Wesley, Edwards, and their contemporary George Whitefield, were men whose ministry had been saturated in contemporary learning. Many of the great hymns of John's brother, Charles Wesley, may have been set to modern tunes, but they reflected his patristic studies at Oxford.

Edwards and John Wesley, to different degrees, were also the heirs of sixteenth-century German Pietism, which stressed the importance of the emotions, assurance of salvation, and self-conscious awareness of God. This Pietism, we might argue, found it difficult to grow in the soil of traditional Calvinist Puritanism, because the latter's emphasis was on right beliefs and right morals, rather than on right religious experience. In fact, the Puritan Covenant of New England, founded by the Pilgrim Fathers in 1620, was based on religious conviction and theocratic principles, rather than religious emotion.

Revivalistic emphasis on right emotions was also related to its stress on the importance of the individual, which was so precious to the Enlightenment philosophers. Perhaps the emergence of literary culture encouraged the individual to stand out from the crowd because of the interiorization of reality that is facilitated by literature. By contrast, the poetry of earlier oral culture was tribal and formal, ritualistic and communitarian. We might also add that German Pietism in its Wesleyan form encouraged an anthropocentric turn – from the transcendent God of Puritanism to the immanent God of religious experience. John Wesley's famous phrase – 'my heart was strangely warmed' – comes to mind.

It is surely not too revisionist to suggest that eighteenth-century revivalism, which set the pattern for nineteenth-century Evangelicalism, was encouraged by pietist and Enlightenment individualism and literary development. If it is true that literary culture was bad news for the Christian story in the universities, it was better news for the story on the streets and in the marketplace, at the open air meetings, and in the burgeoning dissenting chapels.

We should also note in passing that Protestant religious experience since the eighteenth century has tended to be enthusiastic rather than mystical, despite the emphasis on the individual and inner experience.

John Wesley was suspicious of the hermits and mystics and had inherited from John Owen, the great Puritan leader, a strong commitment to the 'gathered' or 'believing' Church as the normative institutional setting for all Christians.

Evangelicals share in common with modern westerners both an emphasis on the pre-eminence of the individual, and the desirability of being with the like-minded in crowds. Camp meetings and American ball parks, Christian conventions and football stadiums – they are sociologically similar in the fact that they celebrate teamwork (togetherness) and individual flair (expressiveness). Revivalism, by definition, involves the notion of mass crowds as the matrix in which God will visit his people individually.

On the whole, the revivals of the eighteenth century were good news for the Christian story for a number of reasons. First, both Edwards and Wesley saw themselves in the catholic tradition of Church, Bible, and creeds. In this respect they were not inventing a new story, but handing on the old one. Unlike Gotthold Lessing, their contemporary, they did not see the Enlightenment as a 'big ugly ditch' that halted the gospel in its tracks. Lessing's 'ditch' was really a chasm or an abyss which was uncrossable, whereas for the great revivalists it was more like a ditch on a cross-country race that could be negotiated with confidence.

Secondly, the revivals stressed the importance of indwelling the story, or appropriating the story for oneself. Just as the Middle Ages had ended in paganism or nominalism, so too had the Reformation degenerated into unbelief or legalism. In short, the revivals insisted that orthodoxy in itself was not enough without orthopraxis. Christian praxis was, to be sure, connected to right belief, but belief itself was mediated through personal encounter with God.

Thirdly, the eighteenth-century stress on the heart experience was not simply a case of a new psychological and individualist approach to religious commitment. Edwards's *Treatise on Religious Affections* may have centred the Christian life in the heart, but unlike Schleiermacher, who tended to use the affections to bypass the dogmatic truths of the gospel, Edwards saw the spiritual life as proof of God's revelation to the world in Christ. Furthermore, Edwards's religion of the heart had more in common with the spirituality of the Desert Fathers than with Enlightenment psychology.

Fourthly, the heart approach also had a pragmatic appeal to the uneducated world, which was no longer versed in the Christian tradition, and which had not yet been initiated into modern English literary culture. The beautifully rich and intricate theology of the Caroline divines in the seventeenth century may have had a considerable impact on the courts of Charles I and II in London, but it was of no use to farmers and shopkeepers. Lancelot Andrewes, for example, would often preach in Greek and Latin!

It was no coincidence, therefore, that in England it was the peasantry and the emerging working classes that took to the preaching of Wesley and Whitefield. On the American frontier, it was the Methodist, 'New Light' Presbyterian, and later Baptist itinerant evangelists who were successful, rather than the Episcopalians or straight-laced Presbyterians. The preacher would ride into town, preach the gospel, call for a response, form a church from the gathered responders, erect a building, and then move on. The Methodists added to this approach the genius of the discipleship classes, which were no less than a modern form of the catechumenate. Designed to socialize new Christians into the kingdom of God, these classes also had the consequence of aiding a major rise in literacy among their members.

Fifthly, revivals reintroduced the communitarian significance of oral tradition to Christianity, although this was reinforced by individualistic literary culture. The American nineteenth-century camp meetings, from the 1801 Cane Ridge revival in Kentucky onwards, were certainly times of individual excitement and emotional release, but they also encouraged sharing and camaraderie. Without this kind of 'bonding', to use psychological jargon, it is difficult to find common cause or establish a long-term commitment to the same goals.

Orality, then, crossed the Enlightenment ditch not only as liturgy in the historical Churches, but also as communal storytelling in the revivals. A major feature of the camp meetings was the 'personal testimony' – the little narrations – which became *de rigeur* in holiness traditions and on into twentieth-century Pentecostalism and Evangelical Churches everywhere. Perhaps, also, the establishment of revivalistic preaching re-established something of the epic storytelling of an earlier age. In the 1830s, the New England farmer, William Miller, would even point to the sky, eager to see his Lord on the point of returning in the clouds to claim his throne.

Sixthly, it may be true that by the nineteenth century, organized and routinized revivals, such as D.L. Moody's campaigns, borrowed the techniques of the novelist and the salesman. But they stayed faithful to the gospel in their fashion, and against the tide of middle-class secularism, they succeeded in telling tne story far more effectively than many of their mainstream counterparts.

In the late twentieth century, we might find televangelism repugnant, a changeling offspring of eighteenth-century revivalism, but in itself televangelism is a natural development of the nineteenth-century American urban missions. If you believe that there is a Christian grand narrative, and that it needs to be proclaimed, there is nothing odd about wishing to do so on the airwaves, as well as in the highways and byways.

As Iwan Russell-Jones pointed out in a recent article, we can laugh at the antics and intellectual somersaults of televangelists like Jack Van Impe, and shudder at his dispensationalist and fundamentalist hermeneutics, but at least he has a story to tell – unlike many of us in the mainstream Churches, who have forgotten who we are.

It is difficult, however, to keep a balanced perspective on revivalism and its Evangelical outcrops without registering some concerns. First, as we have noted, the eighteenth-century evangelists were men of great learning and prudence who were not only products of literary culture but major contributors to it. America may never have produced a greater theologian than Jonathan Edwards. The crafting of his sermons – even the notorious 'Sinners in the Hands of an Angry God' – are literary masterpieces. The depth and breadth of the Christian story in 'Safety, Fulness, and Sweet Refreshment, to be Found in Christ' shows us that he was an incomparable narrator of the Christian story, which he typically told in restrained yet sonorous tones.

At the beginning of the nineteenth century, Charles Finney, who founded Oberlin College, was not the literary equal of Edwards or Wesley, but nevertheless he was a man of literary seriousness. By the last quarter of the nineteenth century, however, it is noticeable that in D.L. Moody, who maintained the rhetoric of a fine preacher, we have already passed over into the electronic age of the soundbite, the salesman's pitch, and the adman.

By the beginning of the twentieth century, evangelism began to run the risk of becoming sheer entertainment. The ex-baseball player Billy Sunday, for example, displayed great sincerity and commitment to the gospel, but also great showmanship and financial acumen. He was the first evangelist in history to die a millionaire. In Los Angeles during the 1920s, that great precursor of televangelism, Aimee Semple McPherson, preached a compelling Pentecostalist gospel, but seemed to prefer spectacular stunts – including her own disappearance – to drawing people deeper into the Christian master story.

It is probably a truism that Billy Graham has been the best of the late-twentieth-century evangelists. He has grown in moral and spiritual stature with age and has remained faithful to his calling without gimmicks or pretensions. What we cannot say, however, is that Billy Graham is a significant theologian, or that he is versed in the Christian tradition or literary culture in the way that Edwards and Wesley were.

All this is not intended as a snobbish aside on the decline of high culture. It is a demonstration that the literary culture which facilitated and sustained the eighteenth-century revivals – as it did the Enlightenment – is not a major influence on this strand of Christian ministry at the close of the millennium. It may be true that many mainstream theologians and preachers have either abandoned or forgotten the gospel, but it is also the case that many evangelists today are no longer theologians or teachers, and some of them display little of the mainstream orthodoxy of John Wesley or Jonathan Edwards. In the book, *Charismatic Renewal: the Search for a Theology*, for example, Tom Smail, Nigel Wright and Andrew Walker argue that the so-called 'Faith Movement' of Kenneth Hagin, Kenneth Copeland and others, is probably heretical.

A second worry in assessing the development of evangelism is to note the tendency to separate preaching ministries from Church life. Theological liberalism, as we have seen, was encouraged by the break between denominations and universities. Similarly, certain brands of fundamentalist Evangelicalism have been characterized by the lack of accountability of some evangelists to their denominations. The growth of para-Church evangelistic organizations not only leads to the danger of promoting the evangelist rather than the gospel, but also creates the possibility that the gospel itself will be seen as an adjunct to an organizational lifestyle, rather than a story rooted in Church community.

A third concern about revivalistic religion is the way in which it has sometimes been blown off course by unwittingly adopting the Enlightenment trend to replace narrative by metanarrative. Two examples come to mind: dispensationalism and fundamentalism.

The eighteenth-century revivals, unlike their late-nineteenth-century counterparts, were not adventist or millennial. Edwards had two basic gospel themes: God's love and God's wrath. The fear of eternal damnation was a major spur to the revivals of New England in the 1730s and 1740s, and may partly explain the shaking, trembling, and swooning phenomena that accompanied them.

However, the social cataclysm of the French and American revolutions of the 1780s reawakened the medieval spectre of Christ's imminent return to earth. The fracture of feudal life both in Europe and the New World caused by the revolutionary spirit led many to believe that they were living in the last days. Revivalists everywhere began to read the Bible with a prophetic eye, and millennial theories became all the rage. The historicist meta-theories of progress, espoused by Hegel, Comte and Marx, found their religious counterparts in Edward Irving, John Nelson Darby and Charles Scofield. Arguably it was a Jesuit, Manuel de Lucunza, who gave them the initial impetus for their theories. Irving translated his book into English from Spanish in 1827, and under the Jewish pseudonym of Ben Ezra it was published in two volumes as *The Coming of the Messiah in Glory and Majesty*.

It was Darby's theories of God's historical epochs, or dispensations, however, that had the greatest impact on Evangelicals in the nineteenth century. In the United States Scofield's *Reference Bible*, first published in 1909, was an extrapolation of Darby's dispensationalism. It carried with it – and does to this day – a progressive timetable of historical events, future expectations, and advice on how to read the signs of the times. Dispensationalism works by imposing a grid upon the text of scripture, rather as Marx imposed a dialectic on history, and then reading the text through the grid.

In itself this creates no great harm – although it creates a hermeneutic of suspicion, and a suspicious hermeneutics – but it is a metanarrative nevertheless. Great millennial expectation falls prey to such theories and they become disruptive and distortive of the Christian grand narrative. Fascination with the end times can simply swamp the gospel story, so that it becomes encrusted with fussy and elaborate additions, like the Russian icons mentioned in chapter two, that had all but been overcome with silver filigree.

The less revivalistic end of nineteenth-century Evangelicalism had a tendency to swerve off course in a different metanarrative direction. The development of the doctrine of inerrancy at Princeton University during the last quarter of the nineteenth century, while intended to underpin the story with a sure philosophical foundation, ran the risk of making the story itself dependent on this new epistemology. Christianity's grand narrative claims that the foundation of faith is Jesus himself, and not a theological and philosophical theory about the divine inspiration of scripture. By raising the doctrine of inerrancy above the status of Christian opinion to theological dogma, it began to function remarkably like a metanarrative.

Fundamentalists have continued to tell the gospel story throughout the twentieth century, but – with notable exceptions – not with the theological acumen and learning of their first generation of scholars. This generation included men such as Charles and Archibald Hodge, B.B. Warfield, Reuben Torrey and James Orr. Fundamentalism has also had a tendency to major on its metanarrative because it gets carried away by its truth claims. These are based on the premises that:

- The Bible is inspired by God.
- This inspiration is equivalent to the fact that God is revealed in perfect truth in the text of scripture.
- There can be no contradictions in the text because God cannot contradict himself.

The unintended consequence of this view of revelation is that the Bible becomes the locus as well as the focus of truth, almost as if God was trapped in the text like the genie in Aladdin's lamp. To make the scriptures the locus of truth seems to be at best a form of religious positivism, and at worst idolatry.

Inerrancy has also led to the hermeneutics of harmony, where elaborate attempts have been made to explain away textual inconsistencies in the Bible, such as the differing accounts in the New Testament of the death of Judas after he had betrayed Christ. The creationism of recent times is a child of such fundamentalism. It seeks to defend Genesis chapters 1 and 2 as a scientific alternative to modern biological science, the premise being that Genesis is a literal description of the origin of the cosmos, which is then used as an *a priori* proof that evolutionism is false.

We can call these Evangelical exercises excursions into metanarratives, because they make the story dependent on something beyond itself, just as the Enlightenment grand theorists came to explain reason's course through their own grand schemas of interpretation. If it is a little unfair to insist that fundamentalism functions as a metanarrative – it is not so obvious as it is with dispensationalism – we can at least ironically note that like their enemies, the modernists, fundamentalists seek to shore up the Christian story with an epistemology which will defend it against the charge of irrationalism. At the very least, therefore, fundamentalism from its early days has become philosophically embroiled with 'second order' or foundational issues, from which it has not yet managed to disentangle itself.

It could be argued that the temptation for Evangelicals to adopt Enlightenment-style metanarratives, rather than stick to the Christian master story, was a nineteenth- and early twentieth-century diversion, and has nothing to do with revivalism in itself. However, even if there is no direct causal link between revivalism and metanarratives, it is notable that both dispensationalism and fundamentalism played a major role in the Pentecostal revivals at the turn of the twentieth century. At the very least, we can say that many instances of revivalism have been intertwined with meta-narrations.

We are on surer, and more significant, critical ground when we turn to our fourth and final concern about revivalism: the volatile nature of religious experience. Recently in North America and Great Britain there has been a charismatic revivalism which has been called 'the Toronto Blessing'. Because of its unusual features – laughing, jerking, roaring, barking, swooning – attempts have been made to show the similarities with the revivals of Jonathan Edwards. This exercise has been prompted by the scarcity of biblical data to support the new enthusiasm, and by the fact that such physical manifestations are not typical of the classical Pentecostal tradition or charismatic renewal. The renewal has concentrated on the 'gifts of the Spirit' of 1 Corinthians chapter 12: 'speaking in tongues', prophecy, and so on.

The ever-prudent Jonathan Edwards, while not wishing to condemn the revivals because of their enthusiasm, was sceptical about the spiritual worth and origin of the more extreme physical manifestations. For him, the jerks and barks of the revivals (the barks being caused by the exhalation of air during the jerking exercises) were secondary symptoms, and not central to God's action in the Great Awakening.

In fact, the present participators of the Toronto Blessing have done well to turn to Edwards and Wesley as possible precursors of the new enthusiasm. They will find in their writings a deep commitment to relating the revivals to the catholic tradition of the Church. Neither of them places frenetic excitement and experiential fervour over and above the sacraments and preaching of the word. Nowhere in their recorded ministry can you find an attempt to make religious excitement or physical phenomena the touchstone of orthodoxy.

In many ways, Wesley and Edwards had appropriated the Christian tradition – its grand story – from its oral past and melded it with the best of literary tradition. They neither fell prey to a legalistic and stale bookishness on the one hand, nor to rampant and strident enthusiasm on the other hand. Subsequent revivals have not always been so balanced.

Edwards, being a high Calvinist, was of the view that revivals were entirely a matter for the sovereignty of God. They could not be organized by mere mortals, or manipulated by technique. As revival moved into the nineteenth century, however, and the Age of Reason waned with the ascent of science and technology, rational techniques increasingly came into play. No less a great revivalist than Charles Finney believed that revivals could be organized on rational principles. He makes this clear in his *Lectures on Revival*: 'A revival is not a miracle, or dependent on a miracle, in any sense. It is purely philosophical results of the right use of constituted means as much as any other effect produced by the application of means.' And with D.L. Moody, poised on the edge of the electronic age, technique, organization and showmanship moved centre stage.

This is not to deny the genuineness of modern revivals, but it is to recognize that as Max Weber noted of political charismatic authorities, they can become routinized and subject to various mechanisms of social control. Because religious enthusiasm is a crowd affair, it is always open either to overt or covert manipulation. Modern charismatics, for example, should not expect the crowd dynamics of the football stadium, the political rally and the pop concert to be absent from their revivals.

Perhaps the most subtle problem with experiential religion in the modern age is not the possibility of mass hysteria, or crowd-induced hyperventilation, but the tendency to confuse human emotionalism with spiritual experience. True religious experience is theanthropic – that is to say, it is of divine origin but appropriated through natural, human experience. Having said that, human experience is an uncertain barometer of the divine. 'Feel good' happenings may be therapeutic, but they are not synonymous with 'the peace that passes all understanding'. 'Warm glows' can result from being with the like-minded in crowds, but in themselves they are not diffused or refracted charisms.

We looked earlier at the conjunction in the Age of Reason of individualism, the interiorization of experience through literary culture, and anthropocentrism. Even in Wesley, ever anxious to take his spiritual pulse, we can see the glimmers of self-absorption with experience. In the so-called quadrilaterals, Wesley added experience to Hooker's three legs of the Anglican stool: scripture, tradition, and reason. Subsequent Methodism, however, has not been so foursquare. It has abandoned its revivalism, catholic tradition, and high view of scripture, but has held on firmly to reason, married to a liberal piety. If this holds true for the United Methodist Church in North America, it also holds for many varieties of modern Presbyterianism, and whole swathes of Episcopalianism.

Conversely – and more importantly – when Methodist revivalism moved out of the denomination, jumping ship with the holiness revivals of the nineteenth century, it stuck to the scriptures and a high-octane experientialism, but kept little attachment to reason and tradition. Experience wedded to a biblical hermeneutic that stressed the immediacy of God's presence – no longer mediated through the sacraments or historical tradition – undercut the ability to distinguish the theanthropic from the anthropic, the miraculous from the merely strange, the spiritual affections from the natural but fallen human ones. If this holds true for many American holiness and 'Bible Churches' today, it holds even more so for charismatic ones, including classical Pentecostalism, charismatic renewal, and Independent or New Churches.

This brings us to the extreme irony of the Christian story in the age of literacy. On the one hand, Schleiermacher, Pietist and theologian of experience that he was, took the mainstream Christian tradition down the long liberal path of gospel amnesia, because he unhooked experience from revealed truth. On the other hand, revivalism, while formally predicated on a commitment to revelation, has in practice cultivated the habit of letting the religion of the heart override revelation as it is grounded in the Christian grand story.

Theological liberals are humane, but gospel amnesiacs. Revivalists are religious visionaries, but fey. The Christian story is essential to both groups, for without it liberals will remain forever lotus eaters, estranged from the historic tradition, and revivalists will remain schismatics, estranged from the historic denominations. Arguably, Christianity in the modern world needs the critical rationality of liberalism, because it is short on self-reflection. It certainly needs to harness religious enthusiasm, for the story needs to be told with verve and conviction if it is to be heard amidst the babble of our modern culture.

To turn to our modern world is to recognize that we are now at the 'fag end' of the literary age and in the full glare of electronic culture. We will briefly examine the emergence of this electronic culture in relation to the gospel, before we reflect on the lessons for the Christian story of the three cultural modes of transmission we have investigated.

4

Forgetting the Story

It would be convenient if we could jump straight from the age of printing to the electrical processes of computers and information technology, rather than deal with earlier and cruder electronic devices. When the printed word went electronic in the mid-twentieth century, it might be thought that we were merely speeding things up in the same way that typography altered the hand technology of chirographics. However, the trouble is that while we now know that printing changed the nature of thinking, we do not yet fully understand how the electrification of the word is changing our thought processes and understanding of the world. This problem is compounded by the fact that electronic culture is as much, if not more, about the use of images and sounds as it is about texts.

Electrical processes today refer to an advanced technology that outstrips anything we have known before and is changing our vocabulary as a result: satellite and cable television, telephone and modem hook-ups, microchips, optical fibres, digital electronics. We can now store and retrieve mountains of information in a microsecond. In the international money markets, money can be electronically moved, laundered, and sunk without trace, at the speed of a phone call. We can translate huge bites and chunks of information into the bytes of computer binary language and back into natural language in no time at all.

With the advent of interactive television, virtual reality, and international networks of computing, we are fast creating a global electronic culture where cyberspace may replace the traditional workplace, not to mention centres of leisure. According to French sociologist Jean Baudrillard, electronic culture has already altered the nature of reality, as electronic images draw us into a seduction of simulation where there is no longer any relation between pictures and things – no transcendental or grounded reality – only a world of self-referential images.

Baudrillard also believes that electronic communication is not a logical extension of oral and printed discourse. Electronic processes alter human perception because they do not rely on the symbolic exchange of earlier forms of communication. Instead, they employ processes which are more akin to the montage of film production, and the open-ended, or 'non closure' techniques of surreal art.

Although we might find Baudrillard's view provocative but unproven, what we cannot deny is that electronic culture today refers to a mass culture that is – and has been since the 1950s at least – inviolably linked not only to advertizing and television in particular, but also to consumer economics in general. In short, the sheer universality and power of mass electronic culture suggests that we cannot simply jump from print to film, or from literary forms of communication to electronic ones, because we would be overwhelmed with the material. Perhaps this is why, as we noted earlier, Ong devotes only two pages of his book to 'electrical processes'!

The solution to this problem is to relocate the significance of electronic culture within the framework of a different debate, so that we can understand its role more clearly in relation to the late developments and dissolution of modernity. We will do this in part two, but for now, more modestly, we can say something of the beginnings of electronic communication as a supplement to, rather than a supplanting of, literary culture. In so doing we will see how the new electronic media were welcomed and exploited by Christians, with mixed blessings for the gospel.

The dawn of the electronic age

The electronic age began long before Queen Victoria's reign was over. Early electronic culture consisted of a number of parallel developments that can be said either to reinforce, augment, or complement literary culture. When Samuel Morse invented the telegraph in 1844, for example, in effect he extended the scope of printing. Typography had enabled information to pass beyond a speaker-hearer gathering to a broader and invisible audience of readers.

The telegraph did this too, but much more quickly. It could send information from around the world to any audience who wanted to read it. All that was needed was a knowledge of Morse code, telegraph wires, and the sending and receiving stations. This was of small use for novelists, but of major interest to governments and newspapers.

The invention of the telegraph extended the competitive nature of daily newspapers and heralded the arrival of 'the scoop'. Telegraphy altered the style, layout, and social and political influence of newspapers. From the 1850s, *The Times* began to include international telegraphic information. News generally became snappier, more urgent, and more compelling. As Neil Postman puts it: 'News took the form of slogans, to be noted with excitement, to be forgotten with dispatch.'

In the decade after the Forster Education Act of 1870 in England and Wales, newspapers increasingly began to cater for the newly literate working classes. The tabloid press was begun with *Tit Bits* and the penny dreadfuls. Such newspapers, now carrying photographs, were more like *The Sun* and *The National Enquirer* than we would like to admit. We are used today of thinking of the phenomenon of urban myths as a modern tabloid obsession. But long before stories began about the sightings of dead pop stars, or of beasts on Bodmin Moor, nineteenth-century newspapers were full of tall tales. The story of Spring-Heeled Jack, who mysteriously and frighteningly jumped out at people all over London, lived on in the penny dreadfuls for forty years, and is still alive and kicking in the Rolling Stones song, *Jumping Jack Flash*.

According to Postman, however, the telegraph had a far wider significance than in merely updating newspapers and giving birth to the tabloid press. 'The telegraph,' he says, 'made information into a commodity, a "thing" that could be bought and sold irrespective of its uses or meaning.' Whatever passed along the wires could be sold to anybody who wanted to buy it.

In many respects, the telegraph was not put to the use that its inventor wished. Samuel Morse saw the telegraph as a means not to spread gossip or information about the price of pork, but to ask the question, 'What hath God wrought?' The nineteenth-century revivalists were not slow to answer the question in their own way. For them the newspaper, now thick with the hottest news, urgently demonstrated the perfidiousness of the world and God's response to it. D.L. Moody, like many evangelists after him, preached with the Bible in one hand and a newspaper in the other. For the millennialists, the technologically-enhanced newspaper must have seemed like a godsend.

However, the significance of the telegraph for religion in the nineteenth century was not merely in its ability to relay bad news. As a communications medium, it was seen by the Evangelical movements in the same messianic terms with which they later heralded the arrival of radio and television in the twentieth century. The new technology, it was fervently believed, would spread the gospel story further, quicker, and more effectively than ever before.

The fact that, in the 1990s, Billy Graham is available on the Internet and that 'missions' are already being conducted in cyberspace, should not surprise us. This is an Evangelical tradition that now spans 150 years. If you believe that you have a message to tell the nations of the world, and if that message is made the more urgent by a belief in the imminent second coming of Christ, and if you believe that there is no salvation without hearing and responding to the gospel, then appropriating new technology to enhance your task is as natural as a Reformed Catholic wishing to see the Bible printed and distributed to the masses in the sixteenth century.

The telegraph was not the only new technology to emerge in the 1840s. The same decade also saw the invention of photography. Admittedly, Louis Daguerre's work was not electronic, but the ability to be able to reproduce nature on film brought the image back into the heart of western culture, which had turned its back on vivid iconography since the Reformation. By the 1870s, when literacy rates were up and the invention of the weekend in England meant an increase in leisure time, photographs were not only appearing in art galleries and newspapers, police stations and Victorian drawing rooms, they were also being married to the power of electricity.

Before moving pictures began in the late 1880s, Victorians were being treated to the enchantment of magic lantern shows. In existence since the eighteenth-century, lantern slides originally had to be hand painted and shown by natural or candlelight. But by putting together crafted lenses, electric light and photography, mass electric entertainment was invented. In the early twentieth century, many a church hall and Sunday school watched in awe as the gospel story, missionary exploits, and photographs of God's good creation were projected onto screen or wall.

Moving, though non-talking, picture companies were commercially viable by the early 1890s, and while the cinema brought news, government propaganda and documentaries to the public, it was stories, accompanied by live music, that people wanted to see. These stories borrowed from the techniques of novel, theatre, vaudeville and tabloid newspapers, and added to them a romance, mystery, and seduction of their own.

The significance and seduction of images is clearer now in the late twentieth century than it was 100 years ago. Vivid imagery, through advertizing, television, and film, are now ubiquitous in the modern world. Curiously, however, despite the exploitation of television, sound recording and radio by evangelistic organizations, such groups have been chary about the use of film. Perhaps this is due to the high production costs; perhaps it is because of the association of Hollywood with Babylon. Whatever the reason, although the Billy Graham Organization periodically produces films, and despite the fact that evangelist T.L. Osborn had a number of successful self-promotion films in the early 1960s, the most widespread use of moving pictures by the Churches in the twentieth century has probably been the Moody Institute's 'Fact and Faith' series.

Hollywood itself has dabbled in biblical themes, from the silent *King of Kings* to the risible *The Greatest Story Ever Told*. But if films such as *The Ten Commandments*, *The Robe*, and *Ben Hur* were great box-office successes, this is because they were historical spectacles headed by major stars rather than because they were telling the story as a Christian witness. It is ironic that the movie that is probably the most faithful to the biblical record is Pasolini's *The Gospel According to St Matthew*. Pasolini, an atheist and Communist, was allegedly murdered by a rent-boy a few years after completing the film, although conspiracy theories abound.

Early electronic culture, despite the invention of the cinema in the 1880s, was more oral than visual, and churches found sound recordings less alien than film. The Reformation had promoted words over images, and hundreds of years later, Protestant churches preferred sacred songs to sacred pictures. Edison's phonograph and the later gramophones began a culture of exchange, first in wax and later in plastics and vinyl, that is reminiscent of the spread of early literary culture in the late Middle Ages. With the record, as with the book, you could transfer the original production to many audiences. Recordings of revivalist sermons, hymns and choruses boosted the Pentecostalist movement in the twentieth century just as the pamphleteering of the protesting Catholics aided the cause of the Reformation in the sixteenth century.

However, it was the radio, and not the record or cinema, that heralded the first electronic mass culture. When Marconi used a radio transmitter in 1901 to send signals across the Atlantic, the nature of modern communication was changed irrevocably. Information could now be transmitted all over the world without telegraph wires and without codes. It became possible, even if you were lost at sea, to send distress signals with pinpoint accuracy, beyond the basic emergency Morse code of 'SOS'.

Long before television arrived in people's front rooms, the radio had entered right into the home, with its stories, music, entertainment, sermons, trivia and advertizing. The American president or the British prime minister could speak to you directly, as Churchill did, to millions of people in the Second World War, when he promised them nothing but 'blood, toil, tears and sweat'.

The two-way radio transmitter also meant that 'turn-taking' communication could be facilitated by radio. Only one other form of technology could match such innovation, and that was the telephone. Since the 1870s, when Scotland's Alexander Graham Bell invented the telephone in his adopted America, literary culture found itself faced with a revival of oral culture. The telephone, however, supports a quite different form of oral culture to that of the Middle Ages: it is not a communitarian but a private method of communication. Its typical audience consists of two people, a speaker and a hearer, in which face-to-face communication is prohibited by distance.

In fact, the telephone, telegraph, radio, film, television and video all belong to the genre of what Ong would call 'secondary orality' – for these are technologies that enhance image and spoken words or music at the expense of text. These oralities are not a return to primary orality; instead, they are post-literary technologies that facilitate communication at the expense of community. Until the advent of information technology – with its faxes, satellites and computers – only telephones and two-way radios promoted conversation and dialogue. Television, film, video and radio have all been one-way systems of communication and information aimed at passive audiences.

Electronic culture, despite its conversational limitations, and like literary culture before it, was appropriated by Christian groups from its beginning. We have already mentioned the telegraph, but as early as the turn of the twentieth century you could listen to Moody and Sankey 'sacred solos' and hymns on record. Aimee Semple McPherson's 'Foursquare Gospel' was on radio in the 1920s, while at the same time in Britain you could hear sermonettes by Elim evangelist George Jeffreys on electric or hand-cranked gramophones.

These were religious communicators that we do not usually associate with the mainstream Churches. This is so, we might argue, because the mainstream Protestant denominations do not major on the story in the way that the newer denominations seem to have done. It is the former that have been most influenced by academic changes in theology and the challenge of secular metanarratives. Throughout the twentieth century, they seem to have been strongly motivated by Church unity as mission – support for the World Council of Churches, for example – but without necessarily a strong commitment to telling the story as a spur to mission.

Given this curious disjunction between the mainstream and what we might want bluntly to call the more sectarian Christian Churches, it will be useful to take one more snapshot of electronic culture before we move on.

The medium of television

The key medium to examine is television. This is so because television comes right into our homes and captures our attention, whether or not we are interested in the programmes we are watching. In the United States, the average viewing time for citizens is said to be a staggering seven and a half hours a day. In the United Kingdom it is up to five hours a day.

Television combines the allure of film and music with the immediacy of the telegraph and a domestic cosiness that is all its own. Media promoters encourage this home entertainment by talking of television as a window on the world. Television appeals to the voyeur in us, and also beguiles us into thinking that we are participating in the great historical and cultural events of our times merely by watching them.

What we are actually doing when we watch television is more akin to spectator sports – and even this can be misleading, for we do not have a ringside seat at the action. We are watching carefully controlled, selected, and editorially-approved media events or fictional shows. These shows and events, with their personalities and dramas, become the staple diet of tabloid newspapers and gossip magazines, which filter back into television as further grist to its mill. We, the audience, also become living feedback, appearing on endless quizzes and prize shows, 'fly on the wall' documentaries, confessional and agony profiles, and above all as vox-pop. Any opinion from anyone on anything is welcome on television.

The TV monitor in our home is a not a window on the world, but it is a window open to the consumer markets. The household is a captive audience for the advertizers. Indeed, the shopping channel on American cable is a form of interactive television that has been with us for some time. The monitor displays the goods, and customers orders their choice on the telephone, paying with a credit card.

Before the era of cable and satellite, which heralded deregulation and market-led television, the new medium was hailed in almost as reverential a tone as Samuel Morse lauded the telegraph. Lord Reith, in his famous inaugural lecture for the BBC, looked to the future of broadcasting in terms of a high moral culture, supplemented by cheery and wholesome popular fare.

Part of this wholesomeness on the BBC, American public television, and the main advertizing networks, was to make room for religion. In reality, religion turned out to be epilogues tucked away in the dead of night, or homilies trundled out for the Sunday 'God slot'. In America, constitutionally a secular society, and Great Britain, a *de facto* one, television has fought shy of actually promoting religion, although the mainstream Churches have been given opportunity enough to shout their wares.

Social commentators such as Neil Postman, picking up where Marshall McLuhan left off in his assertion that 'the medium is the message', have insisted that television simply cannot handle religion seriously. In fact, Postman thinks that television cannot adequately deal with politics, philosophy or religion. His view has affinities with Martin Esslin, who believes that 'television as such displays the basic characteristics of the dramatic mode of communication – and thought, for drama is also a method of thinking, of experiencing the world, and reasoning about it'.

Postman accepts the argument that television is a 'dramatic mode of communication', but adds that it is essentially an entertaining medium. It lures, it seduces, it cajoles, it sells, it amuses *ad nauseam* – but Postman doubts if it can seriously educate or even adequately inform. Even the news, he feels, is over-glamourized by the attractive anchormen and women, dramatic music, and hyperbolic presentation of events.

Esslin recognizes that television confuses fact and fiction with news being squashed between realistic dramas. Advertisements are little stories in themselves that punctuate the scheduled programmes – the 'big shows' – with wish-fulfilments. Real events happen only once, but shows on television can be (and often are) repeated; some cable channels only show old and oft-viewed programmes; with the advent of video we can play our favourite shows, news items, amusing adverts, pornographic clips, to our heart's content.

Baudrillard, as we have seen, believes that television breaks down the relation between image, word and deed, so that reality becomes hyperreality, where images have overcome objects in the world. For him, this is possible because images are murderous and take the place of persons, places, events and things. They become simulacrum – shadowy deceptions that refer to nothing at all but themselves. Television, for the French sociologist, is neither a window on the world nor the markets: it is opaque and reflects back only the mirror image of itself.

Baudrillard's oblique style and rhetorical method are difficult to evaluate. Because we are used to older, social scientific discourse, we expect empirical evidence rather than provocative illustrations. Nevertheless, we can begin to see the possibility that television, like writing, may alter the way we appropriate reality. If we follow the less radical views of Esslin and Postman, they provide us with sufficient food for thought to make us wonder what kind of thinking television encourages.

Postman, as we have seen, is quite clear that television is no more than an amusement that promotes personalities but punishes reflective thought and undermines critical thinking. For him, television is an entertaining medium that soothes, shocks, numbs, excites and soothes again in a rhythm of nervous energy. Pornography, gospel preaching, 'soaps', drama and news, appear before our eyes in a series of almost hypnotic and disconnected images – rather in the way that stroboscopic light confuses the visual senses on a teenage dance floor.

If we were to pursue this line, we might think it fortunate that mainstream Christianity sticks to the seminary and the local church, rather than enter the labyrinth of the simulacrum. However, studies of visual culture are a new discipline, and little is yet known about television as a transmitter of culture – although in recent years, semiotics as the study of linguistic signs has been applied to visual media.

It may be that television promotes personalities and is an inappropriate medium for serious philosophy and theology, but it can depict history in a serious way. Perhaps we remember the extraordinary NBC series of the American Civil War, using mainly still black and white photographs, letters and official documents. And the documentary approach can be a useful and serious extension of investigative journalism. One thinks of ITV's *World in Action* and BBC's *Panorama*. Indeed, the BBC's *Heart of the Matter* and ITV's *Credo* have successfully applied the documentary approach to religion.

It is probably true, however, that television has destroyed oratory, just as literary culture obliterated epic poetry. Former president Ronald Reagan demonstrated that the one-liner can be devastatingly successful on television when rhetoric fails. His most famous line, 'There you go again', whenever he disagreed with (or failed to understand) a political opponent, invariably brought the house down, and in letting him off the hook gave the impression that he was the outright winner. Michael Foot, the former Labour leader, was an inspired orator in the House of Commons but on television his jabbing and jabbering approach looked merely eccentric. Neil Kinnock, his successor, also failed to master the 'chatty', friendly technique that the small screen favours. It is also fair to say that neither Kinnock nor Foot were handsome enough for television: in a world of glamorous images, the looks have it every time.

Television and the gospel

All of these factors may go some way to explaining what works successfully on television, but it does not explain why Christian theologians and educators have had so little to do with the new medium. A conspiratorial thesis might suggest that television is essentially a secular medium and that religion is given short shrift unless it can be attacked. Conservative Evangelicals in the United Kingdom, for example, were furious when in the 1980s the BBC's *Sea of Faith*, with Don Cupitt, and ITV's *Jesus the Evidence*, undermined orthodox Christianity. British television has in fact never scheduled a conservative equivalent of such programmes. Nor does it remain totally neutral in its approach to Christian religion.

Before we dismiss this as paranoia, Andrew and Juliet Quicke's study of the politics of religious broadcasting in Britain, *Hidden Agendas*, contains some convincing evidence that television programming is weighted against conservative Christianity. Atheist Tony Currie, former controller of cable television in Britain in 1991, was sufficiently impressed by the research to give it a positive endorsement.

Be that as it may, a more plausible explanation for the absence of mainstream Christianity from the airwaves is its apathetic approach to communicating faith in and to popular culture. Television is a narrative and dramatic medium, and this is why 'soaps', 'sitcoms' and game shows do so well. Intellectual discourse does not do well, unless it is truncated and dramatized. Feminists such as Germaine Greer and Camille Paglia seem to have adapted well enough, as have scientists such as David Bellamy. Our theological educators, however, are not trained in the art of story, or the role of homiletics in a televized world. In such a medium, we wonder, what is a gospel amnesiac going to say?

Conversely, the successors of the great revivals – the millennialists, fundamentalists, Evangelicals and charismatics – have hailed television as 'God's technology for the final generation'. Most of us in the mainstream Churches have stood on the touchline and shouted 'foul' at the antics of televangelists; suppressed barely-controlled glee at the great scandals of the 1980s; roared with disapproval at the heresies and emotional manipulation; gasped at the sheer affront of asking for and getting so much money – but we have remained on the touchline. We have not been involved. It remains an untested thesis that television has no serious role in telling the gospel story in contemporary society, because the majority of us have never really tried it.

Nevertheless, we need to ask, with Baudrillard and Postman, some searching questions about the role of television in modern culture, and especially about what role television can play in Christian mission. In order to do this, we will need briefly to overview the emergence of televangelism, which in many ways is a logical extension of American nineteenth-century urban mission.

When the Texan evangelist Rex Humbard began his television broadcasts in the late 1950s, and Billy Graham started his *Hour of Decision* in the 1960s, religious television coverage was little more than a filmed event of an 'old time' American gospel hour. By the late 1980s, however, the evangelists really had become 'televangelists', changing their style, approach to communication, and sometimes the content of their message for their audience.

Much has been written of how the fundamentalists were denied access to the television channels, and how they took advantage of the new rules of televized deregulation in the 1980s. They availed themselves of the new technologies – cable and satellite – and slipped into the mainstream of American broadcasting, buying 'prime time' with dollars from their audiences. Fundamentalism, which had been sidelined in America since the Scopes monkey trial of 1925, was back with a voice in mainstream culture. The mixture of hard-sell gospel, popular personalities, right-wing or apolitical politics, and light entertainment formats proved to be a winner.

For a time, the Baptist preacher Jerry Falwell headed a 'moral majority' coalition which helped put Ronald Reagan in office for a second term. His *Old Time Revival Hour* was in fact a platform both for a Southern Baptist gospel and right-wing Christianity that influenced the voting patterns of millions of Americans. Evangelist Pat Robertson of *The 700 Club* even ran for president, and religious personalities such as Oral Roberts, Jimmy Swaggert, Jimmy and Tammy Faye Bakker, were scarcely out of the news.

It all seems long ago now. Today we still have 'old timers' such as Morris Cerullo ranting in pre-war holiness style, Pat Robertson chatting in his more modern and amiable manner, and Kenneth and Gloria Copeland busily selling 'health and wealth'. The new boys on the block, Benny Hinn and Rodney Howard Browne, have arrived, with spectacular mass 'slayings in the Spirit', while others, such as the disgraced Robert Tilton, make way for them. These preachers are successful, but not in the same way (Robertson excepted) as in the 1980s. Relative success in this context means that their ratings are not so high.

And here lies the rub of evaluating television as a successful medium for the gospel. What do the ratings amount to? In 1987, there was a sociological consultation in Boston with Peter Berger, David Martin, James Davison Hunter, Steve Bruce, David Docherty and the present author. During this consultation, we realized that it was virtually impossible to assess the Evangelical success of television and radio. Has electronic culture been a major aid to the gospel or not? As a business, televangelism has had success: you can measure it in dollars and cents. You can also measure it in ratings: for a while Oral Roberts and Jimmy Swaggert both topped 10 million viewers in the late 1980s. You can measure it qualitatively by successful formats and performances. Television, like the camp meeting before it, thrives on dramatic anecdote and heart-warming testimony.

However, television as a medium for faithfully telling the story remains difficult to assess. So often, the television audiences of televangelists are already practising or lapsed Evangelicals. Deregulation in North America has meant that the gospel will only reach a limited target audience. An audience is not a congregation, it is an aggregate of viewers. More significantly, it is a market. And a market is a consumers' constituency – somewhere where your products can thrive. Products, however, are commodities, which leads to the question: what commodities are these markets buying? Is it the televized programmes, the merchandise on offer – videos, books, signed photographs of the personalities, 'prayer cloths', religious jewellery – or is it the gospel? Which is the product, and which is the packaging? Is the packaging, as Postman fears, deemed to be the product?

Christian markets, it turns out, are like markets the world over: they are volatile and liable to consumer change. When the great televangelist scandals broke in the 1980s, so too did the markets, scattering and regrouping in random fashion according to taste, commitment and new-found interest.

David Martin has shown in his book *Tongues of Fire* that although American televangelism may boast significant viewing figures in Latin America, its impact seems to be marginal. Quite clearly, the great success of Pentecostalism there is home-grown, and seems to have more in common with eighteenth-century Methodism and nineteenth-century self-help American Evangelicalism, than late-twentieth-century televized evangelism. It remains to be seen whether the televized evangelistic shows in Africa and Eastern Europe will be perceived as telling the story or selling American culture – or whether the people in these regions will think that the predominantly light entertainment formats *are* the message.

More tragically, we have learned over the years that because television promotes personalities and novelties over and above ideas and morals, it may settle for glimmers of glamour rather than glimpses of gospel. After all, Jesus cannot appear on television; the Holy Trinity is not synonymous with the logo of Trinity Broadcasting Network; and the sacraments can only be simulated on TV. The 'electronic Church', we now realize, is an oxymoron.

Television seduces its audience, but it also seduces its programme-makers. Television produces 'stars', not saints. Stars are quixotic and worldly-wise, and fame, not faith, may be the spur to Christian ministry in a culture where fame and success are the highest callings. We should not be too surprised or judgmental when the evangelists we treat like stars begin to behave like them.

However, we need to avoid cynicism. Religious television has had some successes, as 'telethons' and *Comic Relief* have helped a world in need, even if they are media events. God is sovereign over electronic culture as well as over the spoken and written word. *Songs of Praise* in Great Britain links thousands of older men and women, as well as the infirm, to Church services they cannot attend. And we should not assume that people have not been brought to faith through watching televangelism, or that all preachers on TV are crooks or financial opportunists. The big question to ask of television is not whether its preachers will spread heresy or peddle upbeat religious lifestyles, but whether the medium itself can be successfully utilized for the gospel?

For those of us who are still watching on the sidelines and are thinking of chancing our arm and joining in the game, we have had ample opportunity to learn how to play – and how not to – by watching the professionals. Oral Roberts, for example, learned to adapt his hectoring tent campaign style to a folksy conversational tone – something that Morris Cerullo has never done. Swaggert survived as an old-time Pentecostal through sheer verve, a fine singing voice, and good looks. Pat Robertson adopted the news and views format of secular broadcasting and demonstrates to this day that armchair philosophizing works well on television.

The Bakkers' great appeal was not being afraid of displaying their obviously dysfunctional lifestyle, while happily selling us false hopes (and false shares) in their Christian theme park, Heritage USA. One wonders if the Bakkers' somewhat vulnerable and confessional style influenced Oprah Winfrey – or even President Clinton.

Television, in short, offers opportunities to certain styles of communication but closes others down. If we want to engage in extended debate, continue an ongoing dialogue, lecture in oratorical and rhetorical style, then television will not help us. To be 'good' on television is not a moral virtue but a pragmatic one. What works – chatting, confessing, amusing, nudging, informing, shocking, storytelling – is determined by the nature of the communicating medium, and not by the content of what needs to be communicated.

If we in the Christian mainstream intend to take the risk and appropriate electronic culture, through television, for the gospel, two problems remain unresolved:

- How can we faithfully witness to the gospel without swamping the message by the commercial and entertaining tendencies of the medium?
- How do we convince our audiences that the story we are telling is not a 'soap', or even a divine drama to be believed, but a story that they need to indwell by getting up from their couches and joining with fellow Christians in the Churches?

These two problems arise because it may very well be that television is only possible as a form of pre-evangelism. It is noticeable that the advocates of televized evangelism, like the advocates of radio before them, are committed to a proclamation model of mission. If we follow William Abraham's insistence, in his book *The Logic of Evangelism*, that the gospel is always more than proclamation, more than storytelling, we will be drawn to his own model – gleaned from Eastern Orthodox, Methodist, and charismatic sources – that the evangelist's role is not to tell tales but to initiate people into the kingdom of God. Or to use the language of this book: the story once heard has to be broken into, taken by storm, become our own.

Last Things First

Social progressivists adopt an evolutionary model of cultural development: like the master narratives of modernity, primitive stages are replaced by successively superior ones. Traditionalists, and social conservationists, on the other hand, adopt a regressive model: there was once a golden age, but things deteriorated. This golden age may be located in the Bible, if you are a charismatic or a fundamentalist. It could be in the patristic era, if you are an Orthodox. A Roman Catholic may long for the hegemony of the western Middle Ages. American Reformed Christians may think of their ideal society as the Puritan theocracy of New England in the seventeenth century.

We need to reject both the evolutionary and traditionalist models, because they are different sides of the same coin: they are historicist. The Christian grand narrative speaks of two significant developments in the history of humankind. One is the fall, which causes a fall-out of suffering and decay. The other is the incarnation and resurrection of Christ, which, in Lesslie Newbigin's wonderful phrase, leads to a 'fall-out of joy'. Neither event commits the story to a progressivist or regressivist theory of history. On the contrary, the constant factor in cultural development, according to the story, is human nature which is sinful. Human nature does not progress or regress in time, although societies wax and wane. It waits to be redeemed.

Such a view liberates us from having to locate historical processes within progressivist or dissolutionist theories. We can say that some things in the history of the world have got better, but some things have got worse. It would be silly and churlish, for example, to deny the great benefits to human existence that medicine has brought. But medicine, like science in general, has outstripped morality, which seems to be sinking into ever-greater laxity and turpitude.

If we recognize that human history has always been a mixture of good news and bad news, we can adopt this insight into our overview of cultural transmission. We do not have to start by saying that oral culture is best because it is first; or that electronic culture is best because it is last. We might say, if we wanted to hold to a contingent view of history, how fortuitous it was that the gospel came to life in oral culture.

If the gospel had come into existence in electronic culture, it is difficult to see how it could have survived intact. Its textuality – for we must assume that the gospel events would have been written down – would have been subject to the manipulation and infinite manoeuvrability of word processing. With 'hypertext', for example, we cannot only cut and paste documents at will, but rearrange and recreate different texts from the original text. Hypertext is like Baudrillard's hyperreality: it no longer refers to real events or things, but only to itself.

Film would be an even more disturbing medium in which to establish gospel truth. Since the days of the Third Reich and the Stalinist era, we have known that the camera can lie, and that film can be manipulated by script, camera and editor. This pales into insignificance, however, with the advent of digital recording and the new special effects this makes possible. In the 1995 Oscar-winning film *Forest Gump*, our hero shakes hands with President Kennedy, and a skilful montage of fact and fiction is woven together so artfully that it is not technically possible to know how to tell the difference – we can almost hear Baudrillard saying, 'I told you so'.

More sinister, in a way, is the method in the 1994 production of *The River Wild* of using digital computer techniques to fake the stunts on the river. Unlike *Forest Gump*, where those of us who are old enough know that Kennedy did not really shake hands with our hero, there is no historical or outside reference to measure the reality of who was doing what in the whitewater rafting sequences. Unless movie magazines had 'blown the gaff', we would never have known that Meryl Streep had not actually undergone the stunts herself. Such movie magic will soon be so commonplace that no one will bother to comment on it. In such a world, would the empty tomb become a commonplace without comment on it? Would we be shown shaking hands with the risen Christ?

In wondering whether electronic culture would have given the gospel a good start – that is to say, whether it would be honestly represented – we are not denying that such a culture can imaginatively grasp the story as it has been handed down from oral and literary culture, and even help us to inculturate it in the modern age. After the advent of the telephone, for example, the old spiritual announces: 'Jesus is on the mainline, call him up'. Such a metaphor is delightful, for as the song goes on to say: 'he'll be there'.

But when we move beyond electronic metaphors, and even beyond radio and television, into recent electronic culture, we have to wonder how the Church would have been created. How would the community have come together, when MTV, virtual reality, super mega drives and global technology keep us apart? These activities may be widespread, and may soon be world-wide, but they are not typically activities we do with one another. Most people do not have access to such technology, and it is arguable that those who do are living in virtual community, rather than truly human community.

If the Church came into existence today, would it arrive fully-fledged as a televized commercial organization, promoting therapeutic techniques, and with shopping 'signs following'? Would we attract disciples or consumers; congregations or audiences; believing participants or loyal spectator supporters?

Of course, such speculation is idle, because it falls into that most infinite of categories, 'the might have been'. However, it serves one useful service: it throws into relief just how crucial oral culture was for establishing the gospel. It was a necessary precondition – not a sufficient one – for the establishment of the story, because oral culture is the most stable and least changing of human societies. The gospel had space to grow and time to be rooted in community and institution before it was rocked by the technological innovation of typography, and later by telegraphy and television.

Certainly we can, with genuine modern confidence, demonstrate that orality encourages faithful remembrance of things heard and handed down. It is typography and electrical processes, and not orality, that induce forgetfulness. Orality, however, has its limitations: it is incapable of a deep reflexivity without writing. Literary culture introduced a fund of novelty and innovation into human affairs that oral culture was incapable of creating. Furthermore, orality may have been 'gospel friendly' but it was also culturally promiscuous. It promoted the gospel, but it also promoted paganism and any other religious or mythopoeic narratives. Oral cultures, in short, are good news for all religions, and not just Christianity in particular.

However, in one significant sense we can say that what Ong calls primary oral culture *is* primary for the Church, not merely because it came first, or because it is how things began, but because orality establishes community. In this sense, in our world which boasts contiguous cultures of orality, literacy, and electricity, it is an imperative of the gospel community to keep the primacy of orality alive. This is so because oral culture by its nature is personal, and cannot be impersonal – unlike literary and electronic cultures. Primary oral culture knows of no other form of communication except face to face.

The Christian story is insistent that God is personal by nature. Indeed, the trinitarian relatedness of God's being as a unity of love is the ontological foundation of the Christian story. In this book, it is our first narration, or chapter, of the gospel, as we saw in chapter one. We learn right from the beginning that God exists in a dynamic movement of intimate and related personhood, and his vision and purpose is to share that life with all humankind. Admittedly, oral culture is not divinized culture, but it reflects something of the communicative medium of God's love. Oral community – and not cognitive individuals, as St Augustine thought – may be the true location of the *imago dei* in the world.

Given the primacy of oral culture for the Church, orality can never be replaced, but only augmented and supplemented. In this respect, literary culture, and electronic culture as the secondary orality, have a legitimate role in Christian life. Liturgy, however, as it has always been, remains our primary oral and personal medium of communication. It is not merely something that Churches used to do in olden times; it is the lifeblood of Christian community. The eucharist, in particular, helps us to remember God's decisive action in Christ 'till he comes', but it also feeds us, binds us together, brings us closer to God. There can never be a virtual communion, never a literary rendition of a material supper. A common meal is a meal to be shared, together with the immediate company of saints, but on behalf of the world.

Theologically speaking, it is doubtful that oral culture was contingent history for the coming of the gospel. God wanted to come and meet us face to face, in human form, in Jewish flesh, in transparent culture. He came to die for us, and therefore he had to be with us. It is difficult to be vulnerable on film, wounded in hyperflesh, to be killed in *Mortal Kombat* on the Super Nintendo. God, since the beginning of the world, has always met us in the relatedness of an 'I and thou' conversation: it is the very basis of divine and human communion. He cannot meet us in books, although he can speak to us through them; nor in cyberspace, although he may reach in to pluck us out.

From the beginning of the Christian Church, chirographic culture added reflective and mediated wisdom to direct and immediate communication, and opened up oral discourse to broader horizons. Strictly speaking, therefore, the spoken gospel has always been underwritten by sacred texts – words of power in hallowed form. With the invention of typography, books may have broken up communities, but they also broke down prejudices. It was during the apotheosis of literary culture, the Enlightenment, that the Church began to realize that God loved the whole world so much that he wanted to abolish slavery, remove dominion between fellow creatures, and set people free from the tyranny of the world's principalities and powers. The dreams of freedom in the Enlightenment were no less than intimations of immortality, which the philosophers mistook for precepts of morality.

In principle, electronic culture extends literary culture on the one hand – word processing, computer language – but reintroduces a secondary oral culture on the other hand – radio, telephone, television, film. We note in particular, with this secondary orality, the return of the dominance of the image in the modern world. Such a return has major repercussions for the telling of the story in our culture.

Christian oral culture, as we saw earlier, was as iconographic as it was chirographic. Modern imagery, however, has something of the sacred yet decadent nature of late medieval Catholicism and the early Renaissance. Florentine musculature and Californian 'bodies beautiful' have a certain elective affinity. Both reflect the western aggressive eye which hardens beauty into a brazen, shameless talisman of sexual power. Some years ago, C.S. Lewis commented that 'serious sex worship – quite different from the cheery lechery endemic in our species' was abroad.

Contemporary images, especially through advertizing, may be soaked in sex, but since the advent of television, to echo Baudrillard again, all images are murdering the word. Ironically, even word-processing cannot begin in most computers until you click on an icon and open a window onto the electronic text. Surely now is the time for the gospel to recapture a true iconography in a world where the image is replacing the written word. The Church needs images to enhance and promote the word, rather than humiliate it; it needs images to set the story in colour and space; it needs icons not as windows on text, but as windows on heaven.

Electronic culture, as the second orality, is a great challenge and opportunity for mission. Fleeting images, transient meanings and a world of simulations needs to be measured against images that are truly referential.

Liturgical renewal is necessary to reinstate the image as part of the divine drama of salvation in an electronic world that understands spectacle and drama but wearies of texts. The recognition that a true iconography is necessary for mission is reflected not only in the more catholic traditions of Christianity, but also in the movement known as post-Evangelicalism. As Roy McCloughry wrote recently, God does not always want to be doing 'a new thing'. He also points us to the past, and to what he achieved once and for all on the cross. 'The tradition of the Church,' says McCloughry, 'is also the history of the movement of the Holy Spirit in previous generations.'

Liturgy, as divine drama, tells again the old, old story. It is not play-acting, but an acting out of God's love for the world. This sacred dramaturgy demands words and images of wisdom and power, theologically significant body language, lights and colours, smells and food. If we are asking our contemporary culture to 'come and see', we must have something to show them as well as something to say. Liturgical renewal is not archaeological and antiquarian, not the restraining of the Spirit in a formal straitjacket of tradition. It is nothing less than a preparation for mission in a world where literary culture is moribund.

That mission can only proceed, however, if we put first things first. To renew liturgy is to recapture the gospel handed down to us from oral culture, through literary culture, until today. The handed-downness of things reminds us that they have a history, an embeddedness in past cultures: they are a treasury of blessings to be appropriated by every new generation. The gospel comes from the past to us as a sacred and precious deposit of faith. We do not offer the world a new doctrine, but that which we have received from the beginning.

Yet in a profound sense the gospel which we have received from the past also comes from the future, from the end. It is not the 'first things' (*protologia*) which give us faith in our future, but the fact that the 'last things' (*eschatalogia*) have already begun. Christ's resurrection, witnessed to by the apostles in the past, is in fact the beginning of the end, the ground of hope for the world. Eschatalogical time entered the universe in the incarnation and is now drawing natural time after itself like a magnetic bullseye capturing a wayward arrow. Those of us who believe in the gospel know that 'the one short tale we feel to be true' leads home.

PART TWO

The Gospel in the Twilight of Modernity

5

The Modern Age and the Gospel

Having briefly traced the history of the cultural transmission of the gospel from orality to electronic culture, and having argued for the recovery of the gospel as story for the modern world, it is time for us to turn our attention to this world and its future. To reiterate what we said in the prologue: while Christian mission needs to be driven by the content of the gospel, too little attention to cultural context leads to a failure of communication. The problem of getting our message across has been an endemic one for Christianity in the modern era.

Of even more pressing concern for the gospel is the fact that the modern era itself seems to be coming to a close. This does not in itself indicate that we are about to be plunged into a new Dark Ages (although we could be), or that we are about to be flung upon the final shore of Armageddon (which is not impossible), but it does suggest that modernity – the scientific-rationalist-industrial world order of the last 200 years – has finally run out of steam.

Classical modernity

Modern western culture has been above all an industrial society committed to progress and the pursuit of happiness, and no one can doubt that it has been a double century of extraordinary human achievement. And yet as we face the twenty-first century and the third millennium, we do not do so with the confidence with which we faced the twentieth century in the second millennium. As the writer Saul Bellow recently wrote of American society: 'For the first time probably in the history of the Republic, parents doubt that their children will live as good a life as they have done.'

This pessimism, shared today by so many intellectuals in Europe and America, was sensed by Bishop Lesslie Newbigin when he returned to Great Britain after thirty years as a missionary to India. He felt that coming back was not a homecoming to the motherland of faith, but a return to a fretful culture that was itself in desperate need of mission. For Newbigin, the First World of advanced industrial society was a land without hope; one perhaps in permanent decay. Or, as we will argue, a culture in transition.

The difficulty of talking in this way, however, is that we are not dealing with self-evident facts, but with that nebulous but nevertheless real business of assessing the significance of contemporary change. It is only with hindsight that we can safely say that we have passed from one era to another, or that our culture used to be that but now it is this. Furthermore, a culture does not cease to exist by rational decree or through prophetic punditry: it lingers on until it eventually becomes absorbed into the new one or atrophies. Feudalism, for example, did not suddenly disappear with the birth of capitalism in the Protestant countries of sixteenth-century Europe. On the contrary, life for the European peasant in the seventeenth century was very little different from peasant life in the seventh century.

Cultural change, even when it is as rapid as the transition of Tsarist Russia to the Soviet Union, is a matter of continuities with the old order as well as discontinuities. The Soviets, for example, may have put an end to 'Holy Russia', but they adapted and reinforced the Tsarist centralized bureaucracy as part of the new order, and kept the secret police. Similarly, we should not expect the future to be a violent break with our modern culture, but rather an adaptive reaction to it.

To talk of future cultural continuities and discontinuities with our present culture is, of course, not strictly possible, as the future has not yet arrived. We can, however, legitimately speculate about its possibilities if there is strong evidence of significant cultural change taking place now. Such evidence does exist, but in order to understand it, we have first to understand our present cultural context.

In this chapter, therefore, we will look at modernity as the cultural epoch which has characterized the modern world of the last 200 years to the present time. We will identify some of its foundational features that can be said to characterize its classical or early phase and see how they have hindered or helped the Christian story. Not all our examples will come from the recent past, for many contemporary aspects of modernity have their roots in these foundational features.

So much has been written about modernity in the last few years that it might seem that there is nothing new to say about it. It is vital, however, not so much to say something new as carefully to characterize it, for if we misconstrue its nature we will miss its significance for the gospel. This is the case among many intellectuals, who tend to see modernity in terms of ideas, the project of the philosophical Enlightenment, or even as ideology. Walter Brueggemann, for example, for once misses the mark when in his *Biblical Perspectives on Evangelism* he sees modernity as 'the large intellectual environment of the Enlightenment'.

The reason why such a description is worrisome is that it may lead us to think that if we could only change the intellectual environment then the gospel would run free again. Or again, we may be tempted to construe modernity as secularism, or as televangelists loved to say in the 1980s, as 'secular humanism'. In the language of this book, we might be tempted to think that modernity is no more than rampant metanarrative.

Modernity, however, cannot be understood simply as a fallout of Enlightenment ideas. It is a composite reality that encapsulates the economic, technological, social and philosophical conditions of the modern world. In short, we would be wiser, as we anticipated earlier, to construe modernity in terms of a cultural era or epoch in which we recognize, in the words of James Davison Hunter, that there is 'a dialectic between moral understanding (e.g. the value of reason, the

105

supreme importance of individuality, the value of tolerance and relativism), and social institutional life'. Such an overall cultural understanding allows us to see modernity as an era in which reason is applied and transmitted through institutional carriers.

To identify this applied reason and its institutional carriers is to search through modern culture for a series of indices that will sensitize us to its complexities. By focusing on these indices, we will be able to measure whether they themselves have changed over time – we will do this in chapters six and seven – hence indicating that modernity as a cultural era is now drawing to a close.

Of course, we have to recognize that identifying a list of indices is in itself superficial. Thus we could say that pre-modern Europe was rural, traditional, communitarian and agricultural, and we could compare these indices with modern ones. If we did this, however, we would immediately recognize that modernization has come in two forms: first, and outlasting the second form, we have western capitalist modernity, which has been urban, rational, individualist and industrial; second, and lasting less than a century, we have had Soviet-style modernity, which has been urban and rural, rational, collectivist and industrial.

Such indices may be useful for a cursory glance at modernity, but they will not allow a deeper analysis, precisely because they do not identify the institutional carriers of modern culture. It is important also that we do not fail to recognize the historical dimensions of the new era: cultural epochs are time-bound as well as geographically located. Thomas Oden sees modernity coming into existence in 1789 with the storming of the Paris Bastille, and coming to an end with the fall of the Berlin Wall in 1989.

Symbolically, Oden's schema is suggestive, but we cannot guillotine history in such a neat way. Modernity emerges in embryonic form in the humanism of the Renaissance. It slowly develops with the individualism and freedom of conscience of the Reformation, and the rise of merchant banking in the sixteenth century. It matures in the philosophical

Enlightenment of the eighteenth century, and becomes socially and economically inculturated in the nineteenth and twentieth centuries. Approaching the third millennium, we can legitimately say that modernity has grown old but has not yet passed away.

Oden's French Revolutionary origination of modernity does serve one very useful purpose. It is not until that time that we can say that modernity 'hit the streets' and entered the public domain – political, social, and economic. Until that time, the modernization programme of the new cultural era had been little more than the gossip of the great houses and salons of the European aristocracy, and the more philosophical concern of its intellectual elite.

Keeping in mind these historical and public dimensions of modernity, the indices of modern culture we will investigate are those most associated with the sociology of knowledge of Peter Berger and his colleagues. We will proceed in this way because their insights give due weight to the composite nature of modernity and avoid the abstract philosophical tone that sometimes accompanies talk of the modernization process. These indices will be:

1. The rise of the nation state.
2. The establishment of functional rationality as the *modus operandi* of the modern state.
3. The emergence of structural pluralism.
4. The emergence of cultural pluralism.
5. Whether modernity has a world-view and an ideology.
6. The growth of individualism.

In addition to the insights of Berger and others, we will divide modernity into its high or classical phase in this chapter, and leave its waning or late phase to the next two chapters. By doing this we will be able to show how consumerism and mass culture, which began in the 1950s, have arguably changed the nature of modernity, paving the way for its dissolution or disappearance as a cultural era.

1. The rise of the nation state and the Christian response

One of the problems of being weaned on cinematic views of history is that we have fallen into the habit of imagining that nation states have always been with us. *Robin Hood, Prince of Thieves*, starring Kevin Costner, for example, following in the romantic literary tradition of Sir Walter Scott, projects Englishness back into the Middle Ages as if England in the twelfth century was somehow like 'old Blighty' in the mid-twentieth century. Or again, the 1993 remake of *The Three Musketeers*, like all Hollywood versions, presents France in the eighteenth century as a fully-fledged nation state *à la* de Gaulle.

North Americans are more realistic than Europeans concerning their national status. They know that the United States of America had no existence as a nation prior to the establishment of the union. The British, on the other hand, having been born into a recently extinct empire, still feed off the vestigial memories of that empire – folk memories created in the Victorian and Edwardian ages, strained through the historical 'factions' of William Shakespeare and the Arthurian myths of Malory and Alfred Lord Tennyson.

Even the British history taught in secondary schools reflects the linear storytelling of nationhood: from King Alfred burning the cakes at Alfreston in the ninth century, to 1066 and the Battle of Hastings, through the Plantagenets of the Middle Ages, the Tudors of the sixteenth century, the Stuarts and the Civil War of the seventeenth century, and on and up to the modern age. However, just as the Nigeria of eighteenth-century slave trading was a series of disconnected and competing tribes, so Britain was throughout much of its history a collection of shifting regional collectivities in continual flux.

The same picture holds for most of Western Europe. Normandy conquered England in the eleventh century and alienated the Celts and the Anglo-Saxons, who were already in opposition to each other. For a time, England conquered swathes of French territory and alienated indigenous clans who did not want to be French or English, but merely to be left alone. The state of Burgundy came and went. The Germanic tribes failed to cohere or co-operate in any national way at all until the nineteenth century. The Italian city states stood in opposition to each other – some would say to this day.

Certainly there were distinct languages and local and regional folk cultures within broad, though shifting, cultural boundaries, but nation states as we have known them in the last 200 years were unknown. As for the institutional transmission of culture in the pre-modern age, this was achieved through the Church, the regional and local feudal landlords and their rural estates, the villages and families, the court, and the few cities with their guilds, freemen and aristocrats.

In times of external threat, geographical areas with urban centres could become the focus of national identity, such as Moscow under the Mongolian invasions. Or powerful feudal kings could raise taxes for holy wars through their barons and bishops, as did Richard the Lion Heart in England in the twelfth century. On the whole, however, national identity was alien to the localized rural communities of feudalism. As in biblical times, nations in practice were tribal and cultural allegiances based around warfare (the Goths and Huns, for example), or agriculture (the later Saxons and Gauls, for example).

It cannot be said, prior to modernity, that nascent nationhood was predicated upon race or language – although ideologically, in our era, Nazi Germany and Afrikaner South Africa have made precisely these claims. The United Kingdom is a classical case in point. It was Latin, Saxon, French, Welsh, Cornish, Scottish, and Irish-speaking; long before modern multiculturalism began, its racial origins were Celtic, Anglo-Saxon, Norman, Gaul, and Viking Danish.

Significantly religion has played a major role in nationhood, providing a major spur to the development of sovereign nation states in Europe. The doctrine of *cuius regio, eius religio* – 'to each country its own religion' – was the pragmatic outcome of the Protestant and Catholic wars of the sixteenth and seventeenth centuries.

De facto, therefore, some European states evolved through an extended ceasefire. The beginnings of the modern secular states that emerged after these religious wars have echoes of the early Christian Church, where the bishops maintained their own control of designated territories (sees), and would brook no interference from the outside. Unlike the early Middle Ages, however, there was no longer any universal sense of one faith and one Church recognized in diversity, where disputes could be settled through episcopal collegiality and ecumenical councils.

In the mid-seventeenth century, Thomas Hobbes, a royalist, foresaw the rise of the modern state in terms of contractual agreements between king and people. But it was not his *Leviathan* that became the Bible of modern nation statehood, but the republican doctrines of the eighteenth century. Under the influence of natural law theories, and in particular through the French and American revolutions, nationhood became not so much a territorial, linguistic, or religious category, but was recast as a populist ('we the people') national sovereignty.

Eric Hobsbawm, however, claims that even in the nineteenth century, people still classified themselves as peasants or townsfolk, preferring local rather than national identities. And if it is true that France and Britain were modern states by the late eighteenth centuries, Germany achieved no national identity before Bismarck at the end of the nineteenth century. We could argue, Mussolini notwithstanding, that Italy has never created a truly national identity.

The supreme irony of the modern state, however, is not so much that it is the midwife of modernity, but that it is its child. Or shall we say that the emergence of sovereign nation states from the eighteenth century onwards was only truly brought to life by modernization. Nation states were made viable by democratic and/or centralized government, bureaucratic and rational controls in public life, and successful means of social control through the cultural agencies of religion, family, work, police and the armed forces. Since the last half of the nineteenth century, the modern state has been able to thrive through modern transport and technological means of communication.

So dominant has the nation state become in the modern world that sociologists and cultural analysts tend to focus on the nation as the primary crucible of cultural reality: American culture, French culture, British culture, and so on. Politically sovereign states, and their (usually) legitimate governments, now monitor and direct their peoples' international and national security, their economies, their health and welfare. In the modern word, the state is the single most powerful institutional force in the international community, and probably the most successful institutional carrier of the modernization process.

With this power and cultural sway have come great dangers. Nation states have precipitated and presided over the two greatest and most horrific wars that the world has ever seen. Nations went to war before the twentieth century, but not with the technological and governmental power of modern states. It was also the nations of America and Soviet Russia that throughout the Cold War threatened to bring the world crashing down about its ears. Nations, of course, also divide Christians from one another, even though they may be in the same denomination, or share the same ideals.

The relationship between nation states and Christianity has been ambiguous in the modern era. On the one hand, sovereign states with a monopoly or established religion can usually count on those religions to support the *status quo*. This may be counter-productive for the gospel. In Germany, for example, the Lutheran establishment, under the strong influence of the German school of liberal theology, of Ritschl, Harnack and others, supported the expansionist plans of the Kaiser during the First World War. In the 1930s, a more conservative Lutheranism supported Hitler, and under the influence of Bishop Müller even declared that Jesus was not a Jew!

The Catholic Church supported the fascists in Spain, and tacitly backed Mussolini in Italy while turning a blind eye to Hitler. The Dutch Reformed Church in South Africa, until very recently, supported apartheid by insisting that black people were the descendants of Noah's cursed son, Ham.

These are, of course, extreme examples, but they demonstrate that national states do focus the attention of religion on territory, sovereignty, and national priorities, rather than on the physical, moral and spiritual health of the human race. In more recent years, the political influence of established Churches has declined, noticeably in Protestant countries, but increasingly in European Catholic countries too. This, we would suggest, is not so much because denominations such as the Church of Scotland or the Church of England have decided to become the Church *for* Scotland or the Church *for* England – such missionary and disestablishmentarian forces are still minority influences. Instead, the decline in political influence reflects the decline of institutional religion in public life generally.

Ironically, it is in the United States, formally a secular state from its inception, that we find the greatest religious influence in national affairs in the West. This demonstrates at the very least that freedom of conscience, religious pluralism, and national secular agencies do not destroy religion, but seem to enhance its growth. It also demonstrates how powerful the national legitimating habit is ingrained in Christian religion, even when monopoly or established religion is banned by law. It is virtually unknown for American mainline religion not to support its governmental agencies and, the Vietnam war excepted, its country's superpower status.

Having granted these concessions to the potentially negative influence on Christianity of nation states, there have been genuine cases in international affairs when Christians can without cynicism say of their countries that God has been on their side. The celebration of VE day in May 1995 was a reminder of that reality. Furthermore, the nineteenth and twentieth centuries are replete with stories of how Christians have put the gospel before national interest, from the movement to abolish slavery, to the opposition of imperial and capitalist exploitation of vulnerable and ailing economies in the Third World.

It would be unhelpful, therefore, to see the emergence of the modern nation state as intrinsically evil. After all, although we may now

live in an era when we stress the global nature of our problems –
including the environment and poverty – and the desirability of
international or universal approaches to common human problems, we
tend to stress co-operation from the luxury of established national
sovereignty. Many peoples in the world – the Kurds, Palestinians,
Armenians and Georgians, to mention but a few – are still struggling to
establish the right of self-determination. This struggle is partially due
to the fact that they have largely been bypassed by the processes of
modernity.

2. Functional rationality and the displacement of religion

The emergence of sovereign nation states may be modern, but it is the
modernization process itself that has enabled them to become the
dominant cultural domains of the present era. A key factor in this
process is what has long been called by sociologists 'functional
rationality'. This does not refer to what might be understood as
'ontological rationality'. For Hegel, for example, as for Paul Tillich in
the twentieth century, there is a sense in which humankind can be said
to participate in the mind of God. Rationality, as the *nous* of Greek
antiquity suggests, is not only an intellectual reality, but the highest or
most virtuous faculty. For Kant, also, practical rationality is a universal
treasure of the human mind. For the Enlightenment philosophers
generally, rationality was both a mental critical process and a goal of
human endeavour.

Functional rationality, on the other hand, echoes the medieval
understanding of *ratio*, which suggests a notion of calculation,
technique, orderliness. In other words, while a purely intellectual
understanding of rationality may be pertinent to philosophy or pure
science, modernity as a cultural epoch has been predicated upon a
process of rationalization, where we have seen, in Davison Hunter's
words, 'an infusion of rational controls through all spheres of human
experience'.

These controls have been institutionalized in two ways. First, through the structural institution of technological production – capitalist or communist – and the development of bureaucratic organizations. Bureaucracy is based on rational, legal procedures. Banking and financial markets function through the logic of cardinal numbers, rule-bound computation, and the probabilities of speculation.

In the early part of the nineteenth century, Thomas Carlyle and his friend Edward Irving raged against the coming of the world as an orderly machine. While they could be accused of a reactionary feudalism, their romantic critique of early capitalism as a betrayal of true rationality is echoed in the mid-twentieth century by the left-wing Jürgen Habermas and the critical school of sociology.

On a famous occasion in 1826, when Irving was invited to address the burgeoning Protestant missionary societies in London, he accused them of capitulating to the rationalist spirit of the age with their prudent financial programmes and committee mentality. His alternative suggestion was to rely on the sovereignty of the Holy Spirit!

However, functional rationality has not only been institutionalized by structural institutions: it has also been symbolically institutionalized. The establishment of rational controls in government and industry were dispersed throughout society by a commitment to the values of utility and rational order. This symbolical, institutional carrier of modern culture was spread through government and its agencies, schools, the workplace, and eventually the Churches themselves.

It was in the light of these modern infusions of rational control that many of the metanarratives of modernity arose. But even if sociologists such as Emile Durkheim and Max Weber did not go as far as Auguste Comte in their hymn to the glories of technology, science and 'positivist' values, they were convinced that the process of rationalization as we have described it would put an end to religion.

For Weber, this was so because for him the core elements of religion were magic, myth, tradition, and either charismatic or traditional authority. None of these were conducive to the process of rationalization. On the contrary, rationalization was committed both symbolically and structurally to overcoming those agencies of culture that were opposed first to radical change, and second to rational control. In Weber's telling phrase, modernization through rationalization led to the 'disenchantment of the world' with things of the spirit.

For Marx, Comte and Durkheim, this disenchantment was all to the good, a sign of a maturing and evolving humanism that through rational assertion would lead people out of the darkness of superstition and ignorance into the light of a self-sufficient and triumphant humanity. Only Weber, probably the greatest of the classical sociologists, doubted the long-term benefits of this functional rationality. He wondered how and where human beings would find space for wonder and awe, for a morality that would not be constricted by the language of means and ends, utilities, and pragmatic possibilities. Unlike the theologian Rudolf Bultmann, who found it incredible that anyone could believe in New Testament spirits in a world of wireless and electric light, Weber mourned their loss:

> With the progress of science and technology, man has stopped believing in magic powers, in spirits and demons; he has lost his sense of prophecy and, above all, his sense of the sacred. Reality has become dreary, flat and utilitarian, leaving a great void in the souls of men which they seek to fill by furious activity and through various devices and substitutes.

In the modern world, we are dominated by the clock and by money: indeed, in the world of today, time *is* money. For years, workers have 'clocked-in'. Clocks divide time into orderly, countable and accountable segments. Money is subject to arithmetic control: we can divide it, multiply it, count it. The mathematization of things is part of the process of functional rationality. We see it in the drive to compute and count things other than money, from government statistics to the development of empirical sociology. Today, we even measure the health of churches by their exponential growth.

The ticking of clocks and the clacking of money evokes images of efficiency and a well-ordered machine – or, for the Luddites among us, the mechanical oppression of Fritz Lang's film, *Metropolis*. Such a world of *ratio* is light on *nous* (mind) and void of *pneuma* (spirit). We find that rational processes, and especially bureaucratic and technological ones, do not need religion to go about their business. Christian grand narratives belong to the myths and traditions of the past. Modernity is a spanking new machine that is oiled by rational principles, not spiritual ones. What functional rationality achieves, therefore, is more insidious and pervasive than philosophical atheism: it squeezes God out not by argument but by busyness. Modern men and women are not atheists at heart: they just don't have time for religion.

This is at least true in the public world of work, and arguably, as we will see later, it is the division of the modern world into the public realm of work and the private domain of home and leisure that has had one of the most negative effects on the Christian gospel.

3. Structural pluralism and the relocation of Christian belief

We usually associate the word pluralism with cultural diversity, or competing moral and theological world-views. The idea of *structural* pluralism, however, came about precisely because of the dominance of functional rationality in the public life of modernity. Structural pluralism refers to the radical and unique dichotomy of cultural life into two separate hemispheres.

The public hemisphere in figure 1 refers to the institutions and agencies of the modern state. These include government, state bureaucracies – including education, health and welfare – scientific and technical bureaucracies, the workplace of professions and unions, and what C. Wright Mills called the 'military estate'. It is in this hemisphere that functional rationality reigns. But such rationality in structuring social relationships in terms of expertise and a rational division of labour also alienates human beings and reifies cultural existence into impersonal modes of being. People relate only in terms of ascribed roles in the labour market, or according to their function in the organization, and they have little experience of primary personal relationships.

These relationships, which as we saw in part one are natural in oral societies, are left out of, or left over from the public world. These form the second hemisphere of figure 1 and may be defined as the creative arena of establishing personal identity and the symbolic pursuit of meaning. Such searches take place within the family, in voluntary agencies (including religion), the private world of peer group activity, and the world of leisure pursuits. In this private hemisphere, subjective and expressive modes of discourse flourish, and particularity and individualism are highly valued.

Pre-industrial societies, before the advent of modernity, did not experience the world divided in this way. Women worked with the men

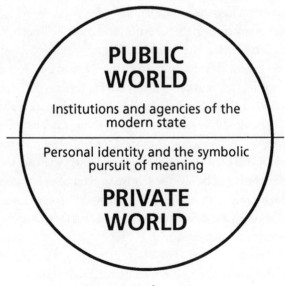

Figure 1: Modern society

in cottage industries or in the fields. The church was the focal point of the rural village or hamlet, which was itself the primary social context in which most people lived their lives. Children were socialized at home, rather than sent away to school. Capitalism was not yet in existence, and so men and women did not yet sell their labour for a wage, or leave home to go away to factory or mine, office or department store.

In this world, tradition, grand stories and traditional authority reigned, rather than the functional rationality of the state and marketplace. In practical terms, Christianity was central to cultural life, even though individuals may not have responded to the claims of the gospel. At the very least, we might say, those claims were public knowledge and normatively binding, not private opinions open to exchange.

To understand the role of structural pluralism in modernity is to grasp the most significant feature of religious decline in the modern world. Religiosity has not disappeared, it has been relocated to the private sphere of cultural existence. Christianity in particular has either voluntarily decamped from the 'public square', or been forcibly removed from it into the private world.

If there is any truth in the secularization thesis, it is not because, as Troeltsch feared in the late nineteenth century, functional rationality would conspire with secularism to stamp religion out. It is because religion as public truth, as communally binding, even as publicly visible, has disappeared. Education has passed from Church to state, and so too has hospital care and welfare. As Foucault showed in his earlier work, under the guise of liberal humanism and the rise of modern medicine, penology and psychiatry, the state came to define and hence to control appropriate forms of behaviour. Christian symbols were replaced by secular logos; priests by psychiatrists; religious figures of authority by 'experts' in human behaviour, or – in more recent times – 'agony aunts' with snippets of subjective advice.

In modernity, telling the gospel story is no longer understood to be a Christian activity concerned with cultural redemption or political authority, because it is now strictly for private consumption only. It is depoliticized. To be sure, in places such as Great Britain, with its monarchy and established religious heritage, religious symbols surface from time to time – during coronations, royal weddings and remembrance days. The commemoration of D Day and VE Day in the 1990s were striking examples of this. But in recent years, these surfacings have been media events and exercises in nostalgia – legitimated public showings of private emotion – rather than evidence of national religious fervour.

Structural pluralism has also meant that religious leaders in the western world are no longer authority figures, but are perceived to be vestiges of an earlier culture in which religion counted. They are therefore anachronisms, to be treated with the respect reserved for extinct species. The government, mass communications, science and education, rarely look to religious leaders for guidance. The mass media will home in on religious gurus if they are controversial or bizarre, but religious leaders do not carry the authority of television personalities such as game-show hosts, or the stars of our favourite 'soaps'. How would the British public react if the Archbishop of Canterbury spoke of national repentance with the imprimatur of a biblical 'thus saith the Lord'? We can be certain that his remarks would not be understood as prophecy, but interpreted as idiocy.

Televangelists often pepper their sermons with such 'King James' flourishes, but this does not offend because it is seen as merely rhetorical. Most significantly, such phraseology is for the consumption of the private market, their followers, for people in the privacy of their own homes. It is not taken notice of in the public square in the way in which the town crier was once heeded in the village square, or the way in which the gospel is intended to be proclaimed as a story of the utmost seriousness and urgency.

In one of the most telling chapters in his book, *American Evangelicalism*, James Davison Hunter shows how modern Evangelicals have unwittingly adapted to the privatized, individualist and subjectivist strains of structural pluralism, and recast Christianity not as an inculturated grand narrative for the modern world, nor even as a domesticated sitcom for the local churches, but as therapy for the lost and the sick, the unhappy and the repressed.

Strictly speaking, he is referring to later modernity, where individualism has been tainted by narcissistic features absent from classical modernity. Nevertheless, what he describes has its origins in the privatization of religion determined by structural pluralism. He trawls some titles from Christian bookshelves, which demonstrate what happens when the grand narrative has been interiorized to the point of disappearance. We could augment them by many similar titles from our own bookstores, the demonic and the dysfunctional figuring more largely these days. At random, some of Davison Hunter's chosen titles read:

> *Transformed Temperaments*
> *Defeating Despair and Depression*
> *God's Key to Health and Happiness*
> *Release from Tension*
> *Feeling Good about Feeling Bad*
> *You and Your Husband's Mid-life Crisis*
> *How to be a Happy Christian*
> *How to Become Your Own Best Self*

This transformation of theology into therapy, where the language of scripture has been translated into psychological discourse, and where stories have been replaced by prescriptions, has prompted Professor Harold Bloom to doubt whether American culture is Christian at all – although as a Jewish agnostic, this causes him no regrets. He argues, in *The American Religion*, that in reality American religion is a mixture of gnosticism and orphism (mystery religions), where the concept of redemption has been replaced by the American wish fulfilment for self-satisfaction. For Bloom, Christianity has become a delicious solipsism where we are never happier when alone with our God. He cites the line from that favourite nineteenth-century Evangelical hymn, 'I come to the garden alone', as being quintessentially what American Christianity in its Southern Baptist incarnation has become.

Bloom's thesis is controversial and exaggerated, but he has highlighted the logical extension of religions of the heart, of piety without normative sanctions, of rampant individualism without community control, of revivalistic fervour slewed-off from the historic tradition, of a grand narrative left behind in the struggle for spiritual satisfaction. In so doing he has touched on the larger question of the communal disconnectedness of cultural pluralism to which we now turn.

4. Cultural pluralism and the loss of Christian distinctiveness

We suggested in part one that most rural societies are homogeneous. A major feature of modernity is that societies become heterogeneous. This heterogeneity refers to a division of national culture into sub-cultures, or sub-societies, that are in many respects culturally distinct. The main structural facilitator of this cultural pluralism is urbanism.

Urbanism, and with it cultural pluralism, existed before modernity, but the differences are both quantitative and qualitative. Multicultural urbanism, such as occurred in imperial Rome or Constantinople, were exceptions to the urban norm, whereas culturally diverse urbanism is normative in modernity.

Furthermore, whereas in the past such cultural urbanity was primarily due to conquest and slavery, modern cultural plurality has been facilitated not only by mass geographical mobility, but also social mobility. A feature of western modernity has been the emergence of social classes whose differing relation to the means of production has created differing lifestyles. And to remind ourselves of social classes is also to remind ourselves that sub-societies are not equal.

For Marx in the nineteenth century, for example, the major classes were either rich because they owned the means of production (the bourgeoisie), or poor because they owned only their labour, which they sold for a wage (the proletariat). To use different language, we can say that different classes have different patterns of consumption because of their unequal access to power and money. It is not too difficult to see that they will also develop different cultural values.

Of course, the cultural pluralism that began with early capitalism and was facilitated by urbanism has since been augmented by massive waves of immigration from differing ethnic groups and national cultures from all over the world. This great diversity of cultural groups in close proximity to each other has been further extended by the emergence of new cultural allegiances, such as the hippies in the 1960s, for example, or gay liberation groups of more recent times.

All of these groups, each competing either for their cultural space or for cultural dominance, are today targeted by mass cultural forces which look upon cultural diversity in terms of potential markets for products, or for promoting new ideas and lifestyles.

North America has been a culturally pluralistic country from the beginning, comprising of indigenous tribes, forced labour slaves from Africa, indentured workers from China, Mexico and South America, and wave upon wave of European immigrants. America's plurality, however, worked in two successful ways until recent waves of immigration and the sheer weight of urban numbers destabilized the situation. The first way of handling cultural diversity was to take advantage of the wilderness and vast open spaces in order to stake out a unique, cultural space. This meant that even religious outcasts, such as the Mormons, could survive by isolation; or unique but fragile cultures, such as the Amish and the Hutterites, could find solace.

In time, modernity has caught up with many of these groups and they have become increasingly urbanized. To be housed in towns, however, and yet remain faithful after a fashion to old cultural ties was made possible by the second way of handling cultural diversity. This was the American tradition of creating separate ethnic zones, such as the Arab quarter created in the 1880s in Witchita, Kansas, for example.

Today, in places such as Detroit and Chicago, you can enter Greektown and Chinatown, while in Cincinnati you can still visit the German quarter. In virtually all the American inner cities you can find dominant pockets of African-Americans, and in California and Texas there are huge swathes of Mexican territory. Since the advent of late modernity, the mass media reach into every home, with windows onto cultural worlds that have little, if anything, in common. In this sense, multiculturalism can enter the home by proxy, even if you live in the remotest rural area.

We might wonder if there is any problem in all of this for Christians. Is not cultural diversity part of God's abundance? The gospel story itself is a tale of reconciliation, of harmony overcoming strife, of a common humanity under one Father in heaven. So what is the problem? One legitimate problem is the natural fear that cultural plurality will undermine established communities, so that in time they become displaced or dispossessed. In North America, the main agencies of displacement have not been urbanism, but cultural imperialism and genocide. The native Americans were driven off their land, to be slaughtered or dispossessed.

This is a reminder to us that talk of cultural displacement may be a thinly-disguised cover for racism. In a world socially partitioned into unequal portions, where power is lopsided, where scapegoats are ready to hand to be sacrificed for the sake of cultural purity or national pride, we need to beware of calls for cultural homogeneity.

The main problem of cultural pluralism for the gospel, however, has nothing to do with ethnicity or cultural diversity in themselves. The problem lies in their linkage with structural pluralism, and their joint tendency to fuel religious privatization and gospel amnesia. But before we examine this problem, let us give cultural pluralism its due. If we look at the countries which have declined most in private Christian devotion and attendance at church, it is the countries of Europe. As David Martin has shown in *A General Theory of Secularization,* the more dominant, monopolistic or established a Christian religion tends to be, the more likely it is to set up violent anti-clericalism and strong ideological opposition to Christianity. Here, both France and Greece come to mind.

Conversely, the more open a society is, the more culturally pluralistic it tends to be – without a dominant or established Church – the more institutional Christianity abounds. North America is the empirical proof of this argument. Whereas Europe hovers between 10 to 15 per cent of people going to church, in North America it is nearer to 40 per cent. Admittedly, this figure is inflated by the fact that small towns and rural hamlets – which are legion in the United States – have not yet felt the combined weight of modernization that is focused on cities in the modern world.

Recent revisionist accounts of the Great Awakenings in North America suggest that it was not Jonathan Edwards and the First Great Awakening that led to religious proliferation, but the urban missions of the nineteenth century, aided as they were by the demographic changes in the growing towns and cities of America. John Butler's *Awash in a Sea of Faith* argues most persuasively that the unique blend of American piety and cultural pluralism established the institutional base of modern Christianity in the United States.

However, rapid growth and sustained Christian denominations carry with them a price: growth comes through competition and division. American may be able to boast freedom from a religious monopoly, but her religious history has been schismatic and tattered. And it is here that the endemic problem of cultural pluralism raises its head. In order to understand it, we will borrow Peter Berger's key concept from his sociology of knowledge, the 'plausibility structure'. For Berger, ideas are not freewheeling in space, flying through the ether, or – to extend the metaphor to today – surfing through cyberspace. Ideas and world-views, especially religious ones, are maintained by social support. They are culturally embedded in community.

Cultural diversity undercuts that embeddedness, and social support is either withdrawn or comes under constant attack. Young Christians have been told for centuries that a coal that falls from the fire – the local church – grows cold; but in modernity, blowing hot and cold refers not to being in and out of the Christian faith, but in and out of commitment to anything. The matrix of family, community and church that provided the plausibility structures of Christianity are now interpenetrated by a vast array of competing agencies: other religions, irreligious forces, secularizing institutions, mass media.

Perhaps it may be true, on the level of abstraction, that the autonomy of free choice is preferable to the heteronomy of monopolistic religion, but in reality the sheer level of choice is bewildering and faith-draining. It is similar to the overload we face in late modernity under the sheer weight of information that new technology has forced upon us – information which is often useless, billions of unread words left flopping on outdated software. Faced with too much of a good thing, we become anxious, or find ourselves in what Durkheim would have called a state of 'anomie' (normlessness). Or we suffer from what the social psychologists call 'cognitive dissonance', as we doubt the veracity of our faith one moment, and cling on to it desperately the next.

In short, pre-modern culture was benign to Christianity because it tacitly supported it. We cannot say that this guaranteed Christian commitment, but we can say that the predominant rural culture promoted the cultural homogeneity of the traditional faith. It is true that in the eighteenth century in an English village you could in principle be a Catholic, Anglican or Methodist. It is conceivable that you might have been a Quaker. You could not, however, be a Muslim or a Buddhist, or switch allegiance rapidly from group to group, because these cultural options were not available to you.

No wonder that modernity, faced with mass competition to Christian faith, has also been the epoch of sects and cults. If you cannot find a community or a natural locality to support and reinforce your world-view, then a viable option is to found your own community, or to find one that has learned strategies of survival. With this option, of course, one runs the risk of closed doors, whispers of delusion, remnant and siege mentalities.

In practice, the history of western Christianity in the last 200 years has been one of searching for strategies of survival, because the combined effect of functional rationality and structural and cultural pluralism has been debilitating for the Churches. If we were less timid, we could have found this process liberating, and an opportunity for mission on our doorstep. Instead, the mainstream strategy, on the whole, has been one of conciliation with, or accommodation to, the agencies of modernity. This keeps the door open, but it may allow others to march in and take over, or lead to a mass exodus of the believers inside. Conciliation is a measure of statesmanship, but compromising with competing social and ideological agencies leads to the loss of Christian distinctiveness. In the language of this book, it leads to a loss of memory – gospel amnesia.

Long before Harold Bloom argued that American religion had become orphic and gnostic, Robert Bellah asserted that beneath the veneer of what seemed to be mainstream Protestantism lay a diffuse religiosity which could better be described as 'civil religion'. This was a synthetic mixture of the Deist and Unitarian beliefs of the founding fathers of the American Constitution, mixed with the small-town values of conformist respectability, patriotism, enlightened self-interest, and a smattering of biblicism.

Sectarian strategies, on the whole, have been to resist modernity by putting truth before conciliation. Sometimes these strategies have been used as a weapon to smite others out of existence. Often, however, like the science allegory of Alasdair MacIntyre with which we began this book, sects break up the evangel into morsels or titbits of truth, which they faithfully preserve, while forgetting that they are only part of the larger meal. They fall out not only with secular modernity, but also with the larger eucharistic community. Just as Weber's modernists became disenchanted with religion, the sectarians become disenchanted with the Church. Cut off from the historic tradition, outside the mainstream of the grand narrative, they exaggerate their own importance in the schema of redemption, and fail to recognize that they have become an agency of disruption to the plausibility structure of historic Christianity.

Cultural pluralism is a phenomenon of the private world already created by structural pluralism. Together, they encourage religion towards privatization and the domestication of the gospel. The grand narrative is tamed by refusing it a public hearing, while granting it private rights. As a bedtime story for children, or as a dream-fulfilment for grown-ups, it forms part of the charming mosaic of multi-culturalism. The public, secularizing forces of modernity are quite happy for Christians to believe that the gospel 'is the one short tale we feel to be true', as long as we keep it to ourselves. Faced with the stark choice of being either martyrs or modernists in the modern era, most of us have opted out and settled for the publicly acceptable status of privatized Christian religion – pietism.

5. The world-view of modernity and its dominant ideologies

If we can say that pre-modern countries had a world-view (a *Weltan-schauung*), we need to recognize that here we are not talking about modern metanarratives, or even the common ideology of nation states. There were, as we have seen, few or no nation states in the modern sense, and it is more useful to talk of the medieval orientation to the world, or think in terms of the Christian mythopoeic story, rather than talk of a rational *telos*, and commonly held world-view.

Conversely, with its rational controls in public life, its state institutions, its modern communications and transport systems, modernity can be said to have replaced the sacred canopies of old with a scientific, rationalist one. This is as true of communism as capitalism: both systems of modernity have stressed rational control over social and political life. Soviet Marxism with its 'dialectical materialism', stemming from the later works of Karl Marx and Engels, thought of communism in terms of a scientific socialism.

However, given what we have said about functional rationality, we need to beware of giving too much credence to the idea that science, as the paradigm of critical rationality, has been adhered to in any theoretical sense by the general public. Science for the average man and woman in modernity has been understood as technological advance. Certainly, the power and problem-solving ability of science has percolated down to the masses through the teaching of the sciences in schools, stories in the mass media, and the ever-increasing new inventions made possible by the combined might of technology and industrial production.

As we said in part one, the wonder of science was the celebration of medicine, labour-saving devices, and new methods of transport. It was electric light and penicillin, automobiles and aeroplanes, tanks and television that caught the popular imagination, and not the cosmologies of Newton or Einstein, or the intricacies of Mendelian genetics.

It would be more accurate to say that the intellectual elite have, in large numbers, adopted a scientific world-view. C.P. Snow's famous essay, *Two Cultures*, highlighted the tension in university life between the sciences and the arts, but while intellectuals like C.S. Lewis objected to what we earlier called scientism, virtually no one doubted that science had changed the way that we view the world.

Mainstream Christianity has accommodated to this world-view in seeking to show that miracles are not incompatible with scientific laws. More radically, it has recast Genesis chapters 1 and 2 into mythical or pre-historical accounts of creation, in order to absorb the scientific insights of Darwinism.

Significantly, however, while secular scientists such as Richard Dawkins still argue against religion in late modernity like nineteenth-century positivists, many scientists of the modern era have not found science and religion to be incompatible. And while some theologians such as Rudolf Bultmann seem to have held that belief in the miraculous was inauthentic or inappropriate religion in a scientific world, others have seen science as intricately connected with Christian faith. The works of T.F. Torrance, in particular, have been at pains to show that theology itself, having God as its proper object of study, and adopting a rigorous methodology, can be seen to be scientific and complementary to the physical sciences.

We could argue, therefore, that science *per se* has not posed a threat to the Christian grand narrative, although fundamentalists and modernists would both disagree. What it has done is to replace religion in the public hemisphere as the primary intellectual discourse. Modernity, precisely because it is rationalist, has been scientific – or at least it has given lip-service to science as the most advanced and successful way of understanding reality.

To conclude on these matters, we need to add significant qualifications in order to say that the dominant world-view of modernity has been scientific. First, if it is true to make this assertion at all, it is true only for the public hemisphere and for the intellectual elites. Secondly, the public world of government, its agencies, education, etc., has been committed to rational, rather than overtly scientific, solutions to problems. In other words, the traditional authorities of the past have been replaced by critical rationalities, of which science is the most potent, powerful and praised.

Rather than say that with the coming of modernity, a religious world-view was replaced by a scientific one, we would be on stronger grounds to insist that Christian narrative has been replaced by modern metanarratives. As Lyotard notes, the progressivist doctrines, from scientism to utopian New Age, are ideological in character.

We have already touched on these metanarratives and their effect on the gospel, so we do not need to repeat them here. However, an extended footnote on modernism as the ideology of modernity would be useful in order to assess the ubiquity of postmodernism in late modernity. Straight away, we must insist that just as modernity can only in a limited sense be said to be dominated by a scientific world-view, so it has, in an even more limited sense, been saddled with a modernist ideology.

To be sure, there has been modern art since Impressionism in the final quarter of the nineteenth century. There have been modern movements in literature, from Virginia Woolf to James Joyce, and new philosophies since Russell, Moore and Wittgenstein, from the early twentieth century. George Tyrrell, the Catholic theologian, was called a modernist by the Vatican in the late nineteenth century, and many a Protestant theologian weaned on the higher criticism from Germany before the First World War could properly be called modernist.

Our opening remarks in chapter one were intended to alert us to the fact that theological modernism is inimical to the gospel. Modernism, to be blunt, has been the primary cause of gospel amnesia among intellectuals in mainstream Christianity.

What we cannot claim, however, is that modernism is in any sense either a comprehensive ideology, or a mass movement of modernity. It does not follow, for example, that a commitment to an architecture that rejects classical and traditional forms in favour of a new, rational and progressivist vision leads to turning your back on Christianity. Many of us love the design of the Guggenheim Museum in New York, for example, because it is beautiful, rather than because it is modernist.

Neither does it follow that appreciating modern styles of literature means losing appreciation for the Victorian novel, or no longer enjoying Chaucer's *Canterbury Tales*. Eclectic modernism often means in practice liking some things that are modern, while rejecting others.

There seems to be a useful rule of thumb that states: 'the more purist modernism has been, the less successful it has proved with the masses'. The modern orchestral music of Schoenberg, for example, or any modern art that has not been representational, has remained a minority interest. Modern architecture was hated long before Prince Charles bemoaned the death of classicism.

People have not objected to living in new houses, it is modernist ones they reject. In the late 1950s, for example, 'span' housing was built in the home counties of England, designed as the alternative accommodation to state housing, for the masses who could afford their own homes. Except for the wooden floorboards on the first floor, all the materials were modern, using concrete and glass, and with flat or slightly sloping felt roofs. More radically, the construction was new, with only two structural walls to the sides, and with the front and back walls 'suspended' from girders. The general public showed no interest. Span housing, with its small, neat rooms, landscaped gardens and clean lines, became virtually the exclusive property of modern architects, television journalists, progressivist engineers, and artists.

It is true that the 1950s were affected by modernism. This was a decade that was decked out with new designs in wallpaper that covered over the old William Morris prints. Chrome, stainless steel, Formica and G-Plan furniture replaced the classic horsehair three-piece suites of the 1930s. But this modernist, mass-market trend lasted no longer than its art deco precursor of the 1930s. Once the transition from the older to the later modernity was achieved by consumerism in the 1960s, modernist principles were already old hat. Even when modernist consumerism was at its height in the late 1950s, the dominant trend in American automobile design was 'tail-fin' extravagance, with baroque, customized individuality – a trend that went against all that streamlined modernism stood for.

Modernity may have been a new cultural era, but it did not turn off tradition like a tap, or adopt a universally accepted ideology. This should not surprise us, because structural and cultural pluralism left the masses to their own devices, where irrationality fermented, dreams bred and romanticism was kept alive. Indeed, modernity itself, having banished the Romantic movement out of the public domain and into the private underworld, has remained fascinated with its mythic, emotive, and non-rational appeal ever since. The development of liberal theology in Germany was arguably more Romantic than rationalist. C.S. Lewis, like Coleridge 100 years earlier, wove rational and romantic threads into his Christianity. Lewis's first successful book, *The Pilgrim's Regress*, published in 1933, was subtitled: 'An Allegorical Apology for Christianity, Reason and Romanticism'.

The Third Reich of Nazi Germany was a strange mixture of bureaucratic and technological control, and the dark, hysterical, wayward strains of Romanticism presaged in the nineteenth century by the works of Nietzsche and Wagner. No wonder that René Guenon understood the hideous strength of Nazism to come from the unholy alliance of magic and tanks.

In short, what we are asserting is that to concentrate on modernism as the danger to the gospel, rather than modernity in all its complexity, is to fall back into that lazy habit of mind that imagines that modern ideas are disincarnate poisoned darts from the dreaded Apollyon. Like the software packages of modern computers, which need hardware to make them work, ideas need institutional carriers in order for them to reach us.

Such mental laziness is particularly apposite with the advent of postmodernism. The significance of this movement can be exaggerated out of all proportion to its influence in cultural life as a whole, unless we can demonstrate the social mechanisms of its inculturation.

6. Individualism and the gospel

Modernity can, of course, come in a collectivist form. The infusion of rational controls throughout the nation state, industrialism, and a scientist ideology are at home equally in communist and capitalist societies. The capitalist economic engine, however, when run by democratic controls and fuelled by Enlightenment ideals, will always favour the individual over the collective. To date, the individual has been one of modernity's most enduring creations.

As we have seen, German Pietism, Reformation principles and revivalistic fervour steer Christian commitment in an individualistic direction. But strictly speaking, the modern idea of the individual is far removed from Christian tradition. In ancient Greece, a person was a *prosopon* or 'mask'. The very insubstantiality of this notion led the Church Fathers in the fourth century to adopt the word *hypostasis* (which was originally a synonym of the word *ousia* or 'substance'), so that the person came to mean a distinct as opposed to a fleeting reality. In the Eastern doctrine of the Trinity, a divine person (Father, Son, Holy Spirit) was never understood as an individual in the modern sense, in terms of isolated consciousness. A divine person was a being with a unique particularity, distinct from, but always in relation to, others. In this sense we can say, in John Zizioulas's phrase, that God as Trinity is a 'being in communion'.

Individualism, in its modern sense, is foreign to the patristic world-view. Although, for the Fathers, created persons were separated one from another, in St Paul's words they were nevertheless 'members of one another'. To be a freewheeling, wayward individual, centred on one's own desires and will, was considered a sign of pathology, of sin – a falling away from common humanity. For the Fathers, a person, even a fallen one, was connected to others and was certainly not to be construed, as many Anglo-Saxon philosophers have done, in terms of an axis of body and mind.

Another way to highlight the distinction between persons in the Christian story and individuals as modernly conceived, would be to note that many oral cultures have a built-in sense of natural community. We can see this in numerous African tribal systems – not to mention traditional Chinese culture – where the idea of a person as an individual separate from or potentially opposed to the group is unknown. Whereas Wittgenstein has convincingly shown that a private language is impossible, in some cultures there seems to be no possibility even of a private self.

The philosophical birth of the modern individual came in two forms – psychological and rational. Hobbes's psychological hedonism, with his notion that people are driven by 'desires and aversions', is the precursor of both utilitarian ethics in the nineteenth century and behavioural psychology in the twentieth. We can see his influence even more strongly in modern advertizing and popular culture, where the individual is targeted as a biological organism with wants and needs.

Locke's philosophy reinforced Hobbes's view that human beings were bundles of sensations and emotions, rather than purely rational beings. This not only fuelled the Romantic movement but, more significantly for culture, gave birth to the narcissistic tendency in modernity for people to define themselves in terms of their desires, feelings and sexuality.

We have already alluded to the fact that modernity has not only been modernist, but also romantic. The same holds true for the eighteenth century. It was as much as an age of sensibility as it was an age of reason. This sensibility was not anti-rational, but it was primarily concerned with the higher *feelings* of the self. In that sense, at least, the eighteenth century was an age of finer feelings than the increasingly florid sentimentality of the Victorians. This is reflected in the exquisite taste of Georgian and Regency furniture, its clocks and chinaware, and even in the rational but sensible gardens of Capability Brown.

The aesthetic relationship between consumer goods and definitions of the self is an interesting one. It may be true that capitalism, for the majority of nineteenth-century citizens, was utilitarian, an exchange of commodities rather than luxuries. But for the eighteenth-century elite, fashionable luxuries were already a reality, and the collection of consumer durables was a means both of self-identity and self-expression. An aphorism for late twentieth-century consumer culture could very well be: 'you are what you buy'.

But if Hobbes generated one of the key ideas of the modern self as driven by desires – *je sense, donc je suis*, as Rousseau would have it – then Descartes' *cogito ergo sum*, with its radical dualisms of mind and body, spirit and matter, had the greater effect on the philosophical Enlightenment. The private, thinking self became not only the grounds for Kant's methodological individualism in both science and morality, but also of human self-determination.

Admittedly this is contentious, but in many ways the eighteenth century not only gave rise to the modern individual, but also to the idealization of the modern family as the proper environment of the individual. The aristocratic family by the time of Jane Austen had taken on the aura of almost bourgeois comfortability, in which the gothic emotions of the novelist Mrs Radcliffe were replaced by a more sedate sensibility. Hearth and home became the context of the self, while the family became its protector. In Victorian Britain, family values, and *ipso facto* individual values, usurped the place of the feudal clan, the community, the Church and the aristocracy.

The nineteenth century was a time of struggling free from a stifling social order where everybody knew their place, and where convention and external control ruled social affairs. The great idea of modernity was not merely the tempered sweetness of reason and sensibility, it was also the warm rush of individual freedom. Kant, after all, did not only follow Hume's lead in being sceptical of the possibility of metaphysics, he was also opposed to the imposition of any external power or force which sought to impose morality or law upon individuals.

To be a free individual in early-nineteenth-century society was to be unshackled from the past. This freedom from the past, from tradition and the pre-modern, led people into many different freedoms and directions. But it would take a long time before modern psychology, mind-expanding drugs, sexually satiated bodies, and mass consumerism brought the individual to its present narcissistic status in contemporary society. Standing as we do on the rim of postmodernity, it seems that Hobbes and Rousseau have triumphed over Descartes and Kant.

The individualism of classical modernity, however, had a different character from the modernity of the late twentieth century. For example, the status of the individual that James Davison Hunter notes in his analysis of modern Evangelicalism has come a long way from the days of Charles Finney. Max Weber believed that in the eighteenth and nineteenth centuries, individualism had an ideological power that influenced the modernization process itself. He called this ideology 'ascetic Protestantism', because he was convinced that there was an austere instrumentality in Protestant thought that was the forerunner of what today we call the work ethic.

For Weber, Calvinistic Protestantism in particular was harsh. It was difficult, without a doctrine of assurance, to know if one was redeemed, a member of the elect. Weber saw an unintended consequence arising from this unrequited search for grace: the evidence of God's providence was not to be found in grace alone, but in a 'works righteousness'. Hard work, and the acquisition of material goods, became 'goods' (true ethical ends) in themselves.

Weber's famous thesis, *The Protestant Ethic and the Spirit of Capitalism*, is important not only because it shows that this Protestant instrumentalism was a cause in the establishment of capitalism, but also because it allows us to see that it tempered the more expressive and rampant individualism inherent in Enlightenment ideas. The American union was built not on modern expressive individualism, but through ascetic Protestant individualism. This was the era of early capitalism, of nascent modernity. Cleanliness was now next to godliness; hard work and well-earned gains were next to grace. The Churches in the private world were themselves the institutional carriers of this new individualism.

As Peter Berger puts it, people were not only most sincerely 'washed in the blood of the lamb', they also learned to wash their feet and wash out their mouths, and in so doing joined the social mobility ladder from the working to the middle class. This was the social foundation of what Berger calls 'okay' religion, when Americans began to feel at home with themselves; when it seemed that the progressive doctrines of the Enlightenment and the pietistic aspirations of middle America came together.

In short, ascetic individualism provided an internal policing of the new modernity, and became the hidden carrier of the values of the modern nation state. It was individualist rather than communitarian, but its emphasis was on self-control rather than self-expression. Self-controlled individualism, taught supremely through the family, and reinforced by schools and churches, created the work ethic which was so useful in feeding the hungry, capitalist machine; so necessary in producing a controlled, earnest workforce; and so essential to the orderly dictates of the public world of functional rationality. Late modernity, which came into existence after 1945, with the post-war consumer boom, altered the nature of this individualism, and, along with the communication networks of mass culture, also altered the nature of modernity.

In the next chapter, we will assess these changes which took place during late modernity. In chapter seven, we will revisit the indices of modernity which we have identified in this chapter. We will then be in a position to ask whether postmodernity has arrived, and to assess whether this is good news or bad news for the gospel. Finally, in the concluding remarks, we will return to the theme of telling the story in the twilight of modernity, and in the dawn of a new era.

6

Late Modernity, Consumerism and Mass Culture

Defining late modernity: some theoretical considerations

To talk of late modernity creates problems for us. They are similar to the problem of appropriating the idea of a master- or grand narrative for the Christian gospel: the phrase is already firmly located in an intellectual discourse that is not of our making. So as we had to redefine 'grand narrative' to include the defining narrative of Christianity – its 'one short tale we feel to be true' – so we will have to relocate the phrase 'late modernity' from one context to another. We need to do this because there is a well-established tradition within Marxism that defines late modernity as the transition of *laissez faire* capitalism to monopoly capitalism.

In Marxist critiques of the so-called postmodernist phenomenon, we find that David Harvey and Fredric Jameson, for example, try to understand it as a cultural response to the shift in economic infrastructure from early to late capitalism. They do not think that the intellectual movement of postmodernism heralds a postmodernity. On the contrary, they see it as ultra-, late- or hyper-modernism, which reflects both the monopolistic control of capital in late modernity and the decadent developments of consumerism. Like the Marxist sociologist Alex Callinicos, they cannot bring themselves to accept the possibility that late modernity is anything more than a developmental stage of economic capitalism.

Conversely, the former supporter of the Frankfurt neo-Marxist school of critical theory, Zygmunt Bauman, wants to claim that postmodernism is more than a cultural reflection of the inexorable development of capitalist hegemony (to use the jargon). He argues that postmodernism signals the end of both capitalism and modernity as we have known it. Bauman has done what many of his left-wing fellow travellers have failed to do, which is to recognize that modernity is not the modernization programme of western capitalism, but modernization itself, whether in capitalist or collectivist guise.

For Bauman, therefore, the collapse of Communism can be interpreted as the beginning of the end of modernity. This is because collectivist socialism has in many ways been more deeply committed to planned, rational and technological modernization than western democracies. If such centrally-planned rationalization could not flourish, then for Bauman, modernity itself is virtually over.

Jean Baudrillard wants to go the whole hog and claim that modernity has been over for some time. He argues that we are already living in a world that is no longer modern in the sense in which we defined it in chapter five. Nor is it late modern; it is postmodern.

What Marxists, centre-left sociologists, conservative social scientists, full-blown postmodernist thinkers, and many other cultural commentators do agree on, is that classical modernity has changed and that the crucible for change emerged after the Second World War with the advent of the consumer society in the 1950s. Late modernity may be understood in different ways by social commentators – and it is certainly called different names – but there is at least a consensus that we are talking about the post-war period, with an accelerating pace of cultural change since the 1960s.

Ironically, many Christians are attracted to Marxist critiques of this cultural change. Marxists, as we have seen, interpret it in terms of the logic of late capitalism, viewing the postmodernist movement almost as a kind of decadence created by what Marx himself would have called a commodity fetishism. So, for example, both Harvey and Jameson seem to be on the side of high Enlightenment ideals – not to mention high culture – and against hedonistic consumerism, the loss of meaning, and the collapse of intellectual form and content into purely consumer aesthetics.

What many Christians fail to notice, however, is that the powerful and scornful Marxist attacks upon postmodernism as mere cultural fashion are predicated upon a refusal to budge from the dogma that the capitalist economy and its concomitant class structure determines cultural life. Marxism turns out, after all, not to be scientific, but a Procrustean bed. Admittedly, many Marxists have become more realistic about the survival and flexibility of capitalism, but most of them still cling to a Hegelian concern with dialectical struggle and synthesis – the class war resolved by socialism. Consequently, they cannot recognize that it is inappropriate to divide late modernity into opposing social classes, or to divide the owners of capital from labour. In short, no amount of empirical evidence that shows that consumerism has altered the social nature of society, or that the movement from mechanical production to electronic production is altering the nature of economic structure, seems to carry any weight with many Marxist thinkers.

Marxists are ideologues welded to an unquestionable metanarrative of revolutionary change. A dictate of that metanarrative states that culture is merely the loosely-fitting skin of external social appearance. The underlying reality, the skeletal and organic framework of culture, is economic.

There is an unmistakable reductionism in this historicist grasp of culture: culture is created by social structure, which is determined by the economic base of capitalism. For Jameson, for example, the shift from early to late modernity, from *laissez-faire* to monopoly capitalism, caused a ripple in the thin skin of culture, and consequently a different configuration of symbolic meaning emerged – or, if you prefer, culture sports a new look. While many people see this cultural shift as worrying, Marxists see it as merely cosmetic change. This is so, because for them a true capitalist crisis – which leads to the overthrow of the class system – is determined only by the logic of capitalist production.

There is something altogether surreal in all of this. Here we are in a world in which Marxism has collapsed as surely as the Berlin Wall came tumbling down. Everywhere socialism is in disarray, and capitalism – in one form or another – has clearly carried the day. And yet Marxists can still talk of capitalist crises and cling to a discredited nineteenth-century neo-Hegelian metanarrative, as if nothing had happened. It is rather like Christians insisting in the resurrection after someone has unearthed the unmistakable bones of Christ!

In 1976, a politically and socially conservative sociologist, Daniel Bell, published a book on *The Cultural Contradictions of Capitalism*. It claimed that with the coming of consumerism in American life, the ascetic individualism of classical modernity had been altered to an expressivist or hedonistic one. He saw this hedonism as a kind of cultural modernism that was counter-productive to rational development and the American way of life. Bell, taking his cues from Durkheim and Weber, rather than from Marx, insisted that changes in the cultural sphere were destined to fracture the credibility and stability of modernity. Bell, more than anyone, was responsible for talking of the new phase of capitalism as 'post-industrial'. However, American and European left-wing sociologists dismissed his analysis out of hand, because it was written by a conservative, and also because the Marxist thesis insists that social structure determines culture, and never vice versa.

From the perspective of the 1990s, Bell's thesis seems to be prophetic. Unconfined by the political correctness of Marxism, he identified more than just a glitch in modernity's progress. He spotted a contradiction in its development that is quite separate to the apocalyptic belief in the crisis and inevitable collapse of capitalism, so dear to Marxist theorists. To begin with, Bell, like Peter Berger and his colleagues, did not insist on an artificial distinction between the social and the cultural. Because he did not hold a determinist theory of social change, and had little interest in economics, Bell noticed that the private world created by structural pluralism was not only running out of control, but also threatened the orderly, functional rationality of the public world.

To be sure, Bell's thesis had weaknesses. He underestimated the impact and cultural power of new technologies. His lack of interest in economics meant that he did not notice the structural changes emerging in capitalist enterprises and organizational life. His social conservatism tended to reinforce the Republican and Conservative conviction that if you leave the market to its own devices, but encourage good citizenship and the classical moral virtues, modernity will right itself again and a new, rational stasis will be maintained.

Such a view seriously underestimated the structural causes of poverty and the institutional racism of American society; neither did it recognize that the pace and changing configurations of cultural pluralism would not allow things to be 'okay' again. Ironically, however, the conservative Bell, and postmodernist radicals such as Bauman, have recognized that consumerism and popular culture have folded back into capitalist production in such a way that they have arguably altered its nature. This, as we have seen, contradicts Marxist dogma.

This has raised the probability that late modernity cannot be reduced to the logic of monopoly capitalism, nor can it be seen as the latest phase in bourgeois development. It is more useful to think of late modernity as a transitional phase in our cultural era that may herald its demise. Late modernity has an historic boundary at one end – the 1950s – but it is open or dissolvable at the other end. For our purposes, we can say that late modernity came into being with mass consumption, which with new technology heralded the truly electronic age. We can also say that late modernity suggests a radical change that should not be interpreted in terms of the metanarrative of progress. On the contrary, late modernity suggests closure, a fading, a twilight.

Bauman argues forcibly that late modernity is already passing into postmodernity, but that we cannot yet see this as a new cultural epoch, but rather as the absence of the defining features of the old one. That is what postmodernity is. We are beginning to notice the modern world, as we have known it, disappear in our rear-view mirror as we move on into the unknown.

The arrival of consumerism

The defining moment in modernity, when it passed from its early to its late phase, was not the permissive 1960s, or the microchip wizardry of the 1990s, but the burgeoning consumerism of the 1950s. Beginning in the United States, and heralded in the 1940s by Henry Ford, consumerism has become the dominant cultural force of the last half of the century. 'Fordism' was the application of mechanical mass-production methods to create consumer durables for a mass public at affordable and competitive prices. This 'Fordism', with its skilled and semi-skilled workforce, paved the way for the first phase of the consumer society.

In the eighteenth century, consumption was restricted to the aristocracy, and production was handcrafted in cottage industries. Nineteenth-century production methods changed all that, but the earliest mass markets were not consumer-led but driven by industry and government. After the Second World War, rising standards of living, full employment, technological advance, and innovative marketing spear-headed the American revolution that has led to its cultural dominance and imitation ever since.

The 1950s was the American dream in a bubble. It was a dream of innocence and naughtiness rolled up together, like Pinocchio and his friends 'letting rip' on Pleasure Island, before the fun turned sour and they turned into braying asses.

It was not a dream which included African-Americans or independent women. For white, married women, the dream was of 'the dream kitchen', with its stainless-steel and Formica surfaces, built-in ovens, refrigerators and dishwashers. For white men, the dream was of a niche in the corporation, expense accounts, and the car, complete with gleaming chromium. For the nuclear family of mom, dad and 2.4

children, it was the dream of a crime-free environment, motoring holidays, and barbecues in the great outdoors.

It was a dream of middle-class, 'okay religion'; a middle America at home with itself and on top of the world. This dream of the modern home in a civilized society was reinforced by the establishment of supermarkets where the shelves groaned under the weight of pre-packaged food. Even the perishable goods could be purchased to store in the freezer back home.

Parking meters made their first appearance, to signal the orderliness and functional rationality of the public world, while people went about their private business, buying what they chose from the supermarket treasure store. Purchasing was enhanced by the credit card, which was invented to make spending simpler. If cash was not available, this could be taken care of by hire-purchase agreements. Such rational simplicity, however, also pandered to a hedonistic 'impulse buying', as the 1950s witnessed the beginning of the 'live now pay later' era of late modernity.

To register the dream-like quality of the 1950s is important, because it demonstrates that right from the beginning, the consumer revolution was predicated not only upon a built-in obsolescence of consumer durables, but also on the fact that selling goods was the selling of a lifestyle. Consumer products were not value-free, but came packaged with an association of ideas. Middle conservative Americans in particular were receptive to suburban wish-fulfilments. Ascetic individualism still lingered on in those days, and the 'burbs', with their gleaming cars and shining respectability, seemed a fitting, albeit secular, fulfilment of the earlier Puritan vision of America as the 'city set upon a hill'.

However, dreams are determined by desires, and desires are legion. Modern consumerism soon discovered that blue-collar workers and young people had dreams too, and these were different to those of suburban housewives and corporate executives. Jeans and t-shirts, rock 'n' roll and aviation sunglasses, were also the inventions of the American 1950s. So too was the 'beat generation', with its 'reefers', and the subterranean counterculture of Jack Kerouac's drifters, 'on the road'.

Relying on new theories, themselves often derived from psychological hedonism, Madison Avenue and the admen became a force to be reckoned with in the modern world. To be sure, Vance Packard warned of the *Hidden Persuaders*, and Reyner Banham as early as 1955 bemoaned the establishment of 'a throwaway economy', but the new consumerism was sanitized by commercialism, which on the whole was jolly rather than sinister.

In the United States, advertizing, especially in the midwest, meant outsize billboards in the great outdoors. America became quite literally the place of the signs. Even today, although states such as Vermont ban billboards, commercial signs dominate the skyline across America. Driving along the highways, or entering the smallest midwest town, is to be confronted – 'in your face', as the Americans say – by the towering signs of fast-food joints, motel chains, liquor stores and evangelistic promise. The small towns change, but the signs remain the same, like a familiar and reassuring skyline: McDonalds, Arbys, Waffle House, Motel 6, Holiday Inn, Word of Faith, Best Western.

But advertizing in the 1950s also moved into the home, where a captive audience sat goggle-eyed in front of the technological marvel of the modern age: the TV. Indeed, so eager were Americans to acquire televisions, that this broke down resistance to hire-purchase agreements, as it was to do in Britain a few years later.

The television commercial was an opportunity to link products to lifestyle, and front them with famous personalities. Tobacco companies took advantage of this, using for example the comedian Phil Silvers – from the TV sitcom *Sergeant Bilko* – to sell Camel cigarettes. Hollywood cowboy star Roy Rogers did more than identify with somebody else's brands: he used his own TV show as a base to promote a range of Roy Rogers products to children, including Roy Rogers boots and Roy Rogers 'genuine felt hats'.

Once TV, film, and consumer products were linked together, merchandizing took a new turn: fads became fashions that sometimes turned into a craze. One of the earliest revolved around Walt Disney's film, *Davy Crockett*, which spawned a host of imitation racoon hats, plastic muskets and Red Indian knives. Before the 1950s were over, people had learned to buy products because they were thought to be good in themselves, enhanced a desired lifestyle, and were associated with a favourite film, television programme, or famous personality. It was as if the glamour and fame of the 'stars' could rub off on you like pixie dust when you bought products tagged to their names.

Eventually, this process was also made to work in reverse. Some of today's films are now carried on the back of merchandizing. Children's toys such as 'Care Bears' and 'Transformers' were products first – with televized cartoons acting like the promotional videos of pop stars – before they became movies. The Hollywood films, *Super Mario Bros*, *Street Fighter* and *Mortal Kombat*, all first existed as interactive computer games. Piggyback selling also works through televized advertizing. One of the most extraordinary examples in recent times was the selling of the coffee product Gold Blend. This was promoted through an extended advertizing campaign on British television, where the adverts became a serialization of a couple's developing romantic relationship over their shared love for Gold Blend. On the back of this much-watched and admired advertizing 'soap', came the book *Love Over Gold* in 1993, which became a bestseller!

Modern admen have gone one stage beyond this approach and now talk of 'synergy', as they seek to produce a film with a bestselling soundtrack, that generates a video with clips from the film, that helps sell the album, which is promoted on MTV. This is precisely how the 1992 film *The Bodyguard* was developed – as the central core of a multimedia extravaganza, which netted over 80 million dollars.

In the 1950s, however, before the bubble burst in the late 1960s, there was a certain innocence in the new dream toys of consumerism. They were fun, and they were material compensation for the hardships of depression and war. They proved that you were somebody. A television series such as *I Love Lucy*, and, in the successive decades, *The Dick Van Dyke Show* and *The Brady Bunch*, were all part of the 'good clean fun' and joyous celebration of having found a niche in the American dream.

However, we now realize that there was never any innocence, goodness or moral cleanliness in the promotion of commercialism. American entrepreneurs and their Madison Avenue 'shrinks' had discovered that people could be made to want things. As J.K. Galbraith pointed out in *The Affluent Society*, consumerism meant the replacement of basic needs with the implantation of 'wants' that you did not even know you had until the advertizers told you so. Keeping up with the Joneses, for example, was a deeply-felt anxiety of Americans who were jostling for their place in the sun. Advertizing both plays on this created anxiety and offers promises of self-esteem and pleasure to those who purchase the goods.

It was a long time before Europe caught up with American advertizing techniques and products. In Great Britain at the end of the 1950s, for example, half the cosmetics, most of the foundation garments, two out of every three cars, and nine out of ten razor blades were supplied by American-owned firms. Since that time, we have imported, adopted and adapted American music, game shows, television sitcoms, and teenage fashions of dress and behaviour. France has resisted the colonialization of American culture better than Britain but, like everyone else, even France has submitted to the takeover of the consumer society as the designer culture of the modern world.

Consumerism has proved itself insatiable. It is for ever seeking new markets for new products and, more insidiously, imposing its mind-set upon high culture and religion. As early as the 1960s, it was clear that consumerism was politically open. It did not object to any particular political dream, as long as it did not threaten to interfere with the market. Even the revolutionary and anarchic potential of 1960s counterculture was domesticated by mass-produced music and fashion. Real revolutionaries such as Che Guevara became cultural icons of radical chic. With his red beret and Jesus Christ beard, Che's iconic representation on a million t-shirts murdered the real image.

Today's cultural icons, scattered across the world on billions of t-shirts, are rarely political figures cut down to size. They are more likely to be cartoon figures brought to life, like the 'toons' in Walt Disney's *Who Framed Roger Rabbit? Wicked City* and *Akira* from Japanese Manga videos vie for attention with *Batman, Beavis and Butthead* and *The Lion King*. Whereas Che Guevara was made to look like a pop idol, now pop idols have become the revolutionary symbols of 'cool' culture. Madonna is not just a soft-porn queen, she is a post-feminist; rap bands are not sexist, racist, or anti-police, they are the authentic voice of oppression; Seattle grunge is not drug-addicted downdressing, it is 'real people'.

There is no longer a leader of the pack, but merely lost leaders in a consumer market of hits and misses. This is so because over time consumerism has become multi-faceted, a mosaic, as it seeks to reflect the cultural fragmentation it helped create. Any fears by High Tories that consumerism would create a uniform popular culture of the lowest common denominator has been proved wrong; high culture can no longer be clearly distinguished from popular culture, because both have been consumerized. Niche marketing, from the National Rifle Association for patriots and bigots in America, to the yuppie concerts of Pavarotti in Great Britain, are a recognition in late modernity that 'you pays your money and you takes your choice'.

There is now only one market, but this one market has become like the supermarket of the 1950s: virtually everything is on sale for anyone who will buy. The recognition by the producers in the 1990s, however, is that buyers are fickle, personality types are legion, wants and wishes are whimsical, and cultural times keep a-changing.

Once the market sold us novelties to keep us buying the old products, and to keep us loyal to established brands. Now the idea of novelty itself has become so successfully implanted in consumers, that it drives us towards difference for its own sake. Brand loyalty is notoriously difficult to maintain. We demand ever new products. So demanding have we become, that in some areas of economic life –

popular music, for example – that it is the consumer and not the producer who calls the tune.

The rapaciousness of modern consumerism in generating new markets, technologies and lifestyles has arguably altered the structure of capitalist production. Desktop publishing, for example, blurs the boundaries between production and labour, producer and consumer. More obviously, consumerism has shifted the balance from traditional industries to new ones. Heavy industries such as coal, steel and shipping have declined, while technologically 'light' and electronically-driven production forces have become dominant. The service sector of late capitalism in many countries now outweighs the significance, in terms of GNP, of manufacturing production. Charles Handy tells us that between 1960 and 1985, employees in the service sector of the United States economy rose from 56 to 69 per cent, and in Italy from 33 to 55 per cent.

Of course, giant manufacturing corporations are not a mirage. Companies such as Sony, IBM and General Motors are real enough, but they do not single-handedly hold countries to ransom, or control the private social reality of citizens in the modern world. Furthermore, the giant corporations of the 1950s are in retreat. ICI, for example, has voluntarily divided. More pertinently, we are witnessing the descaling, restructuring, or 'downsizing' of bureaucracies. With the advent of new technologies and tighter fiscal controls, the middle management of industrial and government corporations are being stripped away. *Company Man*, as Anthony Sampson has shown, belongs to the first great boom of consumerism in the 1950s, but is now destined for rapid decline in the twilight of modernity.

Marxists may still be able to argue that capital is concentrated in the hands of oligarchies – indeed, increasingly so – but monopoly capitalism in its institutional form is being deconstructed before our eyes. Deregulation means the end of corporate loyalties and the breakdown of differences between ownership, managers and workers. Symbolic analysts, computer programmers, and the technologically literate are emerging as a new 'class', divorced from the old loyalties of workers and unions, middle class and management.

Perhaps a more telling symbol of late modernity than the giant national or supernational economic conglomerate is the shopping mall of America. Malls have not merely replaced smaller stores and former supermarkets, but have become America's prime leisure contexts. American teenagers, for example, spend more time in malls than any other cultural space outside the home. Malls are the cathedrals of late modernity, where people come to gaze and wonder in the sacred space, to offer homage and pay their dues to the gods of mammon. In Dallas, Texas, one major Baptist Church has been built to look like a mall, and has created space to 'hang out' and shop in, as well as providing sanctuaries for worship.

From consumption to mass culture

Mass culture is the social interface between global technology and capitalist production. Just as nineteenth-century technology went hand-in-hand with capitalist development – with steel furnaces and steam trains – so late modernity has maintained this partnership, but at an accelerated pace. Nineteenth-century technology was mechanical; late-twentieth-century technology is electrified. The most significant electronic technology in late modernity – the bridge between consumerism and mass culture – is in the development of mass media.

Since the 1950s, the mass media have grown by geometric progression. By the 1960s, the old 'steam' radio had become transistorized and portable. Old '78' records were replaced by vinyl 45s and long-playing 33s. Black and white television entered virtually every home, and colour televisions were almost universal by the end of the decade. Tabloid newspapers and glossy magazines achieved mass circulation, and the growing number of large, clumsy and expensive computers already hinted at new forms of functional rationality.

If we can freeze this development for a moment and turn to the larger social context, we notice that as the 1960s progressed in both culturally and politically revolutionary directions, the relative orderliness of the old social order began to break down. This process was not so much a growth of social anarchy as a dwindling of social taboos. The invention of the fertility pill, an abandonment of the commitment to marital and premarital chastity, the *Lady Chatterley's Lover* trial in 1963, which opened the way both to nudity on stage and film and explicit sexuality and expletives in fiction – all of these things might seem to suggest moral breakdown. We can also note that after the assassination of President Kennedy in 1963, and Martin Luther King in 1968, hero worship was increasingly relocated from political figures to pop stars, fashion models, television and film actors, and sportsmen and women.

Traditional Christians were understandably worried by these changes, which were reflected in the Churches, too. This can be seen in new attitudes to sexual behaviour, death of God theologies, and the demythologizing of biblical miracles. What perhaps we missed at the time in the midst of this social and moral sea change is that the 1960s was the first real decade of a mass culture. Generated by consumerism but facilitated by new media technology, a culture began to emerge that became increasingly self-referential, if not incestuous. People became cocooned in a web of interconnected media. New ideas and practices spread like wildfire, and everyone had access to them.

You would see a Hollywood film and then read in glossy magazines about the filmstars and the film's background. Television not only gave us news, but it also *became* news. Its programmes, personalities and foibles became daily reading in the mass newspapers. Rock music, the fashion industry, film, TV, radio, the tabloids and magazines all fed into each other. Together they helped foster fashions and crazes, fads and follies. Between them they manufactured the legend of the 1960s as 'swinging'.

The mass culture of the 1960s may have been a web of interconnected media creations, but the spider in the web was consumerism.

Without consumerism there would have been no mass culture. But as time has gone on, this metaphor has grown rather thin. We have now arrived at a place where the spider and its web have fused into a living symbiosis. It is difficult now to perceive consumerism outside of an electronically sustained mass culture. It is difficult for mass culture to perceive life outside of itself.

The self-referential world of mass culture has increased exponentially with each new technological breakthrough and each new cultural fad. Not that getting bigger means getting better. Just as George Steiner wonders about diminishing creativity in academic scholarship, with its backlog of unread works, much-cited bibliographies, and weary secondary literary sources, so we may wonder whether mass culture is not essentially a scavenger – plundering its own discarded debris to produce a 'spin' on an old idea here, a novelty from a long-dead tradition there.

This is not simply a question of film and television. Along came theme parks in the 1950s, for example, for all the world like some postmodernist precursor of kitsch architecture and art. So we visited Disneyland in California and travelled through adventure lands, fantasy lands, and future lands. Or later, we attended Busch Gardens in Williamsburg, Virginia, and rode on the Big Bad Wolf rollercoaster, or, better still, the Loch Ness Monster. To confuse us, however, we soon found that the cardboard lands and artificial thrills of Disney are little different from the grown-up Disney of Las Vegas. There, the flashing neon signs and the cut-out architecture – complete with carnival-style happenings and novelty rides – are the real thing. The signs signify nothing but themselves. Or, if you prefer, the signs that stab the sky are nothing more than architectural style.

Today, architecture in London and New York has taken on this fluidity of forms, this riot of styles, the scavenger culture, the world as theme park. There is a shopping precinct in Richmond, Surrey, for example, that reminds one of the fake Transylvanian frontage to the Vampire ride at the Chessington World of Adventures, or of the Alpine scene at the foot of the Avalanche rollercoaster in Blackpool's Pleasure Beach.

And it is not only architecture that refers us back to theme parks. We visit the cinema to see *Jurassic Park*, the remake of *The Fugitive*, and *Speed* – and the cinematic thrills are like taking a 'white knuckle' ride or a journey in a simulation machine. And when we visit Universal Studios in Florida, we can take a fantasy ride to remind us of watching *Back to the Future* – then we watch *Back to the Future* on video at home, to remind us of the ride of the film. We might even read the paperback of the film, and even if we do not, the paperbacks on airport shop corners are full of garish thrills. With their film-script style and the rush of sex, their words are used as if they were really images from the world of film, tumbling together on the page to give us a good read, just as we enjoy a good ride at the theme park.

Of course, all of this has been thrown into overdrive with the Nintendo and Sega Megadrive games consoles, the beckoning, alternative universe of virtual reality, and the world of personal computers. As we stand at the dawn of interactive television and multimedia experience, it is clear that we have barely yet begun to live in cyberspace as the very real space in which we will live much of our lives. And yet mass culture has already claimed more space in our minds than we often realize. We watch so much television that we fail to notice how images of the sacred are thrown into the advertizing mix of sex and fantasy, escape and wish-fulfilment. A frame or two from a concentration camp, someone being shot in Vietnam, an Orthodox priest baptizing a baby, surreal landscapes, bump and grind, historical comedy and tragedy, a bite of gospel narrative... all spun together and edited with music in an endless hijack of other people's lives. This is reality plundered, simulated and remixed for mass consumption.

All this is not the world of tomorrow, but the existing world of hard-sell advertizing. It is the world of MTV. Already beamed across the world, MTV imperially imposes its message across the globe. Its images are picked and mixed to arouse and sell, to excite and amuse. They signify nothing in the sense of a coherently meaningful discourse, or a representation of isomorphic icons to events or places in the world. MTV sells rock'n'roll, and all imagery, both sacred and profane, is grist to its mill.

It is true, of course, that not all mass culture is so cynical. We are not always bombarded with jangled sights and sounds for the sake of the product. And yet, increasingly, even cinema cannot resist picking over its past triumphs in endless pastiche. Watching Steven Spielberg's *Close Encounters of the Third Kind*, we see Cecil B. de Mille's *The Ten Commandments* flickering on TV to remind us of miracles and wonder. Woody Allen's *Manhattan Murder Mystery* interacts with *Double Indemnity*, and ends with a shooting in a cinema playing *The Third Man*. For the Coen brothers, all their films from *Blood Simple* to *Barton Fink* are mixtures of horror genres, *film noir*, and clever in-jokes. The opening shot of Robert Altman's *The Player* is a homage to the opening shot of Orson Welles's *A Touch of Evil*.

One director, Mel Brooks, has built his whole career on directing spoofs of famous films and recognizable genres. *Robin Hood: Men in Tights*, for example, cannot function successfully as a film unless you are familiar with Robin Hood films in general and Errol Flynn's 1938 version in particular.

Mass culture is often attacked for being vulgar, flouting tradition and standards of decency, and playing to the gallery – but this is missing the mark. Mass culture would be moral and uplifting if these things were profitable. Hollywood would (and may) follow Michael Medved if it thought it would make money. The market, however, is morally neutral. As it becomes increasingly deregulated, it will pander to whoever pays the piper. Commercialism, as we noted earlier, feeds off dreams and desires; and degenerate dreams, so the Christian story says, are more likely to claim our attention in a fallen world.

The true dangers of mass culture are not really seen in true perspective from the aesthetic distance of high culture. High culture can be evil too, and even 'good culture' cannot redeem like the good story

– 'the one short tale we believe to be true'. Mass culture is not ultimately dangerous because it has promoted a yobbish culture, or even a yuppie one. It threatens social order because it has not promoted any popular culture – a common culture of the populace – but instead has helped to fragment society into increasingly polarized, isolated and unstable units. Late modernity in the West has encouraged a mass culture of nonconformity, a culture of difference rather than common cause or communal aspiration.

We sometimes fail to recognize this because we have confused the ubiquity of mass cultural hardware – film, telephone, radio, and microchip technology, augmented by optical fibres and digital electronics – with a common global culture. There is no global culture, only a global *market* of consumption. This market may be morally neutral in the sense that it does not desire evil over good, but its instinct is greedy, its hunger relentless, and its very neutrality stems from the fact that as an organism it is blind and non-discerning. Consumption is the driving force of mass culture, but it is not an organizing or controlling force. We may want to say that it is the malign equivalence of the invisible hand of capitalism, but this is misleading, for there is no moral will at the heart of the beast, no ghost in the machine, only raw power pulsating through its every cell.

We talked earlier of consumerism being the spider that through technology spun the web of mass culture. We also suggested that spider and web had become enmeshed together to form the dominant cultural form of late modernity. In other words, consumerism and mass culture may be analytically distinct, but they have joined forces. Together they have altered not only the social nature of modern culture, but also the very nature of cultural transmission. This, more than anything else, has changed the nature of modernity and paved the way for its demise.

Figure 2 represents cultural transmission in terms of a trickle-down model. Society is represented as a social pyramid: the cultural elites at the top dominate and determine cultural values, which in turn sprinkle down, spraying like water from a shower head on the classes below. Such

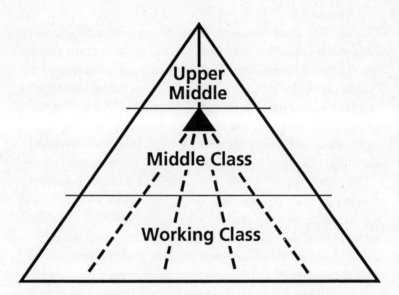

Figure 2: Cultural transmission in classical modernity

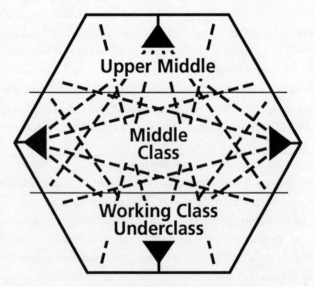

Figure 3: Cultural transmission in late modernity

a model may have been appropriate in classical modernity, when the middle classes appropriated both the power and the values of the aristocracy, redefined them, and then handed them down to the working classes. In classical modernity, the middle classes were arguably the main institutional carriers of cultural values, along with education, religion, and the state.

However, this model is contentious, because it underplays the cultural significance of the working classes, sectarian religion, family life, and the residue of feudal values in rural areas. If the trickle-down model did have some credibility in the past, it has very little now. For in late modernity, with the plethora of interest groups, cultural heterogeneity, and the deregulated mass media, cultural transmission needs to be understood in terms of seepage from below, sprinkling from above, and jets from the side. We need a model that is more like a jacuzzi than a shower.

Figure 3 represents cultural transmission within a hexagonal shape – the middle classes have swollen at the expense of the upper and lower classes – with culture emerging from all directions. It is difficult to represent this iconically, but, strictly speaking, the many-headed hydra of mass cultural transmission is Sabellian: there is only one market, with many faces. A great deal of what is called pluralism is really the multi-faceted hologram of a single reality: the market.

The only way to kill the hydra, should you want to do such a thing, is to find the heart. Lopping off heads is a useless exercise, because in mass culture, heads tumble and fall and grow again with the unfailing logic of *Alice in Wonderland*: 'new heads for old' is the catchphrase of mass culture. To rip out the heart is, of course, to destroy the beast, but in doing this – putting an end to consumerism – we will not only foreclose modernity once and for all, but also almost certainly send ourselves into a new Dark Ages. Only Islam seems to have the nerve for such an enterprise.

A note on the world-wide web of electronic culture

We are nearly ready to revisit the indices we established of classical modernity, so that from the perspective of late modernity we can judge whether there has been a sufficient sea change to merit talk of a new cultural era. Our primary purpose for doing this is to find our contextual bearings, in order that the gospel can be carried into the future and inculturated in the new world to come.

Before we look at this, however, we need to register the fact that what we have said so far about consumerism and mass culture has not taken sufficient note of technological advance. We are all aware that the silicon chip has achieved for electronic culture what the printing press achieved for literary culture: the establishment of a new and faster method of communication. But the chip is more than the new printing press. It is part of the overall electronic revolution which is overhauling and overtaking the production processes of modernity.

It is not our task to highlight these changes here. As robots replace blue-collar workers, and computer systems force out white-collar workers from once secure professions, we can foresee what role such technology will play in industrial descaling and reshaping. We can imagine the possible implications for work and travel, urban and suburban life. What we will note before we pass on, is that the electronic revolution has enormous implications for mass culture.

Again, however, we need to distinguish the hardware from its social implications. Let us take one example. In the 1970s, American scientists involved in America's 'Star Wars' defence system developed the Internet, which was a computer network connected to the telephone service. In the event of an all-out nuclear war, messages were guaranteed to get through one way or the other because of the flexibility and connected viability of the 'net' system. Messages, like a 'smart' bomb sneaking through hostile territory towards its target, would seek and search for a way through the network to a delivery monitor, even if whole areas of the United States were destroyed.

In the 1980s, this computer/phone network was opened up to industry and the universities. The ability to 'log on' to any computer in the world – as long as they were in the network – access information, and then download it to the computer on your desk, was enormously appealing. With digital electronics, which now allow us to translate pictures, texts and sounds into telephone-speak, we can access computers throughout the world for the cost of a local telephone call.

Many of us are already use electronic mail which works through the Internet or rival networks such as Compuserve. These networks can be enhanced by optical fibre if you have access to cable TV, which brings telephone links as well as specialized television channels. One optical fibre is capable of carrying 300,000 telephone calls simultaneously.

The phrase 'information superhighway' came into being after 1990, when scientists found a way to establish the network as a graphic as well as a textual means of communication. Today, the highway offers access not only to a world-wide information service, but also to interactive services of shopping, banking and education. Bulletin boards provide a focus for special interests ranging from pornography to the 'Toronto Blessing', while newsgroups meet and talk 'on line'. Electronic communities are springing up all over the world, based not on territory, class or clan, but on mutual interests. Simulation or virtual reality techniques are now being used in medical diagnosis and surgery, and in engineering and building techniques.

Such electronic sophistication already seems to suggest a postmodern world, where new communities 'over the wire' may emerge to combat the isolation already created by existing mass culture. At the very least, it seems to be a step beyond the passive world of television audiences; an advance on the world of 'couch potatoes'. On the other hand, science fiction guru William Gibson thinks that an electronic brave new world will be a worse nightmare than Huxley ever foresaw. Even that great optimist Charles Handy, from the benign comfort of his 'third age', fears the establishment of new, computer-literate elites, and the concomitant establishment of a new kind of class system, based on knowledge and the control of information. To paraphrase a Channel 4 series on the future of society, the vision of the future may be technological heaven but social hell.

We do not yet know whether the information superhighway is good in itself. Nor do we yet know if the majority of the world's people will have access to it. This is not just a question of money, but of computer literacy. This is of crucial importance to mass culture. Technology can bring people together – 'it's good to talk', boasts the British Telecom advert – but it can also drive people apart. Film, television, radio and magazines already cater to a bewildering cultural diversity, so that it is difficult to establish common political, moral and religious conversations in late modernity. Will the superhighway become yet another twist in the spiral of global technology that promotes a culture of mass-media hardware, but denies access to a common culture of shared meanings, aspirations and ideals?

The superhighway offers an ideal environment for countercultures and religious sects: tune in, log on, download, drop out. For anarchists, the superhighway must be electronic heaven, for as yet no one controls it. Will governments and dictators ever be able to control it? In this respect, the Internet looks set to make life difficult for totalitarianism and uniform collectivity, for which we should be grateful. But most totalitarian structures are collapsing anyway, and the future in the West does not seem to involve totalitarian terrors from without, but disinherited terrorists from within.

7

The Coming of Postmodernity

It has taken some time for us to revisit our indices of modernity. However, we can now do this with the recognition that consumerism and mass culture have been recent developments in the modernization process that were absent from classical modernity. We should not be too surprised, therefore, if we notice some changes. We may also be surprised that some changes are not as great as we thought they would be.

1. Revisiting the nation state

There are truly signs that nation states are beginning to lose their overall control of social and economic life. We suggested in chapter five that nation states have been seen as the crucibles of cultural realities in the modern world, but that these crucibles were themselves forged in the modernization process. Over time, however, the state has become more concerned with behaving like a corporate manager than dealing with issues of sovereignty and citizens' rights. It has regulated the market and arbitrated in social disputes.

But while the United Kingdom, and more so the former West Germany, have been content to exercise fiscal control and regulate social and cultural life in a manner that would that have horrified the Victorians, the United States since the 1960s has been shedding its corporate 'New Deal' image. In the era of Reagan and Thatcher in the 1980s, the trend of western governments was to deregulate and to decentralize government. In the end, we might say, nation states themselves capitulated to market forces.

People living in England and Wales can see this clearly with the dismantling of the old corporate welfare system, where the market mechanisms of quality control and quality assurance have entered the National Health Service, as well as social security and education. The Thatcherite ideal of 'rolling back the state' has become an increasingly normative feature of western governments in recent years. We have seen a shift from the administrative redistribution of resources to market-regulated provision. Indeed, the language of entitlements and rights, from the old Beveridge system of welfare, has been subsumed under the umbrella of appropriate provisions – the notion of appropriateness being not so much one of meeting needs, but of satisfying fiscal constraints and market providence.

The sharp slap in the face that President Clinton received half-way through his term in office in 1994, when the Democrats lost control of both Congress and the Senate, was not so much a lurch to the right as a 'no' to corporate government. At the present time of writing, the United States seems hellbent on rolling back the state to a point of virtual disappearance.

It may seem far-fetched to suggest that America will suffer an internal crisis similar to the Soviet Union, but in a federal system, too much privatization, too much deregulation, may lead to a mood of secessionism. Such a view is not so far-fetched if you live in the states of Texas or California. And in the wilderness of Wyoming and Idaho, where the millennial right-wing militias prepare for their self-inflicted Armageddon, it seems that these private armies are prepared to blow up the union in order to achieve the racially pure and morally purged America that they desire.

In Europe itself, we can clearly see the mood of federalism overtaking national sovereignty. Nations such as Norway may say 'no' to European Union, while Great Britain plays the 'push-me-pull-you', but most European nations seem weary of national sovereignty or wary of rogue nationalism. At the very least, organizations such as the EC, or cartels such as OPEC, not to mention security organizations such as NATO and the UN, demonstrate that nations have devolved aspects and agencies of sovereignty to global bodies.

The globalization of world markets and the power of multinational corporations are wresting power from the hands of governments. In the age of the microchip, when information is shipped across the electric sea with consummate ease, governments are often not in control of either market forces or political realities. As the money markets seem to amass more power to themselves than industrial corporations and manufacturing industries, so financial control is being relocated from shareholders to the hands of the modern moneychangers. 'The masters of the universe', as Tom Wolfe called the Wall Street traders in *The Bonfire of the Vanities*, have their counterparts in 'city states' around the world – Singapore, Hong Kong, Sydney, London, New York.

Riccardo Patrella, head of science forecasting for the European Community, sees these city states emerging as the power centres of the third millennium, rather as the Italian city states dominated commercial life in the Middle Ages. Along with writers William Gibson and Charles Handy, he sees the hi-tech, high-salaried 'haves' walled-up in secure castles, surrounded by electric moats, to keep the unsalaried 'have-nots' out. Perhaps it will be difficult for the barbarians to breach the walls, but it will also be difficult for the elite corps of the electronic world to break out.

It is rare to find any postmodern writers, from Bauman to Baudrillard, who see much future for the nation state. It is not so much envisaged that they will be destroyed by wars, but that they will wither away or become irrelevant to people's lives in the light of electronic communities, downscaled industries, deregulated markets, and privatized localities.

There is, of course, a glitch or two in this postmodern scenario. Such a picture of nation state decline fits Western Europe well enough, as it does North America. Arguably, it also fits the new 'tiger cubs' of the Pacific Rim, although Singapore is already a city state by virtue of its island status. However, it is doubtful if Japan and China are quite ready for a devolution of power. Japan is the most corporate and state-protected of capitalist economies, while China has yet to undergo a democratic revolution. Its future could be state capitalism, or chaos and civil war, rather than the rational devolving of state power to cities and regions.

This brings us to the thorny question of Eastern Europe. The Balkans were striving for independence and sovereignty at the outbreak of the First World War. It seems in the twilight of modernity as if they are continuing the same quest which they began at the dawn of the modern era. Russia, as she was in the nineteenth century, is again aflame with territorial aggrandisement and Slavophile insurgence. Anarchy and civil war is a real possibility in that tragic land, and the West should be fearing a resurgence of fascism reminiscent of the Weimar Republic in Germany or a return to Marxism, rather than expecting Russia to fall into line with western developments.

In short, there is genuine evidence for the weakening of nation states in late modernity, but we would be foolish to wager on its demise. For Christians, if such a death were to occur it would not be a disaster. We are people of the story, located in localized communities that may or may not be compatible with a nation state. Karl Barth is correct, as Nicholas Townsend has argued, in saying that nations are not part of God's natural order. The people of Israel were already a chosen covenant people before they begged God to let them have a king and become 'like the other nations'. Nations rise, fall, and re-configure in history, like rivers changing their course over time. They are not fixed territorial or biological entities.

Messianic nationalism has bedevilled both Russian Orthodoxy and North American Evangelicalism. As Bob Dylan's song reminds us, we all want to believe that God is on our side. The Christian story suggests that the God who humbled himself and slipped into the world unnoticed as a little child is on everybody's side. First Rome, then Constantinople, and finally Moscow, all thought they were the chosen city of God. Transfer this concept to the nation, as have Britain, France,

Germany and America in their time, and you have a recipe for delusion. Such a recipe also confuses the Calvinist doctrine of providence, which teaches God's unmerited grace on nations at certain times, with the unbiblical notion of favouritism over time.

The odds on the survival of nation states seem slightly tipped against them. The twin forces of globalization and decentralization may turn them into a no-man's land. But whichever side the scales fall, this is not an issue to lead to a radical change of direction for Christian witness. Perhaps, as we hinted in a previous chapter, what we really need today and tomorrow are Churches *for* Britain, *for* America, *for* Korea, rather than establishment institutions which identify with the state. And if there is to be no state, we will be Churches *for* whatever social and cultural realities take their place.

2. Revisiting functional rationality

Clearly, functional rationality is still with us. If anything, it has extended its domain beyond the public world of government and bureaucracy into mass culture. Mass culture may appear hedonistic and crass, but its values and products are themselves creatures of market forces which in turn are created by functional rationality. As we see government bureaucracies shrink alongside the descaling of industrial and financial companies, it is likely that the computer-enhanced market will become the future institutional carrier of functional rationality.

This might seem to suggest that functional rationality will carry over into the future as long as capitalism and microchip technology thrive. We should not assume, however, that such structured functional rationality is so secure in its symbolic institutionalization. The commitment to utility and rational order have been traditionally embedded in government and industry. They are not the values peddled in mass culture, nor, any longer, in the home. Furthermore, in the 1980s, the more speculative forces of financial markets came dangerously close to destabilizing governments and industry. The stock exchange, with its barely concealed gambling ethos, has increasingly become the over-played wild card in late capitalism.

In 1995, the spectacular collapse of the London-based City bank, Barings, demonstrated how vulnerable markets have become to the gambling instinct and the rogue player. Deregulation, decentralization and unregulated markets feed the speculative side of capitalism and play down the orderly aspects of functional rationality. In classical modernity, functional rationality was pervasive, careful, but boring. The consumer revolution has helped to change that: functional rationality may continue to trickle down through government and the schools, but hedonistic consumer values have been bubbling upwards and seeping through into the public world.

Marx got it wrong. It was not so much that workers were alienated from the product of their labour in the capitalist process, or that social classes were at loggerheads because of their occupational asymmetry. Living and working in a functionally ordered world was alienating in itself. It did not facilitate communication, community or self satisfaction.

No wonder that expressivism came to dominate in the private world. Little surprise, too, that over time neither schools nor the home continued to promote functionally rational values as the bedrock of cultural life.

We can only assume that such disenchantment has filtered back to governments, who maintain traditional fiscal frugality with late modern speculative frenzy. The decision by the British government in 1994 to establish a National Lottery gave legitimate voice to a gambling fever that has infected 80 per cent of the population of the United Kingdom. Ironically, the logic of cardinal numbers forbids the notion of successful predictions in lotteries: random selections follow no logical pattern and do not allow for predictable or rational configurations. It seems, therefore, that in the lotteries as in the markets, irrational forces are at work, as if somehow functional rationality were not enough to sustain cultural life.

To recapitulate, we can say that functional rationality will be even more institutionally secure in the future than it is at present as far as structural organization is concerned. However, on a symbolic level, with the weakening of government, the decline of bureaucracy, and the widespread alienation of people working in the public world, functional rationality will be weakened. We can already see this contradiction at work in the 'techno-freaks' who surf the Internet with consummate technical skill, in search of the wild and the wonderful.

Christians should not be surprised that functional rationality has a soft underbelly which is vulnerable to irrational attack. This is because it is not centred on ultimate concerns, but utilitarian ones. Utilitarian concerns are merely the rational means to desired ends. This is what has happened in late modernity: ethical ends have been replaced by human desires, and rationality becomes any practical or technical means to satisfy them.

3. Revisiting structural pluralism

In our discussion on structural pluralism in chapter five we divided our culture into two hemispheres, the public and the private (see figure 1). Late modernity has demonstrated quite clearly that these hemispheres are not hermetically sealed. This should not surprise us, because we have already seen that both the nation state and functional rationality have become increasingly tentative.

Government itself has been invaded by market forces: to 'roll back the state' is to enlarge the private world. Mass media already straddles the public-private split, and consumerism increasingly squirms its way into the public world.

The decreasing public sector is partly an ideological decision that goes back to the Reagan-Thatcher era. Bill Clinton's attempt to turn the tide, however, has not merely been a failure, but a signal to western governments generally that 'big government' is a thing of the past. Government may be decreasing, but so too, as we have seen, is the corporation and the corporate mind-set. The Internet suggests that work as well as government will be deregulated, and the division between work and home will dwindle.

In time, this may well affect public infrastructure – of roads, transport, industrial plant, city centres. What seems clear, however, is that the decline of the public domain means a victory for the private world and mass culture but a blow against a public, popular culture. Religion will remain privatized. This will not have the same character in the future as it does today, because in a world where structural pluralism no longer operates – one in which the private has virtually squeezed out the public – Christianity will no longer be on the margins of society. Society as a public enterprise, as a corporate organism, will itself have been marginalized.

To be a Christian in the future may very well entail a reclamation of a common humanity and the building of basic communities as part of our missionary task. Indeed, as we will later argue, Christianity will have no future unless we build a new plausibility structure to nurture and sustain Christian commitment.

For now, however, before structural pluralism becomes dissipated in the dawn of a new cultural era, there are already signs that the public world is vulnerable to religious infiltration from below. This is an important lesson to learn, because the final dissolution of the public-private divide may take many years, and Christians cannot sit on the fence and wait to see how postmodernity will turn out before they act. Mission, to remind ourselves, is determined by the gospel, and not our cultural context.

But what is the evidence that privatized religion in late modernity can influence the public world? The answer is chilling, but telling. It is not the gospel *per se* that has slipped through the public security fence, but political and religious activists. Take the religious right: many of us have missed the significance of this, because we have quite properly been dismayed at the confusion of gospel truth with populist, Republican, and sometimes terrorist, politics. The religious right used to mean Jerry Falwell and the moral majority, televangelism, and Pat Robertson running for president. Now, in North America at least, we have entered the culture wars, and religious right also means the millennial militias who wish to save America from government agencies. They consider the FBI, for example, to be 'un-American'. The bombing in April 1995 of a government building in Oklahoma City demonstrates that such paranoia can be real in its consequences.

Or again, the religious right means not only peacefully demonstrating against abortion on demand outside private clinics, but also endorsing (in some cases) the killing of doctors who perform abortions, and their support staff. Such activities are so inimical to the gospel that we have failed to see that they are also examples of *private* protests that have reached the public domain and influenced it. The legitimate pro-life protest, with its coalition of Catholics, Evangelicals, Jews and Mormons, has become a major political pressure group in American affairs.

That direct action can work for centre and left groups was brought home to the British public in June 1995, when Greenpeace was successful in changing Shell's plans to ditch one of its disused oil rigs in the North Sea. Again, the rising power of the animal rights lobby in the United Kingdom has surprised political pundits both by its passion and willingness to take extreme action. If Christians want even greater evidence of a minority group who have come out of the closet and into the public limelight, they should pause to take note of the extraordinary rise of the gay and lesbian lobby in Aids research and legislation – not to mention their visibility and influence in schools, welfare, entertainment and the media.

Structural pluralism may well dissolve, but until it does, Christians need to recognize that they have been marginalized by the forces of privatization. We too have become a minority group. Animal rights and gay activists have recognized their minority status, and so too has Jerry Falwell, who admitted that he built the moral majority coalition in the late 1980s on the Civil Rights protest model of the 1960s. The public door may be formally closed to the private world of religion, alternative lifestyle and moral opinion, but it can be forced open by protest and media attention. Everybody but Christians *as* Christians appears to have tried it – although the 'Marches for Jesus' in cities around the world have been an interesting phenomenon of the 1990s.

Christian activism is not a question of creating a programme for government: it is about standing up in the public square to be counted. Do the public know what the Christian story has to say about moral behaviour? Have we taken the time to tell the story often enough so that people can see that from it flow economic and social consequences? Lesslie Newbigin appears to be right about Christian witness. It is because we have grown timid, lost faith in the gospel, or even forgotten it, that we do not rush forward for our voices to be heard amidst the clamour of competing interests. We must avoid the vain temptation to build another Christendom; but equally we must not shirk our duty to stir the conscience of our nations for as long as they last.

4. Revisiting cultural pluralism

Cultural change, as we noted earlier, is a question of continuity with the past as well as discontinuity. All the evidence suggests that cultural plurality is here to stay. Consumerism and the mass media have accelerated the process. Indeed, in the future, the mass culture created by media and market consumption may very well be the major institutional carrier of cultural pluralism, rather than the urbanism of modernity.

At the present time, cultural pluralism seems to reinforce the postmodernist celebration of difference and diversity: culture has become a kaleidoscope. What is not clear, however, is whether the shifting patterns of culture have bred a concomitant tolerance of diversity.

In the United States, for example, the high tide of Enlightenment humanism has long since passed. America seems to have lost patience with the poor and oppressed washed up on its shores. The Statue of Liberty is a tourist landmark to be seen from the Staten Island ferry, rather than a beacon of freedom.

Cornel West writes of black nihilism in the inner cities. California is closing its gates to the illegal immigrants who for so long provided the cheap labour for the rich in the vineyards and in domestic service. Relations between the black community and South Koreans are at breaking point. When the Oklahoma City bombing occurred in 1995, it was not the Wyoming patriots that were first on the list of suspects, but the Lebanese and Palestinian communities of the midwest.

Racial tension is augmented by the many competing interest groups of North America. They include the gay lobby, the spectrum of right-wing populism, the disenchanted conservatives of middle America, and 'the new class' intelligentsia that controls the media and communications networks.

It is therefore not enough to talk of diversity as being good in itself, unless such diversity can be properly housed and controlled under one roof. Mass culture can spiral out of control because it is blind. It does not have the mechanisms, and governments seem to lack the will and the means, to create a common cultural framework in which diversity can flourish and feel at home. Cultural pluralism will become cultural chaos unless its fragmentary nature can be arrested.

This is a bleak scenario, but it is a necessary one, if only to set beside the romantic future of Internet communities and cultural cliques all finding their place in the postmodern sun. Consumerism, and the mass culture it helped to create, leads to cultural overload, anomie, bewilderment, alienation and disenchantment. James Davison Hunter's *Stop Before the Shooting Begins* is a reminder that cultural diversity, without a moral common ground of tolerance, soon becomes cultural fragmentation, which leads on to cultural polarization and the culture wars.

'Playing it cool', the cultural insouciance of postmodern writers, will be shown to be merely an affectation of style when the bullets start to fly. The indifferent shrug, or playful celebration of difference, will be a barrier to the healing of cultural wounds. Indifference, after all, is not tolerance, but the stance of the Levite in Jesus' parable of the Good Samaritan, who 'looks on' and passes by on the other side. As Ruth Mertens pointed out in an article on postmodernism, the celebration of difference also means an inability and unwillingness to come together for common cause.

If cultural diversity leads to cultural meltdown, then the Christian story of reconciliation will be a voice of clarity in cultural babble. Coming together, despite irreconcilable differences, is possible only on the grounds of a common humanity. Our common fallenness is a reminder to us that we are related, that there is a sameness of human nature as well as a difference of personhood. People may reject the Christian story, but our story will not allow us to reject them. Nothing damages exclusivist, pharisaical religion more than a reminder that God showed total solidarity with the human race by joining himself to fallen flesh.

However, if cultural pluralism continues to proliferate, leading not to wars but to communications breakdown, indifference and separation, it then becomes vital that Christians build again the plausibility structures necessary for the survival of faith in the future. The future cultural context for the Church is likely to be either siege or indifference to the gospel. Either way, we will need structures of survival. Churches as we know them will have to go, for already natural communities are melting away. The future will be our past, because what we will need is something akin to the monastery and the sect.

5. Revisiting the world-view of modernity

We have already cast doubt on the idea that modernity's *Weltanschauung* is a scientific one, for we have argued that the general public's commitment to science has been pragmatic rather than ideological. At the end of the millennium, however, we notice that scientism is draining away, and that science as the paradigm of rational thinking is itself under threat.

The decline of scientism can plausibly be put down to environmental crisis, the failure of technological marvels to build a better world, and the advanced cynicism that seems to be a decadent feature of life in late modernity. Zygmunt Bauman argues that science is no longer held in awe. No longer is science believed to hold all the answers to the problem of life. It may not yet have been deconstructed, but it has been devalued in the eyes of many thinking people.

The breakdown of the scientific world-view is more curious than it appears. It is not because it has been replaced by religion, or any other world-view for that matter. It is certainly not because there are no frontiers left to conquer. On the contrary, science stands at the dawn of a new age of discovery, as bio-geneticists are slowly but surely mapping out the DNA codes for all created life. Some codes for genes that cause congenital disease, for example, have already been cracked. Already on our supermarket shelves there are genetically 'improved' vegetables and other foods. Ahead lies the possibility that human beings will be bred as spare parts for genetically streamed super-sapiens.

So what has happened? Quite simply science has been subsumed under functional rationality. It is no longer viewed as an independent activity, intrinsically good in itself. Instead, science has become the handmaiden of government, industry, commerce, private laboratories working in the commercial field, and the leisure industry. Increasingly, scientists have become adjuncts of the market. Pure research no longer stands out as innovative, daring or ground-breaking. We might say that the intelligentsia has caught up with the view that the general public has held for years: science is technology and skilful technique that achieves marvellous things.

We do not know for sure, but it seems likely that the disenchantment with science is part of the decline in the plausibility of all metanarratives. Certainly, the myth of progress is now dead in the water. We await the third millennium with trepidation or a cock-eyed enthusiasm. The collapse of Communism has scuppered the left, and while capitalism is now universally accepted, economic power is lurching inexorably towards the Pacific Rim, and the West may be in permanent decline. Perhaps this anxiety is partly a function of pre-millennial tension, and partly the result of long-term economic recession; but whatever the case, progress as metanarrative is discredited. Modernity may go out with a whimper, afraid of its own shadow.

Ironically, one important area of pure science has maintained a vestige of metanarrative, and we should note this to counterbalance Bauman's dismissal of science as the outdated paradigm of rationality. Science may no longer hold the key to utopia, but it still offers clues to cosmology. It was the theological and mystical aspects of Stephen Hawking's book, *A Brief History of Time,* that caught the public imagination: it was almost New Age meets the new physics. Physics may now be running second to biology in public esteem, but speculative cosmology still attracts, and points to otherness in a way that no other branch of science can match.

And so we turn to modernism as the ideology of modernity – and find that it has gone. Since the 1960s we have witnessed its demise in architecture and art. Postmodern art in all its forms has abandoned universal form and originality, and replaced it with pastiche. Jeff Koons is perhaps the best-known postmodern artist. His work consists of reproductions of kitsch and Rococo objects, often made to the finest specifications in exquisite material. His reproductions sometimes seem more real than the originals, calling to mind Umberto Eco's *Travels in Hyperreality*, where imitation objects in the United States are made to seem more real than the real thing itself. Koons has also designed a larger-than-life statue of Michael Jackson in the finest porcelain. Not to be outdone, in 1995 Michael Jackson's album, *History*, was launched with accompanying thirty-foot statues of the star!

Postmodern art and architecture, and increasingly film and literature can be said to be postmodernist because they abandon modernist principles. We have suggested in this book that the coming of consumerism and the commodification of culture has led to a collapse of aesthetic values into market ones. Without strain, we could say that late modernity has become a consumerized, pluralistic culture, where there is an ever-increasing tendency to abandon truth claims and objective values of truth, beauty, and justice, for relative and pragmatic ones.

But we have a problem here. All this could be said to be the *de facto* reality of popular culture, but is it a new popular ideology? The problem is compounded by the fact that 'postmodern' language has become fashionable chic. The not-altogether-accurate description of post-modernism as 'nihilism with a smile' is regularly trotted out at the cocktail parties of the smart set, who want to show their familiarity with the latest trends. Postmodernism, however, remains for the time being an intellectual discourse, not the ideology of the middle classes.

The problem is greater still, because in academic circles postmodernism is usually synonymous with the post-structuralism of the French writers Derrida, Lacan, Baudrillard, Lyotard and Foucault. Their impact on the humanities and social science has been colossal in the last few years. Philip Sampson, in his very fine introduction to postmodernity, notes that in the *Social Science Citations Index*, the number of entries for the word 'postmodern' and related terms rose from seventeen to 276 in the five-year period leading up to 1991. We can skim through sociological journals such as the *Sociological Review*, or even educational ones such as the *Journal of Educational Policy*, and find that Marx has been replaced by Foucault, and the language of international socialism by that of deconstructionism. We can walk into any academic bookshop in Britain or America, and post-structural or postmodern titles will leap out at us from the shelf.

In an age of cynicism and scepticism, it is not altogether unfair to note that post-structuralism reared its head only after the failure of the 1968 student protests in Paris. Both Marxism and Existentialism seem to have been abandoned by a significant number of French intellectuals, who could see, correctly as it turned out, no future for socialism. In

Great Britain, it was the fall of the Berlin Wall that led Marxists to
abandon their ideology with the unseemly haste of the Gadarene swine.
Marxists were only too eager to plunge into a critique that masked the
shame of a failed idealism.

Less cynically, we need to distinguish the specific claims of Derrida
(who in attacking Enlightenment epistemology, denies the metaphysical relation between words and things-in-the-world), and the
overall tenor of postmodernist thought. Speaking loosely, postmodernism turns its back not only on modernism, but also on the
Enlightenment. The search for universals – in science, morality and
aesthetics – are abandoned. As we will see in our next section, that great
Enlightenment construct, the individual, is itself deconstructed, the self
de-centred, the transcendental ego abandoned.

Postmodernism has a hard core of post-structuralism in the middle,
but its much fuzzier edges suggest that it is more of a mood than a
method, a disenchantment with the Enlightenment rather than the
embracing of a new programme. Postmodernism is itself fragmentary,
partial, modest, 'cool', playful, pluralistic. As a series of intellectual
exercises, postmodernism reflects the pick'n'mix of popular culture.
Under its rubric, we can detect Goffman's sociology, Wittgenstein's
later philosophy, Rorty's pragmatism, Derrida's philosophical
linguistics, Foucault's archaeological and genealogical sociology,
Lacan's psychoanalysis, Saussure's semiotics, and the self-referential
electronic world of Baudrillard.

They are in fact very different postmodernisms in many ways. What
they have in common is not nihilism – although it is a common feature
of many French writers – but a commitment to a world that has
abandoned Enlightenment certainties and settled for a reality that is
textually or discursively created. This is a place where language games
or forms of life replace quests for universal knowledge. Knowledge and
truth, meaning and understanding, have come to be seen as situated,
discursively contingent, unstable and fluid.

Perhaps what makes postmodernism seem to be the ideology of the moment is that, as we have already suggested, it reflects the pluralistic changes of late modernity. There is a definite affinity between mass culture, with its pastiche, consumer values and changing fashions, and the playful relativism of postmodern writing. Bauman himself thinks that postmodernism is not an ideological loose canon on the deck of sinking Marxism, but a real response to a changing and disappearing modernity. He wants sociologists to abandon the search for foundations, laws, general principles and metanarratives, and adopt a more modest and interpretive role. For him, a postmodern sociology should work according to the logic of the cultural form in which we now find ourselves, because he is convinced that postmodernity has already arrived. Bauman says that the main feature of postmodernism is:

...the permanent and irreducible pluralism of cultures, communal traditions, ideologies... Things which are plural in the postmodern world cannot be arranged in an evolutionary sequence, or seen as each other's inferior or superior stages; neither can they be classified as 'right' or 'wrong' solutions to common problems. No knowledge can be assessed outside the context of the culture, tradition, language game, etc., which makes it possible and endows it with meaning. Hence no criteria of validation are available which could be themselves justified 'out of context'. Without universal standards, the problem of the postmodern world is not how to globalize superior culture, but how to secure communication and mutual understanding between cultures.

Bauman is worth quoting at length because he encapsulates the postmodern spirit. He accepts that there is no privileged discourse any more, no superior way of knowing. For him, the intellectual's role is to interpret the world and promote understanding. We note here that Bauman draws back from the nihilistic implications of what he has said, and we can still detect the humanist at heart. Indeed, the same observation holds for Don Cupitt's postmodern theology.

As Christians, there are two things for us seriously to ponder when assessing postmodernism. First, we can see that postmodernists, in abandoning Enlightenment metanarrative, allow the legitimacy of pre-Enlightenment narrative again, but only as a glittering gem in the mosaic of pluralistic culture. It is as if they are saying, in Wittgenstein's language, that we may have our 'form of life' – or, in Lindbeck's emendation of Wittgenstein, they will let Christianity's way of life be determined by the gospel, by its own set of linguistic conventions and normative rules, but we must abandon all truth claims. In short, we may have the gospel as long as we keep it to ourselves.

Of course, this we cannot do, for it is not the gospel if we keep it to ourselves. We are the guardians and tellers of the story, not its owners. Neither can we abandon the universal claims of Christ, though no doubt they are an offence to pluralist thinking and the new linguistic egalitarianism. We should notice that postmodernist egalitarianism is an abandonment of Enlightenment quests for human justice and dignity – the secular metanarrative of our story – and its replacement by a web of non-privileged discourses. The web is language, and the discourses are different, but equally valid, linguistic constructions of reality.

For postmodernism, there is no way out of discursively constructed realities. There is no iconic means to reach beyond language to a transcendent or empyrean reality that can arbitrate truth claims embedded in language. Christianity, we will be told, can no longer claim to be a rescue mission for the world, because all the world is swimming and drowning in the same sea of words, and there is no one to throw us a lifeline from outside the sea and hoist us on board an ark of escape.

To switch our metaphor from sea to land: it turns out after all that when the great shout went up, and postmodernists brought the Kantian edifice down, we all ended up equal but buried under the rubble. Dead men, they say, tell no tales...

The second thing to ponder in our assessment of postmodernism is more pragmatic. This book has taken seriously the claim that we are a culture in transition. It has utilized postmodern insights from Foucault to Bauman. Bauman in particular has been cited, because he has attempted an account of the coming of postmodernity which can be located in economic and social changes. Crook, Pakulski and Waters offer an even more convincing economic and sociological account of how modernity is transforming before our eyes under a process of postmodernization.

Taking note of the claims of these writers, and with indebtedness to John Milbank's superb thesis on *Theology and the Social Sciences,* we have attempted to take postmodernism seriously while not capitulating to its claims. This is not the same as saying that postmodernism is all that significant in itself. Just as modernity, as a cultural epoch, is a far greater and significant reality than the rather particular and elitist ideology known as 'modernism', so is the transition of late modernity to a postmodernity of far greater importance than the rush of postmodernism that has come upon us in recent years. We need to take postmodernism's spread and permanence with a large pinch of salt.

Our mass popular culture these days is replete with relativistic mores and a denial of universal standards. Youth culture has abandoned idealism and is 'cool' to the point of nihilism. The language and attitudes of middle-class kids demonstrate that they are too laid back to be agitated by anything. Is this postmodernism as ideology, or the abandonment of one-time certainties in the light of consumer culture? No doubt we can say that such culture might be evidence of postmodernity, but it is not postmodernism.

Similarly, in academic and artistic circles, postmodernism may be an *enfant terrible*, but that is all it is. Philosophy has not abandoned all quests for truth claims; postmodernist science is of no interest to hard scientists; and not all English departments have capitulated to Derrida. The fact that post-structuralism has penetrated American universities so deeply is due no doubt to their fascination with French intellectual culture. Yet even here, postmodernisms of art, feminism, sociology, literary theory and the rest have to compete with the powerful lobby of political correctness, where a more entrenched feminist and gay consciousness is far from ready to capitulate to postmodernist epistemological uncertainties.

In architecture, despite what Jencks may say, buildings are not so much an embracing of postmodernism, but an abandonment of modernism. The chattering classes are not wild about pastiche and knock-me-down-styles. Instead, they want elegant Berkeley homes in regency style – something other than span boxes and the concrete correctness of modern form. So too in art and literature. Not everybody warms to Jeff Koons's kitsch, or Damien Hirst's formaldehyde sheep. Traditional and modern art still sells steadily. Martin Amis's quintessential postmodern tale of much ado about nothing, *London Fields*, may be much admired as a wordsmith's artefact, but its empty heart left most people cold. Both high and low literature is still essentially modern in narrative construction and style.

More chillingly, we must wonder that if postmodernity were to turn apocalyptic – if, say, the Russian discord at home led to a new dictatorship, and war abroad – what would postmodernism have to say in the face of tyranny? We know what Heidegger, that great successor of Nietzsche and precursor of postmodernism, did when Hitler came to power: he welcomed him with open arms. Will postmodernists, arms akimbo, grin like the Cheshire cat as terror walks by? Will the postmodernist sociologists, last seen rushing headlong from the Marxist mountaintop, make their way shame-faced back to the summit? Can postmodernism survive in skid row, under the jackboot, in the heat of passion? Will the world, rocked on its axis by war, famine and environmental decay, look to a discourse of tall tales, or long for 'the one short tale we feel to be true'?

Perhaps we should consider the argument that postmodernism is not the ideology of the future, of the Internet, mass culture and cultural pluralism. Instead, it is the language of limbo; the go-between gossip of transition; the discourse of leave-taking, travelling from modernity to the not yet.

6. Revisiting individualism

On the cusp of modernity we encounter a puzzle. On the one hand, that much-loved and outworn construct of the Enlightenment, the individual, is alive and well, and since the consumer revolution has been baptized into hedonism. On the other hand, the individual, as the creative, thinking and moral subject, is itself the focus of deconstructionist forces.

Postmodernism has abandoned the self and replaced it with the selves of linguistic performance. Just as the name of a thing is no more than a slippery convention in a language game, so the individual is no more than a created, changeable product of social discourse. It is language, we are told, that speaks through performative utterances, and not persons. What we used to call the 'real me', the 'I' within, is merely, in Foucault's words: 'a complex and variable function of discourse'. This view is captured best in Lacan's aphorism: 'I am a poem, not a poet'.

On the surface, modern individualistic hedonism seems to be carrying the day against postmodern iconoclasm. This is still the era of self-satisfaction and narcissistic enclosure. It is an epoch awash with the lapping of therapies designed to make us feel better. And if we cannot feel better, then perhaps we can become famous through our therapeutic failings. Oprah Winfrey is the symbol of triumph through dysfunction. Once we craved functional adequacy, now we flout our inadequacy. The 'Hobbesian self', however, is still the centre of things.

The hedonist self is clearly a different creature to the moral ascetic self of classical modernity. Hedonism seeks pleasure and avoids deprivation. It is motivated by desire, not by free choice. 'If it itches, scratch it': this is the slogan of a world encouraged by advertizing and Hollywood to seek immediate satisfaction for sexual and emotional needs. The shopping mall entices us with goods that say to us: 'you must be allowed to have what you want'. This is a long way from the moral individualism of Kant, and even beyond the heroic individualism of Nietzsche or Hemingway.

This is a self given over to what the Church Fathers called 'the passions' – not only concupiscence, but the lust for possessions and self-esteem, envy and greed. It is a self where the still, small voice of conscience is bullied into silence by a cacophony of competing senses. Late modernity, like the Sony Walkman, is designed to bombard us with noise so that we are never alone. Television, film and advertizing fill up our senses with images of glamour and excitement so that we can never be satiated. Unwittingly, we become the consumer self, determined not by free choice but by whimsy. As units of consumption we are victims of fashion. Increasingly, we begin to look less like *homo autonomous* and more like *homo consumptio*. Perhaps the postmodern self is taking over after all.

We might say that we are becoming de-centred, empty ciphers to be filled, more product than consumer. The French word for person, *personare*, literally means 'sounding through', as if we were empty vessels merely waiting to be filled. The modern self seems to be no more than a bundle of sensations with a memory, looking for a persona. Here the language of Goffman comes into its own, as he sees the self constructed through interaction with others, and the 'real me' is really a collection of dazzling performances, a bundle of masks that communicates our many selves. The self, therefore, is like layer upon layer of an onion with no heart or centre: what you get with an onion is what you see.

So we might say of the individual that the thinking and moral self of classical modernity became the desiring self of late modernity, which in turn has given way to the empty self – deconstructed into a series of marvellous, fluid, but unstable performances. In fact, Derrida, Foucault and others have quite rightly seen, as Christians have, that the individual is an historic creation first of the Renaissance, and then of Enlightenment thought. This thoroughly modern invention may be on the way out.

In fact, the individual will not immediately disappear, because you cannot decant interiority overnight. However, as literary culture declines, and the second orality of electronic culture gathers speed, we may increasingly live on the surface of things. It is easier to slip and slide our personalities into different modes of being, when life is dictated by fashion and we are increasingly sucked into the simulacra of self-referential media signs. We can see here the congruence of mass cultural forces and postmodernist theories.

But the self, so the Christian story leads us to say, has to be rescued and transfigured into true personhood, and not allowed to fade away like the 'incredible shrinking man' of the Hollywood film. This becomes a moral imperative for mission in the third millennium. It is not so much that we want to take issue with postmodernist insistence that it is language that 'thinks' man and the world. Nor is it even a question of refuting the outrageous de-ontologizing of human being into functions of language (Derrida collapses ontology into epistemology in order to perform this trick). What is at stake here is that neither mass culture nor postmodernist ideology has any place for the person.

In postmodernism, individuals lose their particularity as well as their interiority. To use an aphorism of our own: 'a person is more than an individual, but is not not an individual'. Recent emphasis in theology has stressed the relatedness of personal community. This is right and proper, for our story begins with the indissoluble and dynamic (perichoretic) communion of the Godhead. But even within the Godhead there is particularity: Father, Son, and Holy Ghost may coinhere, but they are distinct. In creation, humans do have a centred self, a transcendental ego, what the Fathers called a 'gnomic' or moral will. The individual may be disconnected from community, may indeed not be truly personal until the eschaton, but the thinking, creative, moral self is no linguistic chimera or commercial cipher.

This loss of individuality, therefore, may cock a snook at the Enlightenment, but it also removes moral responsibility from the self. The individual now becomes a player in a normative game of discrete social rules that are binding on a discrete 'form of life'. In short, in removing individuality from the cultural stage, we have also removed the moral agent. It is a very strange morality indeed that relocates agency from the self to the lines that the self recites.

Tragically, however, there is worse to come. Postmodernism not only removes interiority from the self, but it denies the commonality of human nature. A person is a connected being: we are, as persons, constituted by each other, just as Christians are constituted by the otherness of the Holy Spirit. It may be true that perfect communion, realized personhood, is an eschatological reality. That is the fulfilment of our story: we want nothing less than that all humankind will be saved, so that together we might become like God. But in the here and now, personhood is predicated upon community, common cause, common humanity. But there is no commonality, no essence of things, no sameness in postmodernist thought – only difference. How does Bauman aim to heal the culture wars with such promethean tools?

Disconnected and empty seems to be the postmodern legacy – out of touch with each other and out of touch with our selves. This is the world that MacIntyre in *After Virtue* foresaw: a breakdown of common linguistic frameworks, a tearing apart of moral rules, a nihilistic emptiness, the triumph of Nietzsche over natural and moral order. Postmodernism may be playful, but the world burns.

Making sense of postmodernity

In itself, postmodernism is the least significant feature of the demise of modernity. If postmodernism as ideology is all we have to go on, we might wonder if it will survive the first full blast of postmodernization. We should also notice that revisiting our indices of modernity is like casting the runes or reading the entrails: we are faced with ambiguity, which we interpret as best we can. Perhaps the nation state will go, but functional rationality seems set to persist as long as markets survive. Structural pluralism is wobbling, but the privatization of religion, and indeed the privatization of the public world, looks set. Cultural pluralism, on the other hand, will escalate, but seems likely to end in fragmentation rather than harmony. Science as a world-view, along with metanarratives of progress, seem already to have been shelved.

Postmodernism has taken the academy, though not the world of mass culture, by storm. Its impact on late modernity is significant, but nowhere near as much, we would insist, as the way in which consumerism and mass culture have altered the nature of our societies. At the very least, postmodernism seems to reflect the diversity and plurality of commodity capitalism, but this does not mean that we have to accept the discredited idea that culture is merely the superstructure of economic capitalism. Individualism has changed from classical to late modernity, and here the postmoderns may be on to something when they descriptively – and sometimes prescriptively – deconstruct individualism as the totem of modern society.

What all this amounts to is evidence of a shift towards a new cultural epoch, but one in which there will obviously be continuities and discontinuities with the old one. We can help clarify this a little with two different models of cultural change. The first, in figure 4, sees contemporary culture as the intersection of two circles. The area of overlap is the transition between modernity and postmodernity. It is both late modern and early postmodern. Modernity, however, we know; postmodernity we do not.

Such a model is not analogous to a paradigm shift in science. The paradigm language of T.S. Kuhn was developed to explain how revolutionary changes in science take place when a superior explanatory model comes to replace an inferior one. According to Kuhn, this replacement is not so much due to logic, as to scientific consensus. Postmodernity, however, does not mean that this new cultural era is better than modernity, or more sophisticated, or even that it is sustained by consensual support. Our shift in figure 4 suggests only that which is to come after modernity. Following Bauman's usage, we can describe postmodernity as the absence of modernity, rather than the presence of something else – although we have tentatively sketched some of the

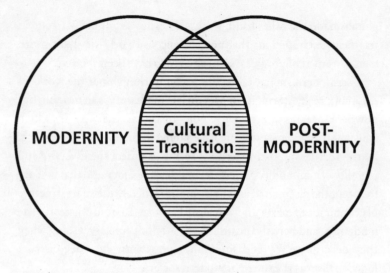

Figure 4: Cultural epoch as paradigm shift

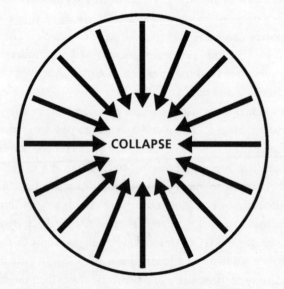

Figure 5: Cultural epoch as implosion

likely features of a postmodern world. Figure 4, however, definitely hints at a movement from X to Y – to something new, and not to something that is merely different.

However, this model of cultural change may be misleading. Figure 5 suggests a different way of describing postmodernity; this time as the implosion of modernity. As Bob Dylan says in one of his songs: 'Time is running backwards'. The instability of late modernity may lead to more alarming scenarios: atomic mishap, the return of fascism, the collapse of the western economy, the return of Marxism, a descent into a new Dark Ages. If city states, decadent imagery and a new paganism are anything to go by, the closest historical analogy to the future is a return to something like an electronic version of the late Middle Ages.

Either model could lead to a new barbarism; either could lead to apocalypse. But then again we might, like G.K. Chesterton's drunken English road, merely meander in a daze to nowhere in particular. Christians need to avoid a rush of blood to the head: we are missionaries, not millennialists. To paraphrase C.S. Lewis, we do not know if we are in the early chapters of our story, or the last one. As indwellers of the story, we are only asked to expect and eagerly await its conclusion, and not to predict when it will occur.

Indwelling the Story

Christians in the future will undoubtedly be involved in many political, moral and social activities which they will consider to be worthwhile in themselves. Ironically, we may find Christians, Jews and humanists of all hues uniting together to defend Enlightenment realities against postmodern ideologies. In the realm of morals, for example, it may be thought that Judaic-Christian-Aristotelian axiologies are preferable to nihilism or unprincipled pragmatism. Enlightenment natural law, with all its faults, may provide a more acceptable base for concerted action and common cause than Bauman's wry suggestion of building bridges between competing and separate pluralities.

Christians also, in the spirit – if not the substance – of Keith Ward's *A Vision to Pursue*, may be active in inter-faith dialogue and concerted efforts to improve race relations, which will be increasingly strained with coming fragmentation. No doubt Christians will be in the forefront of environmental improvement. We can certainly expect major support in Great Britain for the revitalized Labour Party, with its swing towards Christian socialism and its desire to build communities that avoid both collectivism and rampant individualism. The recent work on 'relationalism' and the communitarian philosophy of Etzioni will undoubtedly have considerable appeal.

Engaging in such activities could be seen as an acceptance of Chief Rabbi Jonathan Sacks' thesis that religious people have to be bilingual: both rooted in our faith communities and yet open to a broader ethical and civic discourse for the sake of moral and social order. This thesis is both attractive and seductive. It is attractive because it evokes a high

Enlightenment commitment to civic values, and appeals to an innate 'good sense' of men and women everywhere. It also seems to offer a possible way forward in a world of competing pluralisms. However, it is seductive because it breeds nostalgia for an orderly past which cannot be recapitulated in the present. Such a vision is little more than a restatement of the Enlightenment project, which has not only failed, but has been destructive to Christian belief.

Christians do need to recapture a sense of civic responsibility, but by being the Church again, and not by attempting to become model citizens of a secular society. As Lesslie Newbigin argued in the 1995 Gospel & Culture Lecture, we need to recognize that there is no such thing as a morally neutral state. Secular societies will always fall short of religious ideals. Islam accepts this as axiomatic, but Christians do not seem to believe in the legitimacy of a Christian society any more.

To be sure, we do not want a return to theocratic societies. Constantinian positions always end up confusing the true lights of the New Jerusalem with the bright lights of the earthly city. Neither do we have to settle for an Anabaptist retrenchment, where we run the risk of hiding our lights under a bushel. We can, however, as Vigen Guroian has argued so forcefully, stand up in the public square in order to articulate, and if need be to agitate, for a Christian agenda which is true to its own lights – the truth of the gospel.

It is the gospel that has been at the heart of our concerns. Throughout this book, we have been concerned with its transmission, conservation and mission to the world. It is an axiom of Christian faith that we proclaim the gospel to the world 'till he comes'. In this respect, as the future beckons, evangelism cannot be an option for Christian witness. But missionary work is rather like a long-term plan for creating a vineyard. It is about digging in, establishing roots, and nurturing the young vines in order that others, in time, may harvest the grapes and make the good wine. In the light of this long-term plan, we will conclude by concentrating on three missionary imperatives for the future.

1. Building new plausibility structures

There will be no future for the broad Church in a postmodern world. We will have to return to structures, as we anticipated earlier, akin to the monastery, the religious community and the sect. This may sound like a bleak prospect and a high-risk strategy if we still wish to make an impact on the larger society. Of course, if we were to enter a new Dark Ages, such a proposal begins to look like common sense: when you are under siege, the primary missionary imperative is not to survive but to preserve the gospel. If, however, the world staggers onwards with more consumption, wrapped up in mass culture yet splitting at the seams, we will still need to create sectarian plausibility structures in order for our story to take hold of our congregations and root them in the gospel handed down by our forebears.

Christendom is buried beneath the rubble of its own failure, and late modernity has not provided a benign culture in which Christianity can thrive. When we observe the secularization of religion in the last 150 years, we notice that it is the historic Churches and the mainstream denominations of Europe and the United States that have declined. Max Weber and Ernst Troeltsch saw the Church as 'a sort of trust foundation for supernatural ends, an institution, necessarily including the just and the unjust...' They also saw the Church as religious organization being open to the world, accommodating in tone, universal in intent.

We have already remarked that the mainstream Churches have been influenced by modernist ideology and Enlightenment philosophy to the point of gospel amnesia. Sociologically, however, the Churches have not declined because of apostasy – although 'milk-and-water religion', as C.S. Lewis called it, never attracted many souls. They have broken down because of the increasing irrelevancy of the parish system. Sadly, but true nevertheless, parishes are rarely natural communities any more – they are no longer viable plausibility structures. Local territory is not synonymous with homogeneity. In the inner cities, parishes rarely operate as natural localities.

There is no communal link between schools, homes, churches and geographical territories. Establishment Churches no longer speak for the culture as a whole, or even for the establishment. Some of our neighbours are so foreign to us – in terms of world-view – that they might as well come from Mars. Christian parents know that the chances of socializing their children into the faith are slim, because as soon as they set foot outside their front door, they are entering a pluralistic world of a thousand siren voices. And when they are locked up indoors, watching television in their rooms, they hear the same voices, but this time in stereo and accompanied by seductive imagery.

Of course, talking in this way immediately sets alarm bells ringing, for we sense the dangers of paranoia, exclusivism and separatism lurking behind such a view. It begins to sound as if we are recommending a religion of retreat. Sectarian structures, however, do not in themselves entail social separation, cults, brainwashing or triumphalistic certainty. Weber and Troeltsch, for example, wished only to emphasize the voluntary nature of sectarian structures over and against mainstream Churches, where belonging was primarily a function of being born in the parish. For them, the sect was the 'believer's Church... solely as a community of personal believers of the reborn, and only these...'

In itself, therefore, a Church organized on sectarian lines need not be theologically deviant or cultish. Can Anglicans or Methodists point the finger at Pentecostals, for example, and claim that they have betrayed or distorted the faith more than they have?

Not only did Christianity start life as a sect of Judaism, but it maintained its close-knit communities well into the Constantinian era. Methodism, too, was at its most dynamic in the sectarian stages of its development. Even today, many mainstream Churches operate on sectarian rather than Church lines. The Baptist Union in Great Britain is a paradigm example. In the Church of England, too, the London churches of Holy Trinity Brompton (charismatic), All Souls Langham Place (Evangelical), and St James Piccadilly (Matthew Fox liberal), all operate on voluntarist rather than traditionalist lines. They are success stories within the Church of England in terms of size, vibrancy and growth precisely because they have built up their own communities around the notion of a 'gathered Church'.

Kensington Temple (formally Elim Pentecostal, but now virtually independent) is probably the largest church in Great Britain, with approximately 5000 worshippers. Its great success could be put down to Pentecostal showmanship, professional music and charismatic excitement. No doubt this is true, but it has also, like the American megachurches, created a support network for ethnic groups, single mothers and those who are drug-dependent. To be a member of Kensington Temple or Holy Trinity Brompton is to belong to a church where belief is sustained by consciously inserted social and cultural mechanisms of religious reinforcement.

The House Churches of the 1980s, now more loosely called New Churches, provided strong leadership and charismatic zeal, but again, more importantly, they created their own plausibility structures. Many of us in the historic Churches have looked on in dismay at the growth and ethos of these New Churches, but we have failed to recognize that these organizations offer a genuine resistance in terms of structure, if not content, to the forces of modernity and postmodernity, and in a way that we cannot.

Quite understandably, many Christians do not want to survive in Churches organized in this way. They would feel hemmed in, under scrutiny, isolated from the larger society. But there are other sectarian models of survival. If we look at the successful diaspora Churches in the West, for example, those that have survived and flourished, we notice that they have altered their *modus operandi* from their parent Churches in the old countries. In fact, they have acted quite outside their historical character: they have become sects. This has not been achieved without pain.

Cradle Orthodox, for example, have been challenged by converts who have come in, undergone a proper period of instruction, and by example have encouraged a move away from nominal Christianity.

Orthodox summer and winter camps for children have been established, and social networks have sprung up and survived. The network itself becomes a community, rather than the localities from which the children come. Orthodox families, like the Evangelicals of All Souls, will travel miles to be in the church of their choice.

In North America, the so-called Evangelical Orthodox who have joined the Antiochene Church have created their own communities on the west coast of California, so that in one case, virtually half the town is Orthodox. Those Orthodox Churches in North America and Great Britain which have settled down as if they were still at home with their old plausibility structures still intact, which of course they are not, are haemorrhaging just like the Protestant mainstream Churches. This is particularly true of the Greek Orthodox in Britain, where the Cypriot community is suffering the secularization processes of late modernity and losing its religious heritage.

Committed Christians are not simply those who have had a heart-changing experience, because many Christians have no memory of a time when they were not believers. Today, however, Christian commitment needs to be related to an appropriating of faith and a constant social reinforcement of it. This is hard to do as an isolated individual. Holy Trinity Brompton has instituted a basic foundation course of Christian discipleship, appropriately named Alpha. This is now being augmented by more theologically advanced courses. Significantly, the great success of this course is due to its simple yet effective methodology of small group work and peer assessment.

The Holy Trinity Brompton experiment suggests, like William Abraham's work with the United Methodists of Texas, that Christians in the modern era need to be properly initiated into the Church. The catechumenate of early Christian churches was predicated on a model of the Church as a sect, as voluntary believers. It was seen as axiomatic that pagans and heathens needed to be socialized into the ways of the kingdom. It is precisely that attitude and approach that Christianity needs for the future.

It is not much good to talk of mission and evangelism if Christians do not know what the gospel means, and if Churches are not actively and imaginatively leading their communities into the Christian way – enabling them to indwell the story.

2. Renewing the liturgy

Having begun with sociology – that we need to create from scratch new community structures that will confirm and reinforce Christian belief – we move on to the second missionary imperative: the importance of liturgy (as already signalled in part one, on page 99). Plausibility structures in themselves are the communal bases necessary for any sustained belief. Muslims and members of the Divine Light Mission know it equally well. Christian life is unlikely to survive without social reinforcement, but it cannot flourish unless it is nurtured and sustained by liturgy. There are two reasons why liturgy is important for the Church in the postmodern world.

First, it is the liturgy, as we saw in the earlier section on oral culture, that socializes us into the mysteries of the kingdom of God – that leads us into the life of faith, the wonder of the story.

Liturgy is the regular, unceasing dramaturgical re-enactment of the story. We become more like Christ as together we worship him, feed from him, learn of him. This is essential for maintaining a faithful witness to the gospel. Old Churches can sometimes be run by luke-warm or apostate priests, but however much damage they may cause from pulpit and pastoral guidance, they will always be counteracted by the discipline of liturgical practice.

Conversely, in many of the New Churches, pastors may be enthusiasts for Christ, but be insecurely attached to the historic tradition. Sectarian structures as a sociological reality always run the risk of housing theological sectarians, if they are not linked through liturgy to the gospel story handed down and preserved through past generations. The absence of liturgy leaves the congregation at the mercy of misguided shepherds or itinerant wolves, not to mention successive waves of religious fashion. Without enthusiasm, it is difficult to see Christianity surviving in the future, but if that enthusiasm is not harnessed by liturgy, communities will not learn to indwell the story and become holy. They will live on the edge of their seats, in a state of expectant anxiety, for the next and bigger wave of excitement to sweep them away.

This loops back to concerns raised throughout this book. Liturgy sprang from oral culture, and has become both the institutional and charismatic expression of 'God with us'. Throughout the last thirty years, we have had the charismatic renewal, which has not yet led on to liturgical renewal. The time is now ripe. Postmodernity will be pluralistic and electronic. It will be characterized by the second orality. We will be closed in by the self-referential world of mass culture. It will be the age of the signs. But these signs will not point beyond themselves: they cannot be sacramental, for they point only to other signs like themselves.

Like Derrida's conviction that there is no reality outside the text, no world outside of language, so we will become immersed in images that have no iconic value. Liturgy is the place where not only people, but also all material things, are put in right relation to God. True icons, like holy music, remain what they are – pictures and sounds – but they reach beyond themselves to their source and Creator. As St Paul said, 'The whole creation yearns to be free', and in liturgy, body and mind, spirit and matter, are conjoined in the holy act of transfiguration. We are becoming by metamorphosis new creatures in Christ – we are getting ready for home.

Liturgical renewal in C.S. Lewis's words means a 'baptized imagination', but it also means baptized senses. Liturgy is a school for new creatures, where we learn to worship God in spirit and in truth, in readiness for the day of general resurrection when we will pass over into eternal life. So in liturgy, in a not yet realized but foretasted eschatology, we practise for the great banquet of redemption. We make signs and utter sounds; we eat and make merry; we open our eyes to God's good material creation and look through it, but not without it, as through a window, to the world to come.

In the story of the burning bush, Moses is confronted by the presence of God, and the presence hallows the ground: 'Moses, take off your shoes'. The bush unconsumed is not merely a symbol of otherness, a typological reference to similar events: it is a sign of presence. God's presence hallows our congregations, our liturgies and prayers, our glass and pictures, our bread and wine. God draws near, and as with Moses on the mountain, he passes by. The word 'liturgy' is drawn from the word 'usage'. A liturgy, then, is the well-worn use, the practice of being in the presence of God.

This sense of wonder and mystery – 'sacrament' in the Greek means a holy mystery – is not synonymous with jamboree jolliness or peripatetic performances (although these too have their place). In the second orality that will dominate postmodernity, we need to recapture the practice of holy liturgy, for it is the way to the heart of our story.

Secondly, liturgy is more than mystagogy, more than a guarantee of fidelity to the tradition, it is also evangelism. We could say to the charismatic movement of recent years, without cynicism or taunt, that despite all the enthusiasm and religious experience, the new songs and popular music, it has not resulted in religious revival or a new Great Awakening in the West. One of the reasons for the evangelistic failure of the renewal, as with western Evangelical movements generally in recent times, is its failure to gain the attention of converts from the secular world.

Being 'slain in the spirit', waving your hands, and jumping like pogo-sticks may be exciting to middle-aged, middle-class Christians, whose ancient liturgies creaked through lack of unction, but it is not appealing to an unchurched or younger generation already over-sensitized to electronic culture. Charismatic worship for the middle-aged may be nostalgia for personal renewal, but for their children it is boring and inappropriate worship.

Emotionally intense religion, psychologically speaking, when linked to congregational enthusiasm, theandrical therapy and thaumaturgical promises, may be satisfying at first, but all charismatic activity becomes routinized over time. After a while it becomes much the same kind of potion as pop concerts, raves, New Age mysticism, homeopathic therapies and spectator sports. The charismatic movement becomes a 'scene', an endless round of happenings, where real excitement is hard to find and difficult to sustain. Hype is nearly always followed by letdown, just as stimulants result in a crash after the drug-induced 'high'. In time, cranking up the enthusiasm becomes a chore, or worse, a deceit. Holy Trinity Brompton has part of the answer to this problem: as we have seen, the church has created a workable plausibility structure and is leading its new enthusiasts into the paths of the Christian story.

But this is not the age of the First and Second Great Awakenings, the days of the Clapham Sect and the Welsh revival. We are on the way to postmodernity, and already we are caught in an electronic field of blinding imagery and synthesized sound. Where are our candles, smells and electric bells? Where are our images of light and shade, our music of splendour, our divine dramas, the sacred dance? We have a story, but no one can see it. We tell the story, but no one can hear it. We have a fundamental problem of communication, because we are still bound to an anachronistic literary culture, with its concomitant pietistic interiority.

Of course, there are dangers in new liturgical directions. We may take a wrong turn if we think that all we need is louder guitars, stroboscopic light, religious fashion parades. It is not a question of importing light and colour from the outside, but re-establishing a holy liturgy where the architecture and dramaturgy – with its icons, words and music – tell again, and again, and again, the old, old story. Establishing the right form for the content of liturgy is also essential, for we have learned from televangelism that packaging and style forms part of the content. In this respect, pick'n'mix liturgies run the risk of losing the story through experimentation. If alternative liturgies merely reflect the pastiche of postmodern culture, they will be as much a capitulation to that culture as Schleiermacher's liberalism was to modernity.

We lost our comfortable familiarity with rites and liturgies in the literary age, but we are out of that now. It is time again to sing the sacred song and tell the ancient story to the gathered throng. Christians still doubt this, but New Agers already know it to be true. Already they dream of Avalon, these spiritual nomads looking for home.

Liturgy in postmodern culture *is* mission. The iconoclasm of the seventeenth century is not helpful in the twenty-first. Young people live and breathe signs and wonders; they have been weaned on the electronic image; they have grown accustomed to alternative lifestyles and the sound of distant drums. In this world where icons proliferate but are profane; where texts swarm everywhere but have lost their sting; where images dominate our senses but mirror each other, liturgy is a beacon to show the way out. Instead of abandoning imagery and drama to postmodern popular culture, we must reclaim it for ourselves to be hallowed and offered back to God: 'thine of thine own', in the words of the ancient eucharistic prayer.

Charismatic Christianity has brought back something of divine drama to the Churches, with its religion of miraculous encounter and experience. But it has been fed on interior pietism, anthropocentric prayers and private feelings for too long. In this sense it has been thoroughly modern. The postmodern world, as the second orality, will trust narrative more than feelings, looking for truth in 'forms of life' rather than individual experience. Liturgy both provides the visual and oral content of a living story and reconnects us to the historic tradition. Religious experience that runs ahead of the story, and hence away from it, ends up as charismania – fey, orphic, deluded.

To recapitulate: liturgy is both mystagogy and mission. It nurtures soul and body and draws us 'further up and further in' towards the story. At first we hear the word, accept it, and see that it is true. Then we taste it, and know that it is good. Liturgy is participatory religion drawing us in, taking us deeper, holding us up. It also calls out to a lost world to come and see for itself.

People may be alienated by outdated traditions, but in a postmodern world, liturgy is new and mysterious, numinous and beckoning. To come to the liturgy is to penetrate sameness and the simulacra; to discover for the first time transcendence and otherness; to experience words and images, signs and symbols, that have a reference point beyond themselves.

3. Becoming a holy people

Lesslie Newbigin has rightly shown us that the local congregation as community is the hermeneutic of the gospel. The story is lived by a people; it is to them that it is entrusted. Liturgy by itself, however beautiful and transparent to God it may be, cannot work independently of the *ecclesia*. Christianity will not survive without plausibility structures; it will not deepen and attract without liturgy; but unless it becomes a holy community, it will not be living the story.

Communities are themselves icons. Icons of paint and wood image God and the saints, but so too do holy communities. In the Second World War, Eberhard Arnold and the small bands of Bruderhof communities resisted the Nazi regime. They accepted poverty and refused to bear arms. Such examples of Christian witness are uplifting not merely because of their bravery, but because of their love and holiness. In the nineteenth century, the monks of Optina in Russia were famous not because of their intellectual prowess, but because of their wisdom.

We have belittled such communal expressions of Christianity in the twentieth century. No doubt we will be able to form religious communities on line through the Internet, but it is the bodily expression of the gospel that teaches us what communities are. By all means let us have a vibrant, enthusiastic and outward-looking evangelistic Christianity in the future, but let it not be at the expense of the retreat house, the monastery, the covenant communities, the Christian communes.

Local congregations, however, will remain the most visible, viable and typical expressions of Christian community in the future, even though they will be voluntary associations rather than natural communities. Unfortunately, everywhere we go throughout the remnants of Christendom, we know that we face the same picture: our witness is demeaned because we behave like everybody else. Showmanship might bring people in, liturgy might keep them for a while, but it is more than likely that fellow Christians will drive them out. 'They know that we are Christians by our love' goes the song – but we lie.

The Church in communion is the icon of the Holy Trinity. It is the picture of God which we hold up to the world. Of course, icons are only images of their prototypes: God alone is holy. But pictures are telling. If we are indwelling the story, sharing in God's life, we will mediate God's love through his presence in us to the world. But if we are a backbiting community, arrogant, triumphalistic and pharisaical, we are not an icon of God, but a mirror image of the larger culture. The world will turn back on itself none the wiser for meeting us.

In postmodernity, most people will not live in community, but we Christians must if we are to show the way home. In order to survive, we will have to be close-knit, a 'peculiar people' – but unlike modern sects, postmodern ones must remain open to the pain and separation of the coming era. It is not much use preserving a pure orthodoxy if we are not human, if we do not demonstrate in our communal existence together something of the connectedness of creation. Metropolitan Anthony once told the congregation at the Russian cathedral in Kensington that they should abandon all interest in becoming Orthodox and concentrate instead on being human.

Paradoxically, when we think of what it means to be human, we think of our Lord. We know empirically that humans err, lust, fight and betray each other. But to be truly human is to be selfless, open to the vulnerability of others, loving, kind, patient and forgiving. The fruits of the Spirit (Galatians 5.22-23), which are the proof that the story is being indwelled by Christians who are becoming like Jesus, are touchingly human. They are the virtues of decency made possible only by grace.

This is a reminder to us that the story is not a set of propositional truths, or a manual of systematic theology. It is the story of Christ, that, once written on our hearts, shows us how we should treat each other, how to live together, how to become persons. Ultimately, if we cannot demonstrate the proof of our story by living it, we will never convince people of its truth by talking about it. A story is telling, after all, only if it produces a striking effect on its listener.

Whether we draw people into the story by telling it ourselves, or by our communal actions telling it for us, eventually the point will be reached when all those living the story will meet the author and main character face to face. Ennobled by the encounter, they will be able to say to us, as the Samaritans said to the woman at the well: 'Now we believe, not because of your saying: for we have heard him ourselves, and know that this is indeed the Christ, the Saviour of the world' (John 4.42).

A Story to Die For

No one would die for one of Don Cupitt's stories. Indeed, no one in their right mind would die for the Christian story – unless it was true. To say that it is true is not to demonize other world religions, nor to bind us to some epistemology that is untenable. The fundamentalist theory of inerrancy, for example, binds us not to the story, but to a theory about the divine inspiration of the story which is probably false.

To talk of truth is to come clean and admit to its givenness – the belief in revelation over and against the whispers of reason. This is not to deny the legitimate search for the philosophical foundations of Christian faith, but it is to assert that we may not find them. There may be no going behind the back of Jesus to certain truth claims about him.

In practice, however, Christians come to believe in the truth of the gospel on quite different grounds. Wolfhart Pannenberg, for example, thinks that Popperian science would reveal as a matter of fact that the resurrection did occur as an event in space and time. Others take to the story as a whole because of their trust in the witness of the apostles and the saints down the ages. For some it is a question of experience: Lesslie Newbigin believes that he was saved by grace, and that God rubbed his nose in reality; Metropolitan Anthony is convinced that he was confronted by the risen Christ in his own room.

To say that the gospel is 'the one short tale we feel to be true' is another way of talking about something to which we will commit ourselves; something which for us is of ultimate concern; something – or to be more exact, *someone* – for whom we would be prepared to die. The gospel story is really about a God who poured out his life for the world, and who calls us to follow him by taking up our cross. This is more than a pious invitation to selflessness or ego loss: it is an appeal to our idealism, our best nature, our love for all humankind. St Thomas, after the healing of Lazarus, bravely encouraged the disciples to identify with Jesus on his way to Jerusalem: 'Let us also go, that we may die with him' (John 11.16). To be a Christian, at depth, is to be prepared to die for Christ.

Martyrdom as the ultimate sacrifice, most of us hope, is not something that will be asked of us. But the tragedy of the story in our culture is that it no longer rings with the conviction of absolute truth, because it is not presented as a matter of life or death, hope or despair, heaven or hell. It has been trivialized beyond recognition, to become a success story, a decent story, one of the many stories of world faiths, a tall story – but never a true (or false) story. By contrast, postmodernist society will no doubt allow us to say that the story is true *for us*. It will respect our epistemic distance from the other stories that tell a different tale, so long as we keep our distance and do not encroach upon their linguistic territories.

As modernity fades behind us, we Christians can say that we have passed through it and survived, but in Lesslie Newbigin's words, we have been 'very hard pruned'. We came close to losing our story, the 'one short tale we feel to be true', and if we had done so, we would have had nothing left to offer the future. In the event, chastened by our experience, we have woken up in a world that no longer believes in the God of our fathers, and we find that we have become missionaries to our own culture. In order to prosper in our unfamiliar role, we will have to return to our first love of God, forswear our timidity, and become in the third millennium like the missionaries of the first.

Lord, help us to discover the fervour of the early Christians
And the power of the first evangelisation,
That morning of Pentecost, as it started
In the cenacle of Jerusalem

Where your disciples, with Mary, gathered in prayer,
Awaited, Father, the fulfilment of your promise.
Give us the grace to be renewed
'In the Spirit and in fire.'
Teach us to speak to the world in tongues of fire,
Let us bring to an end this time of uncertainty
Where Christians are timid and mute
Discussing anxiously problems of today,
As in the past on the road from Jerusalem to Emmaus,
Without realising that the Master is risen and alive.

Cardinal Leon-Joseph Suenens,
extract from 'Prayer for the Year 2000'.

Bibliographical Essay

This short bibliographical essay is intended as a guide to further reading. References cited here in abbreviated form are fully detailed in the master bibliography, which contains both the works directly referred or alluded to in the main text, as well as providing the background reading to the book.

Christianity and culture

Two books which proved to be the 'watchful dragons', past which we had to steal in order to begin the present work, are Tillich, *Theology of Culture*, and Niebuhr, *Christ and Culture*.

Despite seeing himself as a theologian on the boundary of Church and culture, Tillich's existential approach remains curiously disengaged from both Christian tradition and contemporary culture. Consequently, as a resource for missiology and culture, Tillich's work is unsatisfactory. Of greater influence has been Niebuhr's classic thesis. His famous taxonomy of the relationship between Christianity and culture has affected – whether directly or indirectly – almost all subsequent considerations of the topic.

Due to the passage of time, however, Niebuhr's sociological categories, mainly derived from Troeltsch, are less convincing at the end of the century than they were halfway through it. His theology, also harking back to Troeltsch, and beyond him to Schleiermacher, echoes the accommodating tone of much liberal Protestantism, which has sought to adapt itself to modernity. For an alternative, resistance model of faith to culture – more in concert with the present work – see Hauerwas and Willimon, *Resident Aliens*.

Lesslie Newbigin, the leading figure in the Gospel & Culture movement, has written several important works: *The Other Side of 1984*; *Foolishness to the Greeks*; *The Gospel in a Pluralist Society*; *Truth to Tell*; *The Open Secret*. Both Newbigin's and the author's works are missiological in intention, but whereas Newbigin relies heavily on Polanyi for his insights into culture, the present work is more indebted to the sociology of Berger.

Two other works from the Gospel & Culture perspective are Osborn, *Restoring the Vision*, and an essay collection, Montefiore (ed.), *The Gospel and Contemporary Culture*.

A fascinating work on cultural appropriations of Jesus is Pelikan, *Jesus Through the Centuries*; his *Christianity and Classical Culture* provides a case study of a crucial period in Christian thought.

Pannenberg, 'Christianity and the West', is an insightful survey and prospect.

The Lausanne Consultation on Gospel and Culture was of seminal importance within Evangelicalism; its papers are collected in Stott and Coote (eds.), *Down to Earth*.

Two semi-popular works worth consulting are: Guinness, *The Gravedigger File*, and Walker, *Enemy Territory*.

Narrative

The thesis of part one of this book arose out of two primary texts: Ong, *Orality and Literacy*, and Price, 'A Single Meaning'. Richly suggestive too is Ricoeur, *Time and Narrative*.

Kelber, *The Oral and the Written Gospel*, is an attempt to apply Ong's work to New Testament studies. On the transition from oral to literary culture in the New Testament world, see Gerhardsson, *The Origins of the Gospel Traditions*, which popularizes his earlier, more detailed work. More recent is Bailey, 'Informal Controlled Oral Tradition and the

Synoptic Gospels' and 'Middle Eastern Oral Tradition and the Synoptic Gospels'.

On the hermeneutics of biblical narrative, Frei, *The Eclipse of Biblical Narrative*, is *de rigueur*; see too his posthumous collection, *Theology and Narrative*.

Two excellent historical surveys of biblical studies are Morgan and Barton, *Biblical Interpretation*, and Neill and Wright, *The Interpretation of the New Testament 1861-1986*.

Heron, 'What is Wrong with Biblical Exegesis?', is a trenchant critique in the C.S. Lewis vein – but better informed – of the atomistic and archaeological approach to biblical studies.

Josipovici, *The Book of God*, is a distinguished literary critic's reading of the Bible; Alter and Kermode (eds.), *The Literary Guide to the Bible*, and Alter, *The Art of Biblical Narrative*, are also notable literary readings. For an application of the narrative approach to the New Testament, see Wright's projected five-volume *magnum opus*, *The New Testament and the People of God*; for a systematic theologian's application, see Fackre, *The Christian Story*.

Works relevant for a consideration of the role of memory in the cultural transmission of ideas include Yates, *The Art of Memory*, Carruthers, *The Book of Memory*, and Thiselton, 'Knowledge, Myth and Corporate Memory'.

On the transition from oral to print culture, see Illich and Sanders, *ABC*. Eisenstein, *The Printing Press as an Agent of Change*, is magisterial – although in the first instance, perhaps one ought to consult her more accessible and easily obtainable version, *The Printing Revolution in Early Modern Europe*.

Modernity and postmodernity

'Postmodernism' and 'postmodernity' are notoriously slippery concepts. Introductory orientations can be found in Hunter, 'What is Modernity?', Sampson, 'The Rise of Postmodernity', Inbody,

'Postmodernism', and Lyon, *Postmodernity*. A useful introduction to the problematic of the postmodern is Lyotard's *The Postmodern Condition*. Ironically, we might note, Lyotard's account could itself be said to be a metanarrative.

Specifically on the relationship between theology and postmodernity, see Ford, 'Epilogue', Loughlin, 'At the End of the World', Brueggemann, *The Bible and Postmodern Imagination*, and the two essay collections, Berry and Wernick (eds.), *Shadow of Spirit*, and Burnham (ed.), *Postmodern Theology*.

A very clear – and in my opinion, the best – sociological analysis of postmodernity is Stephen Crook *et al.*, *Postmodernization*. Bauman's many works on postmodernism are particularly important because they show a shift from neo-Marxist to post-Marxist analyses. A work of social theory which surveys and interacts with many of the social thinkers mentioned in the present work, and which clearly articulates a thesis, is Seidman, *Contested Knowledge*; in addition, Seidman (ed.), *The Postmodern Turn*, anthologizes key works.

Two (neo-)Marxist analyses I have found valuable are Harvey, *The Condition of Postmodernity*, and Jameson, *Postmodernism*. Harvey has many useful things to say about the decadence of postmodern thought, but lacks reflective criticism of the bankruptcy of Marxism.

An intellectually satisfying work, of great importance for its critique of Enlightenment and relativistic ethics, and for its appeal for a reconsideration of Aristotelian ethical categories, is MacIntyre, *After Virtue*.

Sociology

On Comte, Marx, Durkheim, Weber, Berger, Bauman, Bellah, Habermas, Foucault, Baudrillard, Lyotard, *et al.*, see Seidman, *Contested Knowledge*. A brilliant *tour de force* which has already generated much debate among theologians and sociologists is Milbank, *Theology and Social Theory*. It is not, however, an easy read, and perhaps the pervasive motif of violence engendered by modernity (a favourite theme of Bauman's too) is overdone.

On the sociology of knowledge, Berger and Luckmann, *The Social Construction of Reality*, provides a definitive exposition of the theoretical underpinning; a briefer treatment, with a specific application, is Hunter, 'Religion and Modernity'.

Peter Berger has written widely, wisely and wittily on religion and its place in contemporary society. For informed appreciation and critique, see Wuthnow, *et al.*, 'The Phenomenology of Peter L. Berger' (drafted by Hunter), and Hunter, *Making Sense*. Os Guinness's unpublished DPhil thesis, *Towards a Reappraisal of Christian Apologetics*, is also an important study of the theological implications and applicability of Berger's thought. The most profound work on secularization remains Martin's *A General Theory of Secularization*.

On Troeltsch, see the works by Morgan, Pye and Coakley.

There is a growing literature on Habermas and critical theory. Habermas remains as a true champion of the Enlightenment against what he sees as the anti-rationalist tendencies of postmodernism. For an initial overview of his thought, see Wuthnow, *et al*. The new Cambridge Companion, edited by White, is a valuable resource. See too How's monograph.

Since his death, fascination with Foucault the man has burgeoned. For his wide-ranging social thought, see Wuthnow, *et al.*, and the essay collection edited by Gutting.

A great deal has been written about civil religion. Bellah's seminal essay originally appeared in *Daedalus*, and is reprinted in his *Beyond Belief*; the bibliography also notes his ensuing considerations of the topic. In 1982, the winter issue of *Daedalus* was given over to a consideration of religion in contemporary American society; the original contributions were reprinted, together with some additional essays, in Douglas and Tipton (eds.), *Religion and America*.

A trenchant examination of the narcissistic tendency in modernity is Lasch. For a theological reflection, see Torrance, 'The Self-Relation'.

Historical and philosophical theology

There are several standard accounts which detail the early Church's hammering out of an authoritative doctrine of the person of Christ; see Kelly, *Early Christian Doctrines*; Pelikan, *The Emergence of the Catholic Tradition (100-600)*; Young, *From Nicaea to Chalcedon*; Grillmeier, *From the Apostolic Age to Chalcedon*. On the use of the Jesus of history as a starting-point for Christology, see Lash, 'Up and Down in Christology', and Gunton, *Yesterday and Today*, ch. 2. Pannenberg's *Jesus – God and Man* is an outstanding example of this approach.

For the medieval period, Cook and Herzman's reader, *The Medieval World View*, presents a wide range of primary sources. Price, *Medieval Thought*, is a valuable *vade mecum* for more detailed study of philosophy and theology.

In recent years, increasing attention has been paid to the variety and significance of popular religious devotion and practice in the late Middle Ages. Duffy, *The Stripping of the Altars*, is a fine example of this; see too the works by Whiting, Harper-Bill, Collinson, and Kieckhefer.

On the Renaissance, see Brown.

On the Reformation, two works are particularly useful: Cameron, *The European Reformation*, for a historical panorama, and McGrath, *Reformation Thought*, for a theological overview.

For an introduction to the Enlightenment, see McManners. Gay and Cassirer are distinguished older works. A good, wide-ranging and up-to-date one-volume reference work is Yolton, *et al.* (eds.), *The Blackwell Companion to the Enlightenment*.

For the post-Reformation period, see Vidler. For figures such as Schleiermacher, Hegel, Kierkegaard, and Troeltsch, a good guide is Welch, *Protestant Thought in the Nineteenth Century*; see also the essays in Smart, *et al.* (eds.), *Nineteenth Century Religious Thought in the West*.

McGrath, *Iustitia Dei*, is a history of the doctrine of justification by faith; Küng, *Justification*, is a Catholic study of Barth's treatment of the topic.

For studies of atheism and secularization, see Buckley, *At the Origins of Modern Atheism*, and Chadwick, *The Secularization of the European Mind*. The influence of positivism on theology is charted in Cashdollar, *The Transformation of Theology, 1830-1890*.

For a fuller critique of scientism, see ch. 7 of Walker, *Enemy Territory*. Other works on the relationship between science and religion are the collection edited by Russell, and Marsden, 'Evangelicals and the Scientific Culture'. On evolution and the Church's response to it, see Chadwick's essay in Russell, and Moore's detailed work, *The Post-Darwinian Controversies*.

On the theological concept of personhood, see Pelikan, *Christianity and Classical Culture*, and the works by Zizioulas cited in the bibliography. Philosophical issues regarding personhood are addressed in the collections edited by Rorty and Perry, and in Taylor's influential essay, 'The Concept of a Person'.

The philosophical roots of modern individual identity, and the question of what constitutes 'the good life', are examined in Taylor, *Sources of the Self*. On the extent and limits of individualism in American life, and on the difficulties of living a morally coherent life, Bellah, *et al.*, *Habits of the Heart*, is a key sociological study.

The recent emphasis in theology on the relatedness of personal community is exemplified in Schwöbel and Gunton (eds.), *Persons, Human and Divine*; Gunton and Hardy (eds.), *On Being the Church*; McFadyen's *The Call to Personhood*; and Walker, 'The Concept of Person in Social Science'.

Evangelicalism and Fundamentalism

First some general works on Evangelicalism. Bebbington, *Evangelicalism in Modern Britain*, is a solid history of Evangelicalism; Tidball, *Who Are the Evangelicals?*, is a very good survey, covering both history and doctrine. Noll, *et al.* (eds.), *Evangelicalism*, is an important collection. A candid, mutually respectful dialogue between a liberal and an Evangelical is Edwards and Stott, *Essentials*.

Along the fundamentalist-Evangelical spectrum, attitudes to the Bible vary from the pre-critical to the sophisticated and hermeneutically well-informed. See, for example, Boone, *The Bible Tells Them So*; the two collections edited by Carson and Woodbridge; and Goldingay, *Models for Scripture*. On the Princetonians and inerrancy, see Noll (ed.), *The Princeton Theology 1812-1921*, and Balmer's essay.

A particularly influential prism through which scripture is read is dispensationalism, on which see Marsden, *Fundamentalism and American Culture*. Marsden is an indefatigable historian of fundamentalism, as attested by the other citations in the bibliography. Boyer, *When Time Shall Be No More*, chronicles the wide-ranging phenomenon of apocalyptic and millennial prophecy belief in modern American culture. For a wider historical perspective, see Cohn's works.

There is a massive literature on revival and revivalism, particularly in the American context, and there has been renewed interest in Wesley, Whitefield and Edwards. My understanding of the Great Awakening is strongly influenced by the revisionist work of Butler, *Awash in a Sea of Faith* (see also Hatch).

On Wesley, the standard biography is Rack, *Reasonable Enthusiast*. Whitefield's significance is undergoing reassessment, the fruits of which are evident in Stout's biography and Lambert's major essay. Edwards is increasingly being seen as a major figure in American theology and philosophy, as Hatch and Stout's essay collection and Jenson's appreciative 'recommendation' amply demonstrate. Edwards's works on the Great Awakening and on 'the religious affections' take on renewed relevance in these days of charismatic renewal and 'the Toronto Blessing', on which see Smail, *et al.*, *Charismatic Renewal*. For a study of the more independent wing of the renewal, see Walker, *Restoring the Kingdom*, a study of the House Church movement based on participant observation.

Bibliography

Abraham, William J. *The Logic of Evangelism*. London: Hodder & Stoughton; C.S. Lewis Centre, 1989.

Ackerman, Robert. *J.G. Frazer: His Life and Work*. Cambridge: Cambridge University Press, 1987.

Alter, Robert. *The Art of Biblical Narrative*. London: George Allen & Unwin, 1981.

Alter, Robert, and Frank Kermode, eds. *The Literary Guide to the Bible*. Cambridge, MA: Harvard University Press; London: Collins, 1987.

Bailey, Kenneth E. 'Informal Controlled Oral Tradition and the Synoptic Gospels.' *Themelios* 20.2 (1995): 4-11.

'Middle Eastern Oral Tradition and the Synoptic Gospels.' *Expository Times* 106.12 (1995): 363-67.

Balmer, Randall. 'The Princetonians and Scripture: A Reconsideration.' *Westminster Theological Journal* 44.2 (1982): 352-65.

Baudrillard, Jean. *The Illusion of the End*. Ed. Chris Turner. Cambridge: Polity, 1994.

Baudrillard, Jean. *Selected Writings*. Ed. Mark Poster. Cambridge: Polity, 1988.

Baudrillard, Jean. 'Simulacra and Simulation.' *Selected Writings*. Ed. Mark Poster. Cambridge: Polity, 1988. 166-84.

Bauman, Zygmunt. *Intimations of Postmodernity*. London: Routledge, 1992.

Bauman, Zygmunt. 'Modernity, or Deconstructing Mortality.'
Mortality, Immortality and Other Life Strategies. Cambridge:
Polity, 1992. 129-60.

Bauman, Zygmunt. 'Postmodernity, or Deconstructing Immortality.'
Mortality, Immortality and Other Life Strategies. Cambridge:
Polity, 1992. 161-99.

Bebbington, D.W. *Evangelicalism in Modern Britain: A History from
the 1730s to the 1980s*. London: Unwin, 1989.

Beiser, Frederick C., ed. *The Cambridge Companion to Hegel*.
Cambridge: Cambridge University Press, 1993.

Bell, Daniel. *The Cultural Contradictions of Capitalism*. London:
Heinemann, 1976.

Bellah, Robert N. *The Broken Covenant: American Civil Religion in
Time of Trial*. New York: Seabury, 1975.

Bellah, Robert N. 'Civil Religion in America.' *Beyond Belief: Essays
on Religion in a Post-Traditional World*. New York: Harper &
Row, 1970. 168-89.

Bellah, Robert N., and Phillip E. Hammond. *Varieties of Civil
Religion*. San Francisco: Harper & Row, 1980.

Bellah, Robert, *et al. Habits of the Heart: Middle America Observed*.
Berkeley: University of California Press, 1985; London: Century
Hutchinson, 1988.

Berger, Peter L. 'Different Gospels: The Social Sources of Apostasy.'
Different Gospels. Ed. Andrew Walker. 2nd ed. London: SPCK,
1993. 105-19.

Berger, Peter L. *Facing up to Modernity: Excursions in Society, Politics,
and Religion*. New York: Basic, 1977; Harmondsworth: Penguin
Books, 1979.

Berger, Peter L. *The Heretical Imperative: Contemporary Possibilities
of Religious Affirmation*. Garden City, NY: Doubleday, 1979;
London: Collins, 1980.

Berger, Peter L. *Pyramids of Sacrifice: Political Ethics and Social Change*. New York: Basic, 1974; Harmondsworth: Penguin Books, 1977.

Berger, Peter L. *A Rumour of Angels: Modern Society and the Rediscovery of the Supernatural*. Garden City, NY: Doubleday, 1969; Harmondsworth: Penguin, 1971.

Berger, Peter L. *The Sacred Canopy: Elements of a Sociological Theory of Religion*. Garden City, NY: Doubleday, 1969.

Berger, Peter L., Brigitte Berger, and Hansfried Kellner. *The Homeless Mind: Modernization and Consciousness*. New York: Random House, 1973; Harmondsworth: Penguin Books, 1974.

Berger, Peter L., and Thomas Luckmann. *The Social Construction of Reality: A Treatise in the Sociology of Knowledge*. Harmondsworth: Penguin Books, 1979.

Berry, Philippa, and Andrew Wernick, eds. *Shadow of Spirit: Postmodernism and Religion*. London: Routledge, 1992.

Bloom, Harold. *The American Religion: The Emergence of the Post-Christian Nation*. New York: Simon & Schuster, 1992.

Boone, Kathleen C. *The Bible Tells Them So: The Discourse of Protestant Fundamentalism*. Albany, NY: State University of New York Press, 1989.

Boyer, Paul. *When Time Shall Be No More: Prophecy Belief in Modern American Culture*. Studies in Cultural History. Cambridge, MA and London: Harvard University Press, 1992.

Bradshaw, Paul F. *The Search for the Origins of Christian Worship: Sources and Methods for the Study of Early Liturgy*. London: SPCK, 1992.

Brode, J., ed. *The Process of Modernization: An Annotated Bibliography*. Cambridge, MA: Harvard University Press, 1969.

Brown, Alison. *The Renaissance*. Seminar Studies in History. London: Longman, 1988.

Bruce, Steve. *Pray TV: Televangelism in America*. London: Routledge, 1990.

Brueggemann, Walter. *The Bible and Postmodern Imagination: Texts Under Negotiation*. Minneapolis, MN: Augsburg Fortress; London: SCM, 1993.

Brueggemann, Walter. *Biblical Perspectives on Evangelism: Living in a Three-Storied Universe*. Nashville, TN: Abingdon, 1993.

Buckley, Michael J., SJ. *At the Origins of Modern Atheism*. New Haven, CT: Yale University Press, 1987.

Burnham, Frederic B., ed. *Postmodern Theology: Christian Faith in a Pluralist World*. New York: HarperCollins, 1989.

Butler, Jon. *Awash in a Sea of Faith: Christianizing the American People*. Studies in Cultural History. Cambridge, MA: Harvard University Press, 1990.

Callinicos, Alex. *Against Postmodernism: A Marxist Critique*. Cambridge: Polity, 1989.

Cameron, Euan. *The European Reformation*. Oxford: Oxford University Press, 1991.

Carruthers, Mary J. *The Book of Memory: A Study of Memory in Medieval Culture*. Cambridge Studies in Medieval Literature. Cambridge: Cambridge University Press, 1990.

Carson, D.A., and John D. Woodbridge, eds. *Hermeneutics, Authority and Canon*. Leicester: IVP, 1986.

Carson, D.A., and John D. Woodbridge, eds. *Scripture and Truth*. Leicester: IVP, 1983.

Cashdollar, Charles D. *The Transformation of Theology, 1830-1890: Positivism and Protestant Thought in Britain and America*. Princeton, NJ: Princeton University Press, 1989.

Cassirer, Ernst. *The Philosophy of the Enlightenment*. Trans. Fritz Koellen and James P. Pettegrove. Princeton, NJ: Princeton University Press, 1951.

Chadwick, Owen. 'Evolution and the Churches.' *Science and Religious Belief: A Selection of Recent Historical Studies*. Ed. C.A. Russell. London: Hodder & Stoughton, 1973. 282-93.

Chadwick, Owen. *The Secularization of the European Mind in the Nineteenth Century*. Cambridge: Cambridge University Press, 1975.

Coakley, Sarah. *Christ Without Absolutes: A Study of the Christology of Ernst Troeltsch*. Oxford: Oxford University Press, 1988.

Cohn, Norman. *Cosmos, Chaos and the World to Come: The Ancient Roots of Apocalyptic Faith*. New Haven, CT and London: Yale University Press, 1993.

Cohn, Norman. *The Pursuit of the Millennium: Revolutionary Millenarians and Mystical Anarchists of the Middle Ages*. 3rd ed. London: Maurice Temple Smith, 1970.

Collinson, Patrick. *The Birthpangs of Protestant England: Religious and Cultural Change in the Sixteenth and Seventeenth Centuries*. Basingstoke: Macmillan, 1988.

Collinson, Patrick. 'The Late Medieval Church and Its Reformation.' *The Oxford Illustrated History of Christianity*. Ed. John McManners. Oxford: Oxford University Press, 1990. 233-66.

Conomos, Dimitri. 'Orthodox Church Music.' *Sourozh* 8 (1982): 17-30.

Cook, William R., and Ronald B. Herzman. *The Medieval World View: An Introduction*. New York: Oxford University Press, 1983.

Crook, Stephen, Jan Pakulski, and Malcolm Waters. *Postmodernization: Change in Advanced Society*. London: Sage, 1992.

Cupitt, Don. *The Time Being*. London: SCM, 1992.

Cupitt, Don. *What is a Story?* London: SCM, 1991.

Derrida, Jacques. *Of Grammatology*. Trans. Gayatri Chakravorty Spivak. Baltimore: Johns Hopkins University Press, 1974.

Derrida, Jacques. *Writing and Difference*. Trans. Alan Bass. Chicago: University of Chicago Press, 1978.

Dickey, Laurence. 'Hegel on Religion and Philosophy.' *The Cambridge Companion to Hegel*. Ed. Frederick C. Beiser. Cambridge: Cambridge University Press, 1993. 301-47.

Douglas, Mary, and Steven Tipton, eds. *Religion and America: Spiritual Life in a Secular Age*. Boston: Beacon, 1983.

Duffy, Eamon. *The Stripping of the Altars: Traditional Religion in England c.1400-c.1580*. New Haven, CT and London: Yale University Press, 1992.

Eco, Umberto. *Travels in Hyperreality: Essays*. Originally Published as *Faith in Fakes*. Trans. William Weaver. London: Picador, 1987.

Edwards, David L., and John Stott. *Essentials: A Liberal-Evangelical Dialogue*. London: Hodder & Stoughton, 1988.

Edwards, Jonathan. *The Great Awakening*. Ed. C.C. Goen. New Haven, CT: Yale University Press, 1972. Vol. 4 of *The Works of Jonathan Edwards*. Gen. Ed. John E. Smith.

Edwards, Jonathan. *Religious Affections*. Ed. John E. Smith. New Haven, CT: Yale University Press, 1959. Vol. 2 of *The Works of Jonathan Edwards*. Gen. Ed. Perry Miller.

Eisenstein, Elizabeth L. *The Printing Press as an Agent of Change: Communications and Cultural Transformations in Early Modern Europe*. Cambridge: Cambridge University Press, 1979. 2 vols.

Eisenstein, Elizabeth L. *The Printing Revolution in Early Modern Europe*. 1983. Canto. Cambridge: Cambridge University Press, 1993.

Eliot, T.S. *Notes Towards the Definition of Culture*. London: Faber & Faber, 1948.

Fackre, Gabriel. *The Christian Story*. 2nd ed. Grand Rapids, MI: Wm B. Eerdmans, 1984.

Finkielkraut, Alain. *The Undoing of Thought*. London: Claridge, 1988.

Finney, Charles Grandison. *Lectures on Revivals of Religion*. Ed. William G. McLoughlin. Cambridge, MA: Harvard University Press, 1960.

Ford, David F. 'Epilogue: Postmodernism and Postscript.' *The Modern Theologians: An Introduction to Christian Theology in the Twentieth Century*. Ed. David F. Ford. Vol. 2. Oxford: Basil Blackwell, 1989. 291-97.

Ford, David F., ed. *The Modern Theologians: An Introduction to Christian Theology in the Twentieth Century*. Oxford: Basil Blackwell, 1989. 2 vols.

Frei, Hans W. *The Eclipse of Biblical Narrative: A Study in Eighteenth and Nineteenth Century Hermeneutics*. New Haven, CT: Yale University Press, 1974.

Frei, Hans W. *The Identity of Jesus Christ, the Hermeneutical Bases of Dogmatic Theology*. 1967. Philadelphia: Fortress, 1975.

Frei, Hans W. *Theology and Narrative: Selected Essays*. Ed. George Hunsinger and William C. Placher. New York: Oxford University Press, 1993.

Frei, Hans W. *Types of Christian Theology*. Ed. George Hunsinger and William C. Placher. New Haven and London: Yale University Press, 1992.

Fukuyama, Francis. *The End of History and the Last Man*. London: Hamish Hamilton, 1992.

Galbraith, John Kenneth. *The Affluent Society*. London: Hamish Hamilton, 1969.

Gay, Peter. *The Enlightenment: A Comprehensive Anthology*. New York: Simon & Schuster, 1973.

Geertz, Clifford. *The Interpretation of Cultures: Selected Essays*. New York: Basic, 1973; London: HarperCollins, 1993.

Geertz, Clifford. 'Thick Description: Toward an Interpretive Theory of Culture.' *The Interpretation of Cultures: Selected Essays*. London: HarperCollins, 1993. 3-30.

Gerhardsson, Birger. *The Origins of the Gospel Traditions*. London: SCM, 1979.

Giddens, Anthony. *Modernity and Self-Identity: Self and Society in the Late Modern Age*. Cambridge: Polity, 1991.

Gilson, Etienne. *History of Christian Philosophy in the Middle Ages.* London: Sheed & Ward, 1955.

Goldingay, John. *Models for Scripture.* Grand Rapids, MI: Wm B. Eerdmans; Carlisle: Paternoster, 1994.

Gregorios, Paulos Mar. *A Light Too Bright.* New York: State University of New York Press, 1994.

Grillmeier, Aloys. *From the Apostolic Age to Chalcedon (451).* 2nd ed. London: Mowbrays, 1975. Vol. 1 of *Christ in Christian Tradition.* Trans. John Bowden.

Guinness, Os. *The Gravedigger File.* London: Hodder & Stoughton, 1983.

Guinness, Os. *Towards a Reappraisal of Christian Apologetics: Peter L. Berger's Sociology of Knowledge as the Sociological Prolegomenon to Christian Apologetics.* DPhil Thesis. University of Oxford, 1981.

Gunton, Colin E. *Enlightenment and Alienation: An Essay Towards a Trinitarian Theology.* Contemporary Christian Studies. Basingstoke: Marshall, Morgan & Scott, 1985.

Gunton, Colin E. *Yesterday and Today: A Study of Continuities in Christology.* London: Darton, Longman & Todd, 1983.

Gunton, Colin E., and Daniel W. Hardy, eds. *On Being the Church: Essays on the Christian Community.* Edinburgh: T. & T. Clark, 1989.

Guroian, Vigen. *Ethics After Christendom: Towards an Ecclesial Christian Ethics.* Grand Rapids MI: Wm B. Eerdmans, 1994.

Gutting, Gary, ed. *The Cambridge Companion to Foucault.* Cambridge: Cambridge University Press, 1994.

Handy, Charles. *The Age of Unreason.* London: Arrow Books, 1995.

Harper-Bill, Christopher. *The Pre-Reformation Church in England 1400-1530.* Seminar Studies in History. London: Longman, 1989.

Harvey, David. *The Condition of Postmodernity: An Enquiry Into the Origins of Cultural Change.* Oxford: Basil Blackwell, 1989.

Hatch, Nathan O. *The Democratization of American Christianity*.
New Haven, CT: Yale University Press, 1989.

Hatch, Nathan O. 'The Democratization of Christianity and the
Character of American Politics.' *Religion and American Politics:
From the Colonial Period to the 1980s*. Ed. Mark A. Noll. New
York: Oxford University Press, 1990. 92-120.

Hatch, Nathan O., and Harry S. Stout, eds. *Jonathan Edwards and
the American Experience*. New York: Oxford University Press,
1988.

Hauerwas, Stanley, and W. H. Willimon. *Resident Aliens: Life in the
Christian Colony*. Nashville, TN: Abingdon, 1989.

Hawking, Stephen. *A Brief History of Time: From the Big Bang to
Black Holes*. New York: Bantam, 1988.

Heron, Alasdair I.C., ed. *A Selection of Papers Presented to the BCC
Study Commission on Trinitarian Doctrine Today*. London: British
Council of Churches, 1991. Vol. 3 of *The Forgotten Trinity*.

Heron, Alasdair I.C. 'What is Wrong with Biblical Exegesis?:
Reflections Upon C.S. Lewis' Criticisms.' *Different Gospels*. Ed.
Andrew Walker. 2nd ed. London: SPCK, 1993. 86-104.

Hobsbawm, E.J. *Nations and Nationalism Since 1780: Programme,
Myth, Reality*. 2nd ed. Canto. Cambridge: Cambridge University
Press, 1992.

How, Alan. *The Habermas-Gadamer Debate on the Nature of the
Social: Back to Bedrock*. Avebury Series in Philosophy. Aldershot,
Hampshire: Avebury, 1995.

Huizinga, J. *The Waning of the Middle Ages: A Study of the Forms of
Life, Thought and Art in France and the Netherlands in the XIVth
and XVth Centuries*. London: Edward Arnold, 1955.

Hunter, James Davison. 'Accommodation: The Domestication of
Belief.' *American Evangelicalism: Conservative Religion and the
Quandary of Modernity*. New Brunswick, NJ: Rutgers University
Press, 1983. 73-101.

Hunter, James Davison. *American Evangelicalism: Conservative Religion and the Quandary of Modernity*. New Brunswick, NJ: Rutgers University Press, 1983.

Hunter, James Davison. 'Religion and Modernity: A Sociology-of-Knowledge Approach.' *American Evangelicalism: Conservative Religion and the Quandary of Modernity*. New Brunswick, NJ: Rutgers University Press, 1983. 11-19.

Hunter, James Davison. *Stop Before the Shooting Begins*. New York: Free, 1994.

Hunter, James Davison. 'What is Modernity?: Historical Roots and Contemporary Features.' *Faith and Modernity*. Ed. Philip Sampson, Vinay Samuel, and Chris Sugden. Oxford: Regnum Books, 1994. 12-28.

Hunter, James Davison, and Stephen C. Ainlay, eds. *Making Sense of Modern Times: Peter L. Berger and the Vision of Interpretive Sociology*. New York: Routledge & Kegan Paul, 1986.

Hutterian Society of Brothers, and John Howard Yoder, eds. *God's Revolution: The Witness of Eberhard Arnold*. New York: Paulist, 1984.

Illich, Ivan, and Barry Sanders. *ABC: The Alphabetization of the Popular Mind*. Boston: Marion Boyars, 1988; Harmondsworth: Penguin Books, 1989.

Inbody, Tyron. 'Postmodernism: Intellectual Velcro Dragged Across Culture?' *Theology Today* 51.4 (1995): 524-38.

Jameson, Fredric. *Postmodernism, Or, The Cultural Logic of Late Capitalism*. London: Verso, 1991.

Jencks, Charles. *The Language of Post-Modern Architecture*. London: Academy Editions, 1977.

Jenks, Chris, ed. *Visual Culture*. London: Routledge, 1995.

Jenson, Robert W. *America's Theologian: A Recommendation of Jonathan Edwards*. New York: Oxford University Press, 1988.

Josipovici, Gabriel. *The Book of God: A Response to the Bible*. New Haven, CT: Yale University Press, 1988.

Kant, Immanuel. *Critique of Pure Reason*. Revised and expanded translation based on Meiklejohn, 1934. Ed. Vasilis Politis. Vermont: Charles E. Tuttle; London: J. M. Dent, 1993.

Kelber, Werner H. *The Oral and the Written Gospel: The Hermeneutics of Speaking and Writing in the Synoptic Tradition, Mark, Paul, and Q*. Foreword by Walter J. Ong. Philadelphia: Fortress, 1983.

Kelly, J.N.D. *Early Christian Doctrines*. 5th ed. London: A. & C. Black, 1977.

Kenna, Rudolph, and William Grandison. *Somethin' Else: 50s Life and Style*. Glasgow: Richard Drew Publishing, 1989.

Kraft, Charles H. *Christianity in Culture: A Study in Dynamic Biblical Theologizing in Cross-Cultural Perspective*. Maryknoll, NY: Orbis Books, 1979.

Kuhn, Thomas S. *The Structure of Scientific Revolutions*. 2nd ed. Chicago: University of Chicago Press, 1970.

Küng, Hans. *Justification: The Doctrine of Karl Barth and a Catholic Reflection*. Trans. Thomas Collins, et al. 1964. London: Burns & Oates, 1981.

Lambert, Frank. '"Pedlar in Divinity": George Whitefield and the Great Awakening, 1737-1745.' *Journal of American History* 77.3 (1990): 812-37.

Lampert, E. *The Divine Realm*. London: Faber & Faber, 1944.

Lasch, Christopher. *The Culture of Narcissism: American Life in an Age of Diminishing Expectations*. W.W. Norton & Co., 1979; London: Sphere Books, 1980.

Lash, Nicholas. 'Up and Down in Christology.' *New Studies in Theology*. Ed. Stephen Sykes and Derek Holmes. Vol. 1. London: Duckworth, 1980. 31-46.

Levine, L.W. *Black Culture and Black Consciousness: Afro-American Folk Thought from Slavery to Freedom*. Oxford: Oxford University Press, 1977.

Lewis, C.S. *Fern-Seed and Elephants and Other Essays on Christianity*. Ed. Walter Hooper. London: Collins, 1977.

Lindbeck, George A. *The Nature of Doctrine: Religion and Theology in a Postliberal Age*. London: SPCK, 1984.

Loughlin, Gerard. 'At the End of the World: Postmodernism and Theology.' *Different Gospels*. Ed. Andrew Walker. 2nd ed. London: SPCK, 1993. 204-21.

Lyon, David. *Postmodernity*. Milton Keynes: Open University Press, 1994.

Lyotard, Jean-François. *The Lyotard Reader*. Ed. Andrew Benjamin. Oxford: Blackwell, 1989.

Lyotard, Jean-François. *The Postmodern Condition: A Report on Knowledge*. Trans. Geoff Bennington and Brian Massumi. Foreword by Fredric Jameson. Theory and History of Literature 10. Minneapolis: University of Minnesota Press, 1984.

McFadyen, Alistair I. *The Call to Personhood: A Christian Theory of the Individual in Social Relationships*. Cambridge: Cambridge University Press, 1990.

McGrath, Alister E. *Iustitia Dei: A History of the Christian Doctrine of Justification*. Cambridge: Cambridge University Press, 1986. 2 vols.

McGrath, Alister E. *Reformation Thought: An Introduction*. 2nd ed. Oxford: Blackwell, 1993.

MacIntyre, Alasdair. *After Virtue: A Study in Moral Theory*. 2nd ed. London: Duckworth, 1985.

McManners, John. 'Enlightenment: Secular and Christian (1600-1800).' *The Oxford Illustrated History of Christianity*. Ed. John McManners. Oxford: Oxford University Press, 1990. 267-99.

Mâle, E. *The Gothic Image*. London: Collins, 1961.

Marsden, George. 'The Collapse of American Evangelical Academia.' *Faith and Rationality: Reason and Belief in God*. Ed. Alvin Plantinga and Nicholas Wolterstorff. Notre Dame, IN: University of Notre Dame Press, 1983. 219-64.

Marsden, George M. 'Evangelicals and the Scientific Culture: An Overview.' *Religion and Twentieth-Century American Intellectual Life*. Ed. Michael J. Lacey. Woodrow Wilson Center Series. Cambridge: Cambridge University Press, 1989. 23-48.

Marsden, George M. *Fundamentalism and American Culture: The Shaping of Twentieth-Century Evangelicalism: 1870-1925*. New York: Oxford University Press, 1980.

Marsden, George M. *Reforming Fundamentalism: Fuller Seminary and the New Evangelicalism*. Grand Rapids, MI: Wm B. Eerdmans, 1987.

Martin, David. *A General Theory of Secularization*. Explorations in Interpretative Sociology. Oxford: Basil Blackwell, 1978.

Martin, David. *Tongues of Fire: The Explosion of Protestantism in Latin America*. Foreword by Peter Berger. Oxford: Basil Blackwell, 1990.

Medved, Michael. *Hollywood Versus America: Popular Culture and the War on Traditional Values*. London: HarperCollins, 1992.

Milbank, John. *Theology and Social Theory: Beyond Secular Reason*. Oxford: Basil Blackwell, 1990.

Mill, J.S. *Auguste Comte and Positivism*. Michigan: University of Michigan Press, 1961.

Montefiore, Hugh, ed. *The Gospel and Contemporary Culture*. London: Mowbray, 1992.

Moore, James R. *The Post-Darwinian Controversies: A Study of the Protestant Struggles to Come to Terms with Darwin in Great Britain and America 1870-1900*. Cambridge: Cambridge University Press, 1979.

Morgan, Robert. 'Ernst Troeltsch on Theology and Religion.' *Ernst Troeltsch: Writings on Theology and Religion*. Trans. and Ed. Robert Morgan and Michael Pye. London: Duckworth, 1977. 1-51.

Morgan, Robert. 'Troeltsch and Christian Theology.' *Ernst Troeltsch: Writings on Theology and Religion*. Trans. and Ed. Robert Morgan and Michael Pye. London: Duckworth, 1977. 208-33.

Morgan, Robert, and John Barton. *Biblical Interpretation*. Oxford: Oxford University Press, 1989.

Neill, Stephen, and Tom Wright. *The Interpretation of the New Testament 1861-1986*. 2nd ed. Oxford: Oxford University Press, 1988.

Newbigin, Lesslie. *Foolishness to the Greeks: The Gospel and Western Culture*. London: SPCK, 1986.

Newbigin, Lesslie. *The Gospel in a Pluralist Society*. London: SPCK, 1989.

Newbigin, Lesslie. *The Open Secret: An Introduction to the Theology of Mission*. 2nd ed. Grand Rapids, MI: Wm B. Eerdmans; London: SPCK, 1995.

Newbigin, Lesslie. *The Other Side of 1984: Questions for the Churches*. Geneva: World Council of Churches, 1983.

Newbigin, Lesslie. *Truth to Tell: The Gospel as Public Truth*. Grand Rapids, MI: Wm B. Eerdmans, 1991.

Niebuhr, H. Richard. *Christ and Culture*. London: Faber & Faber, 1952.

Noll, Mark A. *A History of Christianity in the United States and Canada*. Grand Rapids, MI: Wm B. Eerdmans; London: SPCK, 1992.

Noll, Mark A., comp & ed. *The Princeton Theology 1812-1921: Scripture, Science, and the Theological Method from Archibald Alexander to Benjamin Breckinridge Warfield*. Grand Rapids, MI: Baker Book House, 1983.

Noll, Mark A., ed. *Religion and American Politics: From the Colonial Period to the 1980s*. New York: Oxford University Press, 1990.

Noll, Mark A., David W. Bebbington, and George A. Rawlyk, eds. *Evangelicalism: Comparative Studies of Popular Protestantism in North America, the British Isles, and Beyond, 1700-1990*. Religion in America Series. New York and Oxford: Oxford University Press, 1994.

Bibliography

Oden, Thomas C. *Two Worlds: Notes on the Death of Modernity in America and Russia*. Downers Grove, IL: IVP, 1992.

Ong, Walter J. *Orality and Literacy: The Technologizing of the Word*. New Accents. London: Methuen, 1982.

Osborn, Lawrence. *Restoring the Vision: The Gospel and Modern Culture*. London: Mowbray, 1995.

Ouspensky, L. *Theology of the Icon*. Crestwood, NY: St Vladimir's Seminary Press, 1992.

Paglia, Camille. *Sexual Personae: Art and Decadence from Nefertiti to Emily Dickinson*. New Haven, CT: Yale University Press; Harmondsworth: Penguin Books, 1991.

Pannenberg, Wolfhart. 'Christianity and the West: Ambiguous Past, Uncertain Future.' *First Things*, Dec. 1994, 18-23.

Pannenberg, Wolfhart. *Jesus – God and Man*. Trans. Lewis L. Wilkins and Duane A. Priebe. London: SCM, 1968.

Panofsky, Erwin. *Gothic Architecture and Scholasticism*. Cleveland: World Publishing, 1957.

Pelikan, Jaroslav. *Christianity and Classical Culture: The Metamorphosis of Natural Theology in the Christian Encounter with Hellenism*. Gifford Lectures at Aberdeen, 1992-93. New Haven, CT and London: Yale University Press, 1993.

Pelikan, Jaroslav. *The Emergence of the Catholic Tradition (100-600)*. Chicago: University of Chicago Press, 1971. Vol. 1 of *The Christian Tradition: A History of the Development of Doctrine*.

Pelikan, Jaroslav. *The Growth of Medieval Theology (600-1300)*. Chicago: University of Chicago Press, 1978. Vol. 3 of *The Christian Tradition: A History of the Development of Doctrine*.

Pelikan, Jaroslav. *Jesus Through the Centuries: His Place in the History of Culture*. New Haven, CT and London: Yale University Press, 1985.

Perry, John, ed. *Personal Identity*. Topics in Philosophy 2. Berkeley: University of California Press, 1975.

Polanyi, Michael. *Personal Knowledge: Towards a Post-Critical Philosophy*. 2nd ed. London: Routledge & Kegan Paul, 1962.

Postman, Neil. *Amusing Ourselves to Death: Public Discourse in the Age of Show Business*. London: Heinemann, 1986.

Price, Betsey B. *Medieval Thought: An Introduction*. Oxford: Blackwell, 1992.

Price, Reynolds. 'A Single Meaning: Notes on the Origins and Life of Narrative.' *A Palpable God*. San Francisco: North Point, 1985.

Pye, Michael. 'Troeltsch and the Science of Religion.' *Ernst Troeltsch: Writings on Theology and Religion*. Trans. and Ed. Robert Morgan and Michael Pye. London: Duckworth, 1977. 234-52.

Quicke, Andrew, and Juliet Quicke. *Hidden Agendas: The Politics of Religious Broadcasting in Britain 1987-1991*. Virginia: Dominion King Grant Publications, 1992.

Rack, Henry D. *Reasonable Enthusiast: John Wesley and the Rise of Methodism*. London: Epworth, 1989.

Ricoeur, Paul. *Time and Narrative*. Trans. Kathleen McLaughlin and David Pellauer. Chicago: University of Chicago Press, 1984-88. 3 vols.

Rorty, Amélie Oksenberg, ed. *The Identities of Persons*. Topics in Philosophy 3. Berkeley: University of California Press, 1976.

Russell, C.A., ed. *Science and Religious Belief: A Selection of Recent Historical Studies*. London: Hodder & Stoughton, 1973.

Rybczynski, Witold. 'Mysteries of the Mall.' Review of John Brinckerhoff Jackson, *A Sense of Place, A Sense of Time* (Yale University Press). *New York Review of Books* 41.13 (1994): 31-34.

Sacks, Jonathan. *Faith in the Future*. London: Darton, Longman and Todd, 1994.

Sacks, Jonathan. *The Persistence of Faith* (the Reith Lectures). London: Weidenfeld & Nicholson, 1991.

Sampson, Anthony. *Company Man: The Rise and Fall of Corporate Life*. London: HarperCollins, 1995.

Sampson, Philip. 'The Rise of Postmodernity.' *Faith and Modernity*. Ed. Philip Sampson, Vinay Samuel, and Chris Sugden. Oxford: Regnum Books, 1994. 29-57.

Sampson, Philip, Vinay Samuel, and Chris Sugden, eds. *Faith and Modernity*. Oxford: Regnum Books, 1994.

Sandeen, Ernest R. *The Roots of Fundamentalism: British and American Millenarianism 1800-1930*. Chicago: University of Chicago Press, 1970.

Schleiermacher, F.D. *The Christian Faith*. 1821. Edinburgh: T. & T. Clark, 1928.

Schleiermacher, F.D. *On Religion: Speeches to Its Cultured Despisers*. Trans. John Oman. Introd. by Rudolf Otto. New York: Harper & Row, 1958.

Seidman, Steven. *Contested Knowledge: Social Theory in the Postmodern Era*. Oxford and Cambridge, MA: Blackwell, 1994.

Seidman, Steven, ed. *The Postmodern Turn: New Perspectives on Social Theory*. Cambridge: Cambridge University Press, 1995.

Smail, Tom, Andrew Walker, and Nigel Wright. 'From "The Toronto Blessing" to Trinitarian Renewal: A Theological Conversation.' *Charismatic Renewal: The Search for a Theology*. 2nd ed. London: SPCK; Gospel & Culture, 1995. 152-66, 175-76.

Smail, Tom. '"Revelation Knowledge" and Knowledge of Revelation: The Faith Movement and the Question of Heresy.' *Charismatic Renewal: The Search for a Theology*. 2nd ed. London: SPCK; Gospel & Culture, 1995. 133-51, 171-75.

Smart, Ninian, *et al*, eds. *Nineteenth Century Religious Thought in the West*. Vol. 1. Cambridge: Cambridge University Press, 1985.

Steiner, George. *Language and Silence*. London: Faber & Faber, 1967.

Steiner, George. *Real Presences: Is There Anything in What We Say?* London: Faber & Faber, 1989.

Stott, John R. W., and Robert T. Coote, eds. *Down to Earth: Studies in Christianity and Culture*. London: Hodder & Stoughton, 1981.

Stout, Harry S. *The Divine Dramatist: George Whitefield and the Rise of Modern Evangelicalism*. Grand Rapids: Wm. B. Eerdmans, 1991.

Studdert Kennedy, G.A. *The Warrior, the Woman and the Christ: A Study of the Leadership of Christ*. 2nd ed. London: Hodder & Stoughton, 1929.

Taylor, Charles. 'The Concept of a Person.' *Human Agency and Language*. Cambridge: Cambridge University Press, 1985. Vol. 1 of *Philosophical Papers*. 97-114.

Taylor, Charles. *Hegel*. Cambridge: Cambridge University Press, 1975.

Taylor, Charles. *Sources of the Self: The Making of the Modern Identity*. Cambridge: Cambridge University Press, 1989.

Thiselton, Anthony. 'Knowledge, Myth and Corporate Memory.' *Believing in the Church: The Corporate Nature of Faith*. The Doctrine Commission of the Church of England. London: SPCK, 1981. 45-78.

Tidball, Derek J. *Who Are the Evangelicals?: Tracing the Roots of the Modern Movements*. London: HarperCollins, 1994.

Tillich, Paul. *Theology of Culture*. Ed. Robert C. Kimball. New York: Oxford University Press, 1964.

Torrance, Alan J. 'The Self-Relation, Narcissism and the Gospel of Grace.' *Scottish Journal of Theology* 40.4 (1987): 481-510.

Torrance, Thomas F. *God and Rationality*. London: Oxford University Press, 1971.

Torrance, Thomas F. *Theological Science*. Oxford: Oxford University Press, 1969.

Troeltsch, Ernst. *The Absoluteness of Christianity and the History of Religions*. 1902. London: SCM, 1972.

Troeltsch, Ernst. *The Social Teaching of the Christian Churches*. Trans. Olive Wyon. London and New York: George Allen & Unwin; Macmillan, 1931. 2 vols.

Vidler, Alec R. *The Church in an Age of Revolution: 1789 to the Present Day*. 2nd ed. Harmondsworth: Penguin Books, 1971.

Walker, Andrew. 'The Concept of Person in Social Science: Possibilities for Theological Anthropology.' *A Selection of Papers Presented to the BCC Study Commission on Trinitarian Doctrine Today*. London: British Council of Churches, 1991. Vol. 3 of *The Forgotten Trinity*. Ed. Alasdair I. C. Heron. 137-57.

Walker, Andrew. *Enemy Territory: The Christian Struggle for the Modern World*. London: Hodder & Stoughton, 1987.

Walker, Andrew. *Restoring the Kingdom: The Radical Christianity of the House Church Movement*. 2nd ed. London: Hodder & Stoughton, 1988.

Ward, Keith. *A Vision to Pursue: Beyond the Crisis in Christianity*. London: SCM, 1991.

Warren, Robert. *Building Missionary Congregations*. London: Church House Publishing, 1995.

Weber, Max. *The Protestant Ethic and the Spirit of Capitalism*. Trans. Talcott Parsons. Foreword by R. H. Tawney. New York: Scribner's, 1958.

Welch, Claude. *Protestant Thought in the Nineteenth Century*. New Haven, CT: Yale University Press, 1972, 1985. 2 vols.

West, Cornel. *Race Matters*. New York: Vintage, 1994.

White, Stephen K., ed. *The Cambridge Companion to Habermas*. Cambridge: Cambridge University Press, 1995.

Whiting, Robert. *The Blind Devotion of the People: Popular Religion and the English Reformation*. Cambridge Studies in Early Modern British History. Cambridge: Cambridge University Press, 1989.

Wiles, Maurice, and Mark Santer, eds. *Documents in Early Christian Thought*. Cambridge: Cambridge University Press, 1975.

Williams, Benjamin D., and Harold B. Anstall. *Orthodox Worship: A Living Continuum with the Synagogue, the Temple, and the Early Church*. Minneapolis, MN: Light & Life Publishing Company, 1990.

Wills, Garry. *Under God: Religion and American Politics*. New York: Simon & Schuster, 1990.

Wittgenstein, Ludwig. *Philosophical Investigations*. Trans. G.E.M. Anscombe. 3rd ed. Oxford: Basil Blackwell, 1967.

Wright, N. T. *The New Testament and the People of God*. London: SPCK, 1992. Vol. 1 of *Christian Origins and the Question of God*.

Wuthnow, Robert. '*Quid Obscurum*: The Changing Terrain of Church-State Relations.' *Religion and American Politics: From the Colonial Period to the 1980s*. Ed. Mark A. Noll. New York: Oxford University Press, 1990. 337-54.

Wuthnow, Robert. *Rediscovering the Sacred: Perspectives on Religion in Contemporary Society*. Grand Rapids, MI: Wm B. Eerdmans, 1992.

Wuthnow, Robert, *et al.* 'The Critical Theory of Jürgen Habermas.' *Cultural Analysis: The Work of Peter L. Berger, Mary Douglas, Michel Foucault, and Jürgen Habermas*. Boston and London: Routledge & Kegan Paul, 1984. 179-239.

Wuthnow, Robert, *et al.* 'The Neo-Structuralism of Michel Foucault.' *Cultural Analysis: The Work of Peter L. Berger, Mary Douglas, Michel Foucault, and Jürgen Habermas*. Boston and London: Routledge & Kegan Paul, 1984. 133-78.

Wuthnow, Robert, et al. 'The Phenomenology of Peter L. Berger.' *Cultural Analysis: The Work of Peter L. Berger, Mary Douglas, Michel Foucault, and Jürgen Habermas*. Boston and London: Routledge & Kegan Paul, 1984. 21-76.

Wybrew, Hugh. *The Orthodox Liturgy: The Development of the Eucharistic Liturgy in the Byzantine Rite*. London: SPCK, 1989.

Yates, Frances A. *The Art of Memory*. Chicago: University of Chicago Press, 1966.

Yoder, John Howard. 'Civil Religion in America.' *The Priestly Kingdom: Social Ethics as Gospel*. Notre Dame, IN: University of Notre Dame Press, 1984. 172-95, 214-15.

Yoder, John Howard. *The Priestly Kingdom: Social Ethics as Gospel.* Notre Dame, IN: University of Notre Dame Press, 1984.

Yolton, John W., *et al,* eds. *The Blackwell Companion to the Enlightenment.* Oxford: Basil Blackwell, 1991.

Young, Frances M. *From Nicaea to Chalcedon: A Guide to the Literature and Its Background.* London: SCM, 1983.

Zizioulas, J.D. 'Human Capacity and Human Incapacity: A Theological Exploration of Personhood.' *Scottish Journal of Theology* 28.5 (1975): 401-47.

Zizioulas, J.D. *Being as Communion: Studies in Personhood and the Church.* Crestwood, NY: St. Vladimir's Seminary, 1985.

Zizioulas, J.D. 'On Being a Person: Towards an Ontology of Personhood.' *Persons, Human and Divine: King's College Essays in Theological Anthropology.* Ed. Christoph Schwöbel and Colin E. Gunton. Edinburgh: T. & T. Clark, 1991. 33-46.

Index

Index

Index